VATICAN CITY

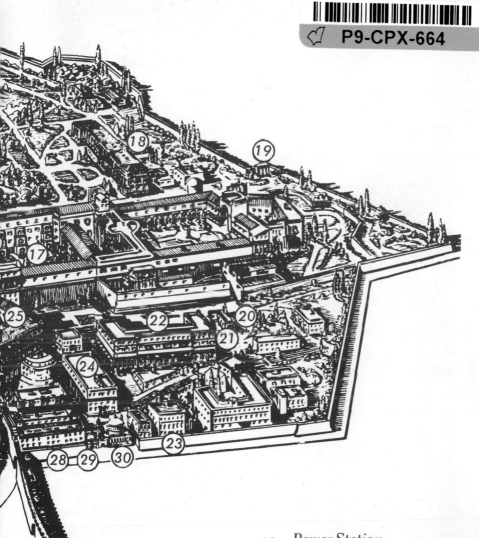

THE WORLD OF

THE VATICAN

HARPER & ROW, PUBLISHERS · NEW YORK AND EVANSTON

THE WORLD OF

THE VATICAN

•

BY ROBERT NEVILLE

FIRST EDITION

H-M

LIBRARY OF CONGRESS CATALOG CARD NUMBER: 62–7295

CONTENTS

CONTENTS

THE WORLD OF

THE VATICAN

I

THE TURN
OF THE TIDE

The long shadows of two millennia of history forever play on the Vatican. Inside the Leonine Walls, which enclose and guard from general view most of the 108-acre enclave on the right bank of the Tiber at Rome, life often seems more attuned to the precepts of a remote past than to the exigencies of the present.

Habits established centuries ago are still punctiliously observed within the Apostolic Palace. Custom and ceremony often date back to the reigns of such early Popes as Leo the Great and Gregory the Great. Uniforms smack more of the Renaissance than of recent centuries, while all sorts of offices and titles, such as Majordomo, Master of the Chamber, and Privy Chamberlains Participating, are holdovers from the imperial households of ancient Rome.

In fact, the norms of the Roman Empire weigh heavily on the Church. In certain respects the Pope himself appears to be the lineal descendant of the Caesars. A good deal of the cherished terminology of the Roman Catholic Church antedates the Christian era. For example, the title of Pontifex Maximus, or Supreme

9

Pontiff, which originally meant "bridge builder" but now simply denotes the Pope, was used to describe the office of the head of pagan cults centuries before the Emperor Constantine recognized Christianity as a legal religion. Julius Caesar, among other notables, was a Roman Pontiff. So were Lepidus and Augustus.

The expression "Roman Curia," which today means the Church's headquarters in the Eternal City, originated in the early days of Rome. It then meant an assembly of tribes; later, during the Republic, it became a virtual synonym for the Roman Senate. The term "diocese," meaning today the territory under a bishop's jurisdiction, was originally an administrative unit devised by the Emperor Diocletian, who was, incidentally, noted for his persecution of Christians.

So steeped in tradition is the Vatican that at times the place seems old-fashioned to the point of obsolesence. Half the offices at the Papal court are vestiges of the times when the Popes enjoyed temporal as well as spiritual power. Many of the titles of honor must be translated in order to be understood today. Thus the Master of the Sacred Apostolic Palace is in reality the Pope's chief theologian. The Furrier of the Palace was once a scout sent ahead to look for quarters for a Papal court on the move; now his major duty is that of leading certain processions.

A group of men called *bussolanti*, whose black tunics and white ruffs are invariably in evidence at the Vatican on ceremonial occasions, were first so named because their primary task was to pull back the *bussola* or heavy curtains that once hung before the Papal antechamber. Their chief labor nowadays consists of accompanying diplomats on their way to present credentials to the Pope, taking part in processions, and being at the side of certain prelates on solemn occasions.

The most numerous group at the Papal Court is the Chamberlains of the Sword and Cloak, who have more or less the same duties as the *bussolanti* but on a higher level. They are divided into four classes: the *Secret* Chamberlains of the Sword and Cloak are supposed to come from noble families; the Chamberlains of the Sword and Cloak of Honor come from the bourgeoisie; the Chamberlains of the Sword and Cloak *di numero* (of number) are nominated for life; while the Supernumerary Chamberlains of the Sword and Cloak lose their jobs on the death of the reigning Pope.

While most of these posts are now bereft of actual power in the Church at large, they still figure prominently in the scheme of things within the Roman Curia and help make Vatican administration a heavy-handed affair. The Secretariat of Briefs to Princes, for example, was at one time kept busy writing letters in Latin to various powerful royal personages of Europe. But today there is little royalty left, and even fewer who would appreciate a letter in Latin. Even so, this Secretariat still exists, and is normally headed by a cardinal, who is a member of the Curia. The most conspicuous latter-day activity of the Secretary of the Briefs to Princes has been to devise Latin terms for such modern appliances as telephones, television sets, and elevators. In some ceremonies, he also replies in the name of the Pope to various supplications addressed to His Holiness on the throne.

The Apostolic Chamber, in the old Papal States which were wiped off the map in 1870, used to operate as a sort of finance ministry. But now the Chamber, headed by a cardinal called a *camerlengo*, comes to life only in the short interregnums between Popes. The Datary, one of the Vatican's five offices, was once a tax bureau, and as such had an important function when the Pope ruled most of Central Italy. But now, not only has Papal territory shrunk to 108 acres, an eighth the size of New York's Central Park, but the fewer than one thousand inhabitants left as Vatican subjects pay no taxes. Still the office remains, headed by a Curia cardinal.

These anachronisms within the Vatican—and the list could be extended—provide both colorful copy and interesting photographs. But they also create a certain atmosphere of sluggish unreality. Ceremony, however brilliantly performed, is no substitute for vigorous administration, and much of the energy of aging Pontiffs and their staff at the Vatican is dissipated in ritual observances.

In a place where tradition is the overriding factor, experimentation and innovation are inhibited. Suggestions for change, even when they come from loyal adherents of the faith, are not only stubbornly resisted at the Curia but are usually treated as tantamount to an attack on the Church itself. A prominent Italian Jesuit, for example, who proposed, among other controversial suggestions, that the forthcoming ecumenical council of the Church might include reforms in the Curia was rebuked in none other than *L'Osservatore Romano*, the Vatican's own daily. The author was constrained quietly to withdraw his book from circulation.

Pope John XXIII has apparently more than once felt the pressures of a tradition-minded Curia. Some of the minor projects he has favored have encountered enough opposition within the Vatican to delay or block their execution. According to reliable bystanders the Pope once declared, a bit in jest but also a bit in earnest: "You see, I am not master even in my own house." Suspicion is rife in Rome that the Holy Father, when he originally called his ecumenical council, had in mind a really grand design of remaking Church administration and policy, but has since been obliged as a result of Curia pressure to settle for what now augurs to be a modest goal of technical reforms. (See Chapter XII.)

Out of this highly developed sense of the past has come, of course, the Vatican's renowned long view of history. Argument can be generated over whether the view is not, at times, too long for the Church's good. Certainly, the headquarters of Roman Catholicism is not a prey to fashion or passing moods. Snap decisions are never made in Rome. Mistakes have doubtless been committed, but not without careful pondering and prudent consideration of what is best for the Church, not especially today or tomorrow, but in the decades and centuries to come. Nobody at the Vatican expects immediate results. If one Pope cannot accomplish all he would like, there is always the next Pope; over the centuries the Church will flourish and finally triumph.

[1] *Concilio; per una riforma nella carita*, by the Rev. Riccardo Lombardi.

The long view of history entails, however, the risk of being permanently behind the times. Some new ideas have taken so long to penetrate the Leonine Walls that by the time they were accepted by the Vatican the world had moved on to something else. In general, opposition to new ways is ingrained and dogged; again and again Rome has opposed new trends that were bound in the end to succeed.

For centuries the Vatican mistrusted science to the point of refusing to acknowledge the results of proven research, let alone trying to reconcile them with religious beliefs or history. Scientists themselves were berated and even persecuted. The case of Galileo comes easily to mind, but there have also been more recent, if less dramatic, instances. For example, the great discoveries of archaeologists of the last century in the Middle East and Near East patently called for a new approach to Biblical interpretation. The Vatican was at first unmoved, however, and insisted that the Bible must be accepted literally. It was not until the pontificate of Pius XII, at the height of World War II, that the traditional view was finally modified with the publication of a little-reported but quite remarkable encyclical by Pius XII on Biblical research.[2] This encyclical granted, among other things, that the Old Testament authors might easily have had different standards for writing history than do historians of today and that at times they might even have indulged in allegory.

The Vatican stand on birth control is put down by many as still another refusal to acknowledge what can only be termed scientific facts. Official statements on this subject, even several recent ones from Pope John XXIII himself,[3] not given to the problems of overpopulation and undernourishment the informed attention they deserve. Many feel the new situation will have to be faced more directly.

[2] *Divini Afflante Spiritu*, published September 30, 1943.
[3] Once, after urging parents not to be afraid of having large families, which are a "sure sign of God's grace," the Pope added: "The world was not created to be a cemetery."

Catholic doctrine, it is repeated ad infinitum, can never accept artificial control of procreation. (On this point many Catholics confuse the debate with extraneous argument; they talk about sterilization and abortion, whereas the real problem is the use of contraceptives in whatever form.) But apparently in many parts of the world Catholic leadership already realizes that the Church's position on this question needs to be restudied in the interest of greater clarity and direction.

The most significant expression on birth control from Catholic sources is found in a pronouncement of an assembly of cardinals and archbishops of France in March, 1961. (Rome frequently permits the Church in France to conduct experiments which would be forbidden elsewhere.) The French statement frankly admits the principle of limiting the number of children in a family. It declares that the Church does not insist on unlimited births at any cost, and asserts that parents must decide how many children can be properly cared for and properly educated. Control by artificial means is still condemned, but regulation of birth by other un-specified means is implicitly permitted. Although this French pro-nouncement is far ahead of anything emanating from Rome, it has been made available to inquiring writers and correspondents at the Vatican.

In the social and political sphere, Rome all during the last century was regarded as the center of incorrigible reaction. The Church had fought hard against the ideological structure of the French Revolution; both before and after that event Catholicism favored autocratic and monarchical forms of government. The Vatican's natural allies of the nineteenth century were the Austro-Hungary of Metternich and the Spain of the Bourbons. Nine-teenth-century liberalism, which now seems so mild, was declared anathema, as was Socialism, not to mention Communism. There was widespread suspicion that democracy and Catholicism would not mix.

Perhaps the most serious charge against the Vatican, which even now finds echoes in many quarters, was that Rome opposed the whole idea of separation of Church and State. In other words, the concept of the secular state was rejected and freedom of conscience in religious worship was denied. At the same time a cynical theory entitled "thesis" and "hypothesis" was propounded and supported in powerful Catholic quarters. (Not, however, in America.) The tenets of this theory were, briefly, that in those countries where Roman Catholics were in a majority "error"—meaning other religions—must not be free to propagate (this is "thesis"); whereas, in countries where Roman Catholics were in a minority, the Church should insist on full religious freedom ("hypothesis"). This theory still has advocates at the Vatican, including Cardinal Alfredo Ottaviani, secretary of the Holy Office, one of the Vatican's most important ministries. (See Chapter IX.)

The net result of thus going against the prevailing thought of the nineteenth century was that Catholicism lost ground continuously on practically all fronts. The Church had little standing among intellectuals. Catholicism certainly had no appeal to revolutionaries. Artists and writers were rarely Catholic. Catholic education, not to mention Catholic scholarship, was suspect. The Church allowed the Socialists in most of Europe to capture the growing trade union movements. The working classes in traditionally Catholic countries became largely apostasized. Government after government fell into the hands of anticlerical parties, not for a few years, but for decades on end. The Vatican's influence at the centers of world power was reduced virtually to nothing.

But today the tide seems to have turned. The last two Popes, Pius XII and John XXIII, have broken through the oppressive Vatican bureaucracy to achieve notable results in putting the Church back into the stream of progress. In many parts of the Occident, Roman Catholicism is now on the upsurge. As a consequence, the Vatican in general and the Papacy in particular are currently basking in the rays of increasing respect and enhanced prestige.

This, of course, is a vastly different Vatican from that of a century or even two decades ago. For one thing, it is much less politically minded. The Vatican now tacitly recognizes that clerical regimes can no longer be established, even though Catholics still command majorities in many places. Catholic dogma no longer has the hold on people's minds that it once had; only a tiny percentage of Catholics now attend services daily. Catholic worship —the same can probably be said for Protestant worship—has become more superficial and less intense as the century progresses. In other words, the "new Catholicism"—the Vatican would rigidly reject the term—embraces much less comprehensive aims than the old. Perhaps it is precisely because the Catholic goal is now relatively modest that the Vatican enjoys such world favor today.

Curiously enough, Catholicism has become strong in places where once it was weakest. In the United States, although the population is still heavily Protestant, the Catholic Church has grown in numbers and in influence to the point where a Catholic President now occupies the White House and many Catholics hold important posts at all levels of government.

Throughout Europe, the commanding postwar roles of the great Catholic parties are evidence of renewed political and social influence. Since 1949 the *Christliche Democratische Union* has been in power in Germany, long the bastion of European Protestantism. In France, ever Catholic but with a strong secular tradition in politics, the once great Radical Socialist party, anticlerical to its last member, has come to the end of its long reign of power, and in its stead can be found statesmen of clear Catholic persuasion. Further gains for the Church have been registered in Austria, Belgium, and The Netherlands. The Vatican counts as one of its most significant postwar victories the new educational policy in The Netherlands, where Catholic schools receive the same state support as public schools. The same can be said, to a modified extent, of the latest French educational act.

Postwar Italy represents perhaps the most dramatic example of a change in the fortunes of the Church. The Vatican and Italy have, of course, a very special relationship. The Papacy has been an Italian monopoly for the past four centuries. The Roman Curia has always been and still is overwhelmingly Italian. The language of the Vatican, despite all the talk about Latin, is Italian.

This closeness has had its effects on both sides. No people have been more devoted than the Italians to the institution of the Papacy, at the same time that they have had no illusions about the qualities of some of the men who have held that highest office. The Vatican, in turn, displays toward Italy an attitude which some might call paternal and others might label intrusive. Whatever the correct term, Italy is the Vatican's window to the modern world. Because of these special circumstances, the story of the change-about in the fortunes of the Vatican in the Italian peninsula deserves telling in some detail.

Until less than a century ago the Roman Pontiff had been the absolute ruler of a populous stretch of central Italy called the Papal States. The usual argument for maintaining this territory under the Pope's temporal rule was not only that it provided needed funds for the Church's headquarters but also that it gave the Vatican freedom of operation. Most Italian historians charge that the Papal administration of this territory was inefficient if not corrupt. However that may be, the Papal States were wiped out in 1870 in an upsurge of clamorous, anticlerical nationalism known as the Risorgimento. It was the Risorgimento which finally unified Italy and which to this day sends a thrill down the spine of patriotic Italians.

Thus after 1870 the Popes no longer ruled either Rome or any other part of Italy. The reigning Sovereign of the time, Pius IX, retired into the Vatican palaces and adjoining gardens and never emerged, considering himself a "prisoner" to the end of his life. His three immediate successors—Leo XIII, Pius X, and Benedict XV—likewise remained penned up in this tiny enclave throughout their pontificates. Although the newly created Italian nation, with its capital now established at Rome, offered to pay an indemnity and even deposited liberal sums regularly to the Vatican's credit, the Popes refused to touch this money.

Some Catholics early recognized that the Vatican's loss of temporal power in Italy was, in reality, a blessing in disguise for the Church. At the very least the hierarchy at Rome could thereafter concentrate on religious matters and not be concerned with day-by-day government of a large area. But officially the Vatican was to mourn the loss of the Papal States for almost six decades. It went further. In an attempt to sabotage the democratic process in Italy, the famous Papal decree called *Non expedit* explicitly forbade all good Catholics to vote in national elections.

The major effect of this ruling was exactly the opposite of what was hoped. It virtually insured the continued rule of an anticlerical government in Italy. For a good fifty years, from 1870 to the close of World War I, Catholic influence was negligible in the government of a country which counted itself 99 percent Catholic. Italians might still go to mass regularly and even line up for confession, but when it came to ordering their national way of life at the polls they displayed a remarkable freedom from ecclesiastical pressure. Just as the Church was officially disestablished, so were the schools secularized. One could now be born, be educated, marry, die, and be buried in Catholic Italy without benefit of clergy. Gradually the absurdity of *Non expedit* became apparent to the Vatican, and the rules were relaxed. But by that time it was too late; Benito Mussolini was on the threshold of power.

The Vatican and Italy finally made up their quarrel and signed, in 1929, the well-known Lateran Treaty. The Vatican agreed to accept a generous indemnity—which it invested with profit—and to waive all claims to the former Papal States.[4] In return Italy agreed to recognize not only the independence of the Vatican but also the special status, with accompanying privileges, of the Church in Rome and throughout the peninsula.

[4] By this time the Roman hierarchy had become convinced that the last thing the Vatican wanted was the responsibility of governing laymen. At one point in the negotiations the Italians actually offered to include in Vatican territory a slice of the populous Roman quarter of Trastevere, where incidentally many citizens in the postwar years have voted Communist. But Cardinal Gasparri politely said, "No, thank you."

Mussolini badly needed the Lateran Treaty to bolster what was then only a mildly successful regime. The Duce was even willing to pose as a good Catholic and be photographed ostentatiously kneeling before an altar in order to curry favor with the Church. He went so far as to regularize in church his own common-law marriage, contracted when he was a disbelieving Socialist. He indulged in the flattery of imitation by organizing the Fascist Grand Council on lines similar to the Sacred College of Cardinals. The Vatican's chief negotiator, Cardinal Pietro Gasparri, sensed Mussolini's anxiety at this period and drove a hard bargain. Historians soon pronounced the Lateran Treaty a brilliant coup for the Church.

Not, however, until World War II had convulsed the European continent and had killed off Fascism could the Vatican really take advantage of the Lateran Treaty and come into her own again as a political and social force in the Italian peninsula. The challenge was now the threat of Communism; but the war had greatly weakened the normal secular institutions that might once have given effective battle. The Liberal party had been virtually wiped out by Mussolini. The Italian monarchy had so compromised itself with Fascism that it had been voted out of office in a national plebiscite. About the only organization capable of standing up to the encroaching Red tide was the Church.

Whereas formerly the Vatican had spurned the ballot box, the Church now went into elections with a vengeance. The chosen instrument in Italy was the Christian Democratic party, a political organization originally known as the Popular party. It was now reorganized with the active encouragement of the Vatican. American money, funneled into Italy through sometimes devious channels, contributed largely to the early financing of this party. A future footnote of history will doubtless record the curious fact that Protestant United States materially helped the Catholic Church to regain its privileged status in Italy. Clerical support for the Christian Democrats was—and continues to be today—undisguised. At one point the reigning Pope, Pius XII, ordered cloister nuns to emerge from their convents and vote the Christian Democratic ticket in a crucial election.

The Christian Democratic party has ruled Italy without interruption since the war, and seems likely to continue for some years to come. In fact, to many Italians it represents the only present alternative to Communist power. The average Italian voter, anticlerical in habit though he may be, is up against the general proposition that he must either cast his ballot for the Christian Democrats (or their allies) or run the risk of Communism. He may grumble against the *preti* (priests), but he votes for their candidates.

In most ways this Vatican-sponsored regime has achieved brilliant results. Italy has become a showcase for industrial progress. The annual increases in production are phenomenal. The lira has become one of the world's strongest currencies. Moreover, unlike regimes of the past with a theocratic stamp, Christian Democracy in Italy has acted with moderation even in the question of civil liberties. Speaking generally, freedom to speak and write has been as well observed in Italy during the postwar years as in most of the world. Movie censorship in Italy, for example, has been infinitely more liberal than in the United States.

All this has been due chiefly to the fact that, by and large, the men of the Vatican have been content to exercise indirect rather than direct control. To an outsider the government of Italy might seem today to have most of the attributes of a truly secular regime; actually, the general rules of conduct are laid down by the clergy. Only good practicing Catholics, trained to take their cue from the Church, have been permitted to rise to top leadership. The most powerful men in postwar Italy have not been the lay politicians with the top jobs but rather the Church's 280-odd Italian bishops. Meanwhile, the Pope himself has come to be accepted as a sort of fatherly overseer of the nation.

The form of government, of course, is republican. A President has been permitted to occupy the Quirinale Palace, once the summer home of the Popes, and a Chamber of Deputies has continued to sit at the Montecitorio Palace, once used as the Ministry of Posts in the Papal States. But this window dressing fools few Italians. Even the lowliest peasant somehow senses that ultimate power rests not in the Palazzo Chigi, where the Prime Minister has his office, or in Parliament, but rather in the enclave across the Tiber. And whereas the old Papal States comprised only a fraction of the Italian peninsula, the present area of effective control extends throughout the country, from the Tyrrhenian Sea to the Adriatic, from the Brenner Pass to the southernmost tip of Sicily.

Why have all these changes, not only in Italy but elsewhere in Europe and America, come about? Partly because of Communism. The successful postwar struggle against the Red tide brought enormous international prestige to the Church. In America to be a practicing Catholic has almost come to be accepted as a certificate of anti-Communism. Curiously enough, the Church's stand has probably helped it even behind the Iron Curtain. Should Eastern Europe soon be liberated from Communist rule, the Catholic Church is likely to emerge there more popular and stronger than ever.

Partly, too, it has been a simple matter of the passage of time. Fashions change in religions as well as in clothes, and sometimes with as little apparent reason. In some countries, such as England, Catholicism has become the religion of a certain elite. In their search for something with which to combat the threat of utter chaos many have turned toward the Church. To some troubled souls Catholicism has offered a longed-for authoritarianism in place of a disrupting and often chaotic freedom.

The psychological climate of the postwar years undoubtedly favored the growth of the Catholic Church. Widespread disillusion with the results of nineteenth-century liberalism had long since set in. Many intellectuals in France, England, and the United States were becoming converts. The literary production of Catholic authors in some countries was beginning to equal, in quality as well as quantity, that of non-Catholic writers. In matters of education, the Church had liberalized its methods and softened its attitudes. In these past years many worthy scholarly enterprises have been undertaken with the blessings of Rome.

Finally, the enhanced position of Catholicism in the world has come about because the Vatican has set about mending its once backward ways. A few of the old guard still dream of the days when Catholic Europe was at the center of world power. Some of the hierarchy even today think in terms of clerical-backed governments with state-supported churches. But most of the members of the Roman Curia, and certainly the present Pope, have long since realized that the world has changed. For better or worse, the secular state is here to stay, and the Church may be better for it. By and large the Vatican has decided to confine its methods to spiritual and moral persuasion.

Adversity forced Rome to do some deep thinking on how society might be ordered in an increasingly industrial and democratic society. In time the reactionary spirit of Pius IX, the long-reigning Pope of the nineteenth century, was discarded; in its stead came the progressive encyclicals of his successor, Leo XIII, considered by many the greatest of recent Pontiffs. Leo XIII produced, among other writings, the famous encyclical *Rerum novarum*, with its bill of rights for labor, and changed the Church's once strong predilection for a monarchical form of government into a partial endorsement of democracy.

Several decades elapsed before this change of attitude soaked into the consciousness of the world. As was perhaps normal, the thinking of Leo XIII influenced not so much his immediate successors as those later Popes who were seminary students at the time he was composing his great messages. Both the late Pius XII and the present John XXIII lived their most formative years during the pontificate of Leo XIII and were inspired by his ideas. The important encyclical of John XXIII entitled *Mater et Magistra*, issued in 1961 and discussed in Chapter VIII, can be considered in direct line of succession to Leo XIII's *Rerum novarum*. The net result is that the Vatican can no longer be considered a center of either reaction or conservatism.

The long reign of Pius XII (1939 to 1958) was decisive in putting Catholicism back into the mainstream of modern thought and action. One of this Pontiff's preoccupations in his later years was to reconcile religion and science. Among other acts, he welcomed to the Vatican all manner of international scientific conventions, even those dealing with spatial exploration and nuclear energy. And he himself unfailingly did them the honor of addressing them. The open conflict between science and Catholicism has virtually ceased to exist.

At the same time the era of mass tourism had a tremendous effect on the Vatican. Heretofore the Popes had always received Catholic pilgrims in audience, but now Pius XII began to hold audiences for tourists of whatever faith. The hitherto strict etiquette for dress was modified in response to an increasingly democratic age. A woman's head must still be covered and her dress must otherwise be modest, but it could now be of almost any color and her skirt could be short or long. Men calling at the Vatican were expected to wear dark suits, but successive majordomos of His Holiness soon recognized that in the age of air travel, with its weight restrictions, gentlemen could not be expected to carry white tie and tails, heretofore considered *de rigueur*. More, perhaps, as a result of the tourist rush than of any other factor, Pius XII became a world figure, as familiar to the masses as any other man of his period.

Popular figures of television, the cinema, radio, and sport were invariably welcomed at Papal audiences (and it mattered little what their personal reputations might be), at the same time that special greetings were in order for the dozens of legislators from many different countries who passed through Rome.

All manner of evidence bears testimony to the increased prestige of the Vatican today. For example, once upon a time rulers and prominent statesmen, especially those from non-Catholic countries, actually shunned meeting the Roman Pontiff. President Emile Loubet, of France, on his state visit to Rome some sixty years ago, deliberately did not call on the Pope, and his Italian hosts of the time did not protest. Kaiser Wilhelm II, when he visited Italy before World War I, stopped at Venice instead of proceeding to Rome, where the question of a Papal audience would certainly have arisen. Even ex-President Theodore Roosevelt declined to request an audience with the then Holy Father when he visited Rome on his famous post-election trip.

But nowadays such things simply do not occur. All the prominent visitors who pass through Rome, down to the lowliest cabinet minister of the newest African republic, want to see and talk with the Pontiff.[5] A list of present-day callers at the Apostolic Palace reads like the *Statesmen's Yearbook*. And it hardly matters whether the country represented is Catholic or Protestant, Moslem or Buddhist, pagan polytheistic or Confucian, whether it is pro-West or pro-East, aligned or nonaligned, or how it votes in the United Nations. The only exceptions are the representatives of out-and-out Communist regimes, but with them there is also no problem. They rarely if ever make official visits to Rome.[6]

The Vatican, at the present writing, has established diplomatic relations with some fifty nations, and the list is growing. Latest to sign up is Senegal, on the West Coast of Africa. Only about half of these nations could be called Catholic. The Scandinavian countries (with the exception of Finland) still decline to maintain missions at the Vatican, and so do the United States and Switzerland, although there is a Vatican mission at Berne. The centuries-

---

[5] The Quirinale, where the President of Italy has his office, and the Vatican now have a reciprocal understanding in the matter of guests. A statesman calling at the Quirinale is expected also to call on the Pope, and vice versa. This agreement was violated in only one recent instance, the visit of Prince Rainier (and Princess Grace) of Monaco, who called on the Pope but neglected to check in with the President of Italy.

[6] Much interest has been aroused at Rome at the prospect of a tour of Italy by the Soviet Prime Minister, Nikita Khrushchev, who has been invited (with no date set, however) to return the visit made in 1959 by President Gronchi to the U.S.S.R. Many in the Italian government see no objection to such a trip, but one of its grave difficulties would be the question of an audience with the Pope. Would Khrushchev want to see His Holiness? And if he did, would the Pope receive him?

old Protestant feeling that Church and State are separate and that the Vatican, being a religious entity, should not be entitled to the privileges of a temporal power still holds in those countries. But these considerations are brushed aside by the newer nations of Asia and Africa. They do not hesitate to exchange ambassadors and nuncios, even though in many cases (as, for example, Pakistan and Japan) their role seems perfunctory. Meanwhile, the Vatican has been voted membership in such nonpolitical international organizations as UNESCO, FAO, and the international atomic energy commission at Vienna.

For the celebration of the eightieth birthday of Pius XII in 1956 a total of fifty countries sent special missions. A few years later, when John XXIII passed his eightieth year, the missions numbered sixty-eight. Many nations that did not have diplomatic relations with the Holy See stepped forward to honor the Roman Pontiff. Among them were Israel, Madagascar, both the Congos, Korea, Iraq, the Ivory Coast, Kuwait, and the United States. Among the personalities heading the various missions were the prime ministers of Austria, Brazil, Ireland, and Italy, the Portuguese Minister of Justice, the Finnish Minister of Education, former Presidents of Lebanon and Switzerland, the President of the Belgian Senate, and the Argentine Secretary for Culture.

On this occasion, too, came a message of congratulations from an unusual quarter. Nikita Khrushchev conveyed through the Soviet Ambassador at Rome his wishes for the best health of His Holiness and for "the success of his noble aspirations to strive for peace on earth through continued negotiations of international problems." The Church is obviously not one of Khrushchev's favorite institutions. Yet his message was quite different in tone from the usual Communist attacks on the Vatican as a tool of capitalism, imperialism, colonialism, and feudalism.

But the most eloquent testimony to the Vatican's renewed prestige is the enthusiastic reaction to John XXIII's call for an ecumenical council in October, 1962. The response has been over-whelmingly favorable, even from sources formerly antagonistic toward Rome. Orthodoxy and Protestantism alike have risen to the idea that this Catholic council may further the cause of Christian unity. In the wake of John XXIII's call many Christian non-Catholic leaders of various countries have stopped off at Rome to pay their respects at the Apostolic Palace. The day is still far off when Christendom might again be united under one head. But meanwhile Rome is regaining at least part of her old commanding position in the Christian world.

II

THE SHELL
OF SOVEREIGNTY

The Vatican is a small but complicated place. It is composed of two chief entities, Vatican State and the Holy See, both of which are subdivided into numerous jurisdictions.

Apart from the fact that the Pope has supreme authority over both, Vatican State and the Holy See are separate and distinct. The Holy See, on the one hand, is the Church's religious headquarters at Rome, and as such will be described in Chapter III. Vatican State, on the other hand, is the shell of temporal sovereignty which, according to the hierarchy, is essential if the Church is to carry out its mission.

Generally when people refer to Vatican State they mean the diamond-shaped enclave to the rear and to the right of the Basilica of St. Peter's, which is the most conspicuous single building in the tiny state. Actually, however, this area constitutes less than half of all Vatican territory.

Besides the Vatican itself a score of extraterritorial properties totaling 180 acres are scattered in and near Rome. The 135-acre pontifical villa at Castel Gandolfo, in the Alban Hills, fifteen miles from Rome, forms a part of Vatican State. So does the Palace of the Apostolic Chancellery, in downtown Rome, as well as the vast Basilica of St. John Lateran, the complex of buildings attached to St. Paul's-Outside-the-Walls, the dozen or so buildings in which the sacred congregations and the various offices of the Holy See do their work, and, finally, the Villa Gabriel, on Janiculum Hill, which has been converted into a training school for Catholic missionaries. Vatican territory will soon be further enlarged by an extensive plot of land near Bracciano, north of Rome on the Cassian Way, which will serve as Radio Vatican headquarters.

In the main area of the Vatican is to be found the Apostolic Palace, a conglomeration of edifices built mostly during the Renaissance, containing an estimated fourteen hundred rooms. On the third floor of this palace, facing St. Peter's Square, is the Papal apartment of nineteen rooms, while other floors contain apartments of such other dignitaries as the Cardinal Secretary of State and the Master of Pontifical Ceremonies.

In this palace are also the great halls where the Pope receives in audience. These include the Clementine Hall, the Hall of the Consistory, and the Hall of the Congregations. The Secretariat of State is located on the second floor overlooking the courtyard of San Damaso, while the Vatican museums, containing perhaps the finest collection of ancient and classical art in the world, are housed in an extension of the big palace, with a separate entrance. The entire palace is punctuated by three main courtyards, plus a series of delightful smaller ones.

The "business district" of the Vatican lies to the far right of the piazza of St. Peter's, and is reached through the Gate of Santa Anna. The road here leads past the parish church and on to the grocery store, the post office, the car pool and garage, the bookstore, the press office, and the offices of *L'Osservatore Romano*. There are three cross-streets in this section—the Street of the Pilgrim, the Street of Typography, and the Street of Posts. To enter the "business district" the visitor has merely to state his business and can then proceed, without a written permit, up to a certain point.

The Vatican's front-door vehicular entrance is through the Gate of the Bells, directly to the left of the atrium of St. Peter's itself.[1] This entrance leads, eventually, to the Apostolic Palace and the Secretariat of State. Dignitaries calling on the Pope or his Secretary of State come through this gate, after which their cars must circle around the rear of St. Peter's and then enter a series of narrow, one-way underpassages to reach the Court of San Damaso. At this gate written permits, signed by a Vatican authority, are normally required.

This entrance also leads to the new area of the Vatican, that part of the hill which the Pope acquired as a result of the Lateran Treaty. All the Vatican's new buildings, most of them of neo-classical design with high ceilings and long corridors, are here, including the governor's office, the studios of Radio Vatican, the Ethiopian College, and the railroad station, now converted into a warehouse.

There is no strictly residential part of the Vatican. Members of the Pope's official family generally live in the Apostolic Palace. Officers of the Swiss Guard have apartments in the "business district." A half-dozen cardinals make their homes in the Palace of the Sacred Congregation of the Holy Office, a brooding edifice just off St. Peter's Square. Altogether nine cardinals live within the Vatican. The canons of St. Peter's have their own living quarters in the Sacristy, a beautiful old building to the left of the Basilica itself.

Three apartment buildings have been erected in the new area to relieve the Vatican's housing shortage. Even so, only seven hundred of the Vatican's one thousand citizens have found living quarters within the premises.[2] Some Vatican citizens, especially

[1] There are three other vehicular entrances which can be opened in case of need. One little-used gate, high on Vatican Hill, is for the special use of the Pope on those occasions when he wants to go or come without passing through the crowded piazza below. The busiest entrance is the Bronze Door, for pedestrians only, which leads to the Scala Regia of Bernini, up various stairways, and into courtyards, and finally to the reception halls of the Palace.

[2] The Vatican's population has almost doubled in thirty years. In 1929, when the state was founded, it was 532.

those who lead an active social life, prefer to live outside, if for no other reason than that the Vatican's gates are shut at 11 P.M. A resident wishing to go to the theatre or opera in Rome must first ask permission and then make special arrangements to return after eleven. Similarly, a dinner guest in a Vatican household must leave before the appointed closing hour.

The Apostolic Palace is one of the most beautifully furnished and decorated edifices in the world, but this beauty does not prevail in the various private apartments. Centuries ago the Princes of the Church were the setters of style and connoisseurs of taste, but nowadays nondescript Victorian seems to be the dominant style.

The furniture of these Vatican homes is likely to come from the giant warehouse known as the Floreria, or flower shop, although it has not functioned as such within the memory of living man. Located a few steps down from the San Damaso Court, the Floreria contains everything that could conceivably have been needed to decorate a home a century or two ago. It has fancy chandeliers and red damask to hang on the walls, curving divans for the center of a room and mirrors large enough to cover the side of a building. Over much of it lingers a heavy coating of gilt. Here have been deposited from time immemorial the outworn possessions of numerous cardinals and Popes. Among the prize exhibits is a deer's head with large horns that once decorated the private library of Pius XII. John XXIII, when he took possession of the Papal apartments, ordered it quickly removed and sent it to the Floreria.

One striking physical aspect of the Vatican is the great number of churches and chapels in the area. Besides St. Peter's, which can easily hold thirty thousand people, there are the parish Church of St. Anna; the Church of St. Pellegrino, oldest of the group; the Church of St. Stephen of the Abyssinians; the Church of St. Martin of the Swiss, which serves as a chapel for the Swiss Guards;[3]

[3] The Vatican has three Guards Units—the Swiss, the Palatine, and the Noble Guards. The Swiss Guards, about ninety in number, are recruited in

the Church of St. Sebastian for the Gendarmery; and Santa Maria in Camposanto, known as the "Teutonic Church," and sometimes used by the German contingent of the Vatican.

There are also numerous chapels. The Sistine Chapel is used not only on high solemn occasions but for conclaves in which a Pope is elected. Within the Apostolic Palace itself are the Paolina and Mathilda chapels; the Chapel of Nicholas V; and the Pope's private chapel, dedicated to the Virgin of Czestochowa, of Poland. The Jesuits who run the Vatican radio also have a chapel, while individual cardinals living inside the Vatican almost invariably have chapels in their quarters.

The Vatican has three cemeteries. The Teutonic cemetery at the left of the Gate of the Bells is small and rarely used nowadays unless a German prelate has expressed a wish to be buried there. Another, this one tiny, is found in the courtyard of the offices of L'Osservatore Romano. It cannot now be used. The third, which is still in use, is under the Church of St. Anna. Only Popes are now buried in the vaults or crypts of St. Peter's itself.

Vatican State has some but not all the characteristics of a sovereign state. As a result of the Lateran Treaty, it can confer citizenship, issue passports, coin money, maintain its own postage system, and is exempt from the penalties of the Italian customs system. Vatican citizens are not subject to Italian taxes on their income, and Vatican State pays neither taxes nor assessments to the Italian or Roman governments. In times of war Vatican personnel as well as all bishops are assured access across Italian territory to the Papal domain.

Some of these prerogatives of the independent state are of limited value. For example, Italian coinage is much more generally used in the Vatican than is Papal coinage (the two have the same value). Freedom from customs regulations has sometimes proved

---

Switzerland for three-year periods and serve with pay at the Vatican full time. The Palatine Guards are not paid. They are generally workers from the streetcar or bus lines of Rome. The Noble Guards come, of course, from the Papal nobility of Rome and are not paid.

an embarrassment. For a few years after the last war, it was easy for visitors to pick up cartons of American cigarettes in the Vatican and sell them for twice the cost in Italian territory. This led to considerable popular criticism and Vatican authorities at length decided to ration items known to be sold more cheaply inside than outside the area. Today most Vatican prices tend to conform to Italian prices.

The Vatican has its own police force, the Gendarmery, recently enlarged to about 150. These young men are recruited principally from small towns and farms in the Alban Hills. But so great are the crowds in St. Peter's Square on important occasions that Italian police are regularly asked to lend a helping hand. Until a few years ago the Vatican had a small jail, but its only occupant was a monsignor caught trafficking illegally in money. He escaped after only a few days, and some time later the jail was closed.

The Vatican is not self-sufficient, and could never hope to be, either in goods or services. A Vatican housekeeper can buy most of her groceries inside the premises, but for such essentials as kitchen equipment, linens, and clothes she must go to neighboring Italy. Water and power come from Rome's sources. The sewerage system empties into the Roman sewers. The greater part of Vatican personnel (as distinguished from Vatican citizens) lives outside the Leonine Walls. Even though the rights and privileges of the Vatican are spelled out in the Lateran Treaty, Vatican State could scarcely exist without the good will of the Italian state.

The government of Vatican State is ostensibly simple. The Pope in theory delegates his powers of absolute monarch to a governing committee of three cardinals, who in turn nominate a governor. Under the governor come the administration of the museums, the maintenance of the Apostolic Palace and other buildings (except for St. Peter's, which is under special jurisdiction), and the management of such facilities as the post office, the gardens and nurseries, the grocery store (called the *Annona*, meaning market in Latin), and the car pool and garage. The governor also has at his disposal a good-sized legal office, a small staff of accountants, and a registry.[4] In practice, however, the system of government in Vatican State rarely conforms to the theory.

In its thirty or more years of existence Vatican State has had only one governor, and he ruled only for a short period before the last World War. The office still exists, however, and is still listed in the *Pontifical Yearbook*.

As for the governing committee of cardinals, it too has seldom functioned according to plan. Early in his pontificate Pius XII named two cardinals to the committee, but never named the third member. The chairman was Cardinal Nicola Canali, who governed actively for a few years after the last war and became the most powerful member of the Roman Curia. As time passed Cardinal Canali became enfeebled, in mind as well as in body, and was increasingly unable to perform his duties. Since, however, nobody is ever retired for incapacity at the Vatican, he remained the nominal chairman.

Meanwhile a Papal nobleman, Count Pietro Enrico Galeazzi (see Chapter IV), had become a close and trusted collaborator of the late Pope. A lay architect and engineer by profession, his job was merely that of director of the Vatican's technical services, or, in general, overseer of maintenance work. But because he had easy and immediate access to Pius XII, Count Galeazzi became the virtual governor of Vatican State, with more unsupervised power than a real appointee.

This situation continued until the death of Pius XII in 1958. His successor, John XXIII, brought back some measure of clerical supervision by naming Cardinal Domenico Tardini, his Secretary of State, as a sort of overseer. Finally, with the deaths of both Tardini and Canali in the late summer of 1961, the present Pope

---

[4] From this latter office emerge some curious statistics from time to time. For example, a total of twelve passports was issued to Vatican citizens during the year 1961. Another item: while deaths among the Vatican citizens have averaged around fifty a year, births average only one every five or six years. One baby was born inside the Vatican during 1954, another in 1960, both to Swiss Guard officers.

was at long last able to appoint a full-fledged committee of cardinals, this time headed by Cardinal Amleto Cicognani, successor to Tardini as Secretary of State. But even this committee has conspicuously failed to nominate a governor. Count Galeazzi, though his power has been severely curtailed, remains the highest-placed layman at the Vatican.

Although the failure to name a real governor over the years probably stems from clerical reluctance to delegate any major power to laymen, the job is eminently that of a layman supervising the work of other laymen.

True, a few menial and clerical services at the Vatican are performed by members of religious societies. The Vatican telephone system, for example, is run by the friars of the Little Work of Divine Providence. The Vatican pharmacy is operated by a group of religious, known as the "Do Good Brothers," who also run a hospital on a nearby island in the Tiber which became famous during the last war as a hiding place for men wanted by the Nazi occupation forces. Still another group of religious, the Salesians, known also as the Sons of St. John Bosco, are bookkeepers, typesetters, and linotypists. They print the many secret and confidential documents of the Vatican and also run the administration of *L'Osservatore Romano*. A group of nuns, known as the "Sisters of Tapestry," specialize in the mending and restoration of the many hundred elaborate and precious tapestries that adorn the walls of the Apostolic Palace, while a few other sisters do nursing service, generally for aging and ailing prelates, within the Vatican.

Otherwise the employees of the Vatican State are all laymen. They include the policemen and firemen,[5] the carpenters and masons, the gardeners and ditch diggers, the painters and mechan-

[5] The Vatican has a staff of fifteen firemen, who, however, have never been called upon to put out a major fire. Years ago the Apostolic Chancellery, on the other side of the Tiber, was heavily damaged by fire, but this was handled by the Rome fire department. The only disaster of any proportion at the Vatican during recent times came during the thirties when the roof of the library fell in.

ics, the garbage collectors and street cleaners, the lawyers, the sales clerks, the stenographers.

The maintenance of law and order is not a major problem of Vatican government. There has never been a holdup on Vatican premises and there has been only one recorded instance of housebreaking within recent years. Picking pockets is fairly common inside St. Peter's, especially on crowded feast days, but this is the work of outsiders, and is usually dealt with by the Italian police force. The nearest the Vatican has come in modern times to witnessing murder came a few years back when an angered Swiss Guard wounded his commanding officer in the hip.

Nor is alcohol much of a problem. Most Vatican residents, from the Pope down, take wine with their meals, but cocktail parties are virtually unknown and heavy drinking is extremely rare. There is only one public bar within the Vatican, and it closes at dusk.

The main duties of the Vatican Gendarmery consist of controlling passage through the two gates and regulating traffic inside the territory. Once this was not much of a problem, but now practically all the highly placed clerics who work at the Vatican have cars, generally Fiats, and these, when added to the Cadillacs and the Mercedes-Benzes of the diplomats accredited to the Holy See, not to mention the private vehicles of visiting cardinals, create a busy stream of traffic inside the Leonine Walls. A large car park has recently been provided, and there is talk of limiting parking time. Even so, traffic jams are rare, and there has been only one minor accident since the war. Incidentally, the Vatican is still without traffic lights; instead, gendarmes are stationed at virtually every turn.

The care and maintenance of the buildings and grounds of Vatican State present special problems and consume a large part of the energy of the laymen employed by the governor's office. Most of the buildings are old and need periodic repairs. Floors must be redone, decorations restored, furnishings renewed, elevators and lighting replaced. The twelve-centuries-old Leonine Walls, sturdy as they are, must be patched from time to time. The piazza in front of St. Peter's as well as the encircling colonnades are heavily taxed by the vast crowds that gather there on big occasions; so are the audience rooms of the Apostolic Palace. They all must undergo frequent repairs.

Vatican State is not plagued by the usual problems of an industrialized society. Economic pressures are virtually nonexistent. There is rivalry, of course, among the clerics, and the stakes are high. A job near the throne may lead to a cardinal's hat, and membership in the Sacred College of Cardinals can eventually lead to the highest office. But at least the livelihood is secure.

Incomes, it is true, are low. Even a cardinal earns only 400,000 lire (about $645) monthly, while the commander of the Swiss Guards earns about $340. An editor of L'Osservatore Romano receives 117,500 lire, or a little less than $200, per month.

But expenses are also low. The only tax is an annual levy of 300 lire (less than 50 cents) a person. Since no real estate can be privately owned inside the Vatican, residents are usually assigned apartments. For these the rents are nominal, amounting generally to 4 percent of salary. Thus a secretary of one of the twelve sacred congregations of the Holy See, with the rank of monsignor, who draws a salary of about $300 monthly, would be expected to pay rent of $12 a month. The sum, of course, is barely sufficient to cover the normal upkeep.

The interests inside the Vatican also differ from those of the society outside. Inside the Leonine Walls people discuss and argue about such subjects as saints and sinners, visions and miracles, dogmas and rites, virtues and vices. Shop talk consists of what the new Pope is doing, how various causes leading to beatification and canonization are faring, and the prospects of a new consistory for the naming of more cardinals. A ceremonial occasion provides much grist for the conversational mill for days to follow. How did the Sistine Chapel choir sing? What was the timbre of the Pope's voice? Did he seem tired? How many cardinals were present and how many were too sick to come?

The pace of life inside the Vatican is, indeed, slow; but there is also an intensity that is matched only rarely outside. Perhaps the nearest equivalent can be found in the atmosphere of a university. The absence of the normal distractions of modern life releases time for sustained thinking. Most of the clerics spend their evenings among their books. Not everybody, but almost everybody, can read and speak several languages. Well-stocked libraries are the rule. The perennial best-sellers at the Vatican remain the writings of the Fathers and the Doctors of the Church.

III

CORPORATE
STRUCTURE

The Holy or Apostolic See at Rome is the central headquarters of Roman Catholicism. In this hallowed city, according to Catholic belief, Peter, primate among the Apostles and holder of the keys, established the Church, and here all but a few of Peter's 263 successors have reigned as Vicar of Christ on earth.[1]

The Holy See functions mainly on the religious level, although a few of its branches are also concerned with mundane affairs. It is with the Holy See, and not the Vatican, that some fifty nations of the world now maintain diplomatic relations. It is the Holy See, and not Vatican State, that maintains a diplomatic corps of some forty apostolic nuncios and delegates either stationed in various world capitals or, as in the case of black Africa, roving about their territory.

But, most important, it is the Holy See that regulates the religious life of every Catholic and makes decisions that affect the faithful the world over. The Catholic stand on birth control, the Catholic approach to Protestantism, how the Church feels about

[1] The question of whether Peter the Apostle was ever really in Rome has perturbed historians for centuries.

Communism must in the end all be defined at the Holy See. Here too all manner of doctrinal questions, ranging from the wording of the catechism to the validity of baptism, are decided. At the Holy See, Church policy and practice are formulated.

In its smallness Vatican State has a certain Graustarkian quality; but the Holy See is both large and sprawling. While the Pope and his Secretary of State live and work in the Apostolic Palace, the various other offices are spread through the city of Rome. Of the Holy See's twelve ministries—or sacred congregations—only four are located in the Vatican proper, and these are the least important. The Holy See's courts are also removed from the Vatican.

The headquarters staff of the Church is normally composed of around twenty-five hundred persons, almost all of them clerics. Only a fraction of these are Vatican citizens. All the cardinals, according to the Lateran Treaty, have a right to a Vatican passport, and so do the Holy See's diplomats, but otherwise a Spaniard or an American or a French prelate assigned to Rome to work in one of the sacred congregations normally retains his own nationality and keeps his own passport.

While all the nations of the Occident and many of Africa and Asia are represented at the Holy See, the overwhelming majority of the headquarters staff is Italian. Virtually all the top posts are held by Italian prelates. The heads of ten of the twelve congregations, for example, are Italian, while the two congregations with non-Italian heads are of relatively minor importance. This Italian preponderance is doubtless due mainly to geography, but there are other factors too. A high official of the Vatican once explained to this writer that Italians were much less prone to error in doctrinal matters than were other nationalities. The great heresies that the Church has had to face came from Africa or Asia or northern Europe, but never from Italy.

There are perhaps two or three hundred Germans working in the Holy See. Some of them are holdovers from the pontificate of Pius XII, who valued thorough and exacting theologians. The French are much less numerous and often give the impression of being unhappy at Rome. They dislike the food and the language and, more important, usually consider the Italian approach to religious problems as not sufficiently intellectual. A few Spaniards, Portuguese, and Latin Americans are also on the staffs of the various congregations, but they do not seem to be active. There is a scattering of Asians and Africans, mainly representing the Eastern rites.

As for the Americans, there are not over twenty or thirty clerics in all. For the first time in history the Curia recently had an American cardinal, Aloisius Joseph Muench, who, however, was too ill to play an important role. He died in February, 1962. The highest-placed American prelate at the Vatican today is Monsignor Francis Brennan, of Pennsylvania, deacon of the Sacred Rota, one of the Holy See's ecclesiastical courts.

The Americans at the Holy See seem not so much unhappy as uncomfortable. A standard complaint is that they must wear cassocks even in the street.[2] The regulations of the Vicariate of Rome for the conduct of priests, especially the rule against attending public spectacles, irk them. They cannot quite understand an Italian clergy which avoids any social contact with the laity. They are a little shocked at the gossip, some of it malicious, in Vatican circles. All in all, the Latin approach to Catholicism is slightly disturbing to American clerics.

At the head of the Holy See is, of course, the Pope. He is not

---

[2] The Council of Trent, in the mid-1500's, made the wearing of a special type of dress obligatory for priests but did not lay down either its color or its shape. In the 1700's the monks' habits of the Middle Ages, copied from the dress of the poor of those times, came more or less to be accepted even for the secular clergy, but the final establishment of the long robe or cassock, reaching down to the ankle, was fixed in the last century by Pius IX. He stipulated that priests should wear such clothes both in and out of the Church. This ruling has been relaxed for the clergy in many non-Catholic countries. In the United States, of course, the Catholic clergy wear black suits when not officiating in the churches. On and off an argument rages at the Vatican over the desirability of modernizing the priestly dress. Many nuns insist that they cannot properly go about their duties dressed in medieval habits. This matter has even been suggested as a proper topic for the ecumenical council.

only first among bishops but all other bishops come under his direct jurisdiction. Theoretically the Pontiff has absolute power over the Church. No decree is valid without his approval. He can write and unwrite constitutions. He can obey or ignore precedent and set aside tradition. He can proclaim dogmas on his own and change discipline without consultation. Only two things he cannot do: he cannot name his successor nor can he bind the successor by his acts. In practice, the Pope is supposed to consult either the bishops of the Church or the Sacred College of Cardinals on most important matters, and he generally does so on theological questions; but on questions of high policy the consultation often comes only after the Pope has arrived at his own decision. For example, Pope John XXIII decided to convene the ecumenical council without seeking the prior counsel of the Curia cardinals.

This writer once asked a Vatican prelate what would happen if a Pope were to lose his mind and reason. What with the tendency to elect increasingly older Popes, this would appear a not impossible eventuality. When a cardinal such as Canali becomes incapacitated, he can be quietly deprived of his power if not of his position. But Popes are elected for life; there is no provision either for recall or for enforced abdication. Nor for that matter is there any machinery for setting up a regency. Convening the College of Cardinals to take over the direction of the Church would be considered illegal. A council of the Church, which once might have resolved such a question, can now be called only by the Pope, who can also decide what subjects to consider. The prelate's answer to the question came back:

"Well, the Good Lord seems to protect the Church from such a catastrophe. Popes just apparently do not lose their mind or reason. But should the impossible happen, I believe the Vatican bureaucracy would act as an effective brake against rash or embarrassing acts."

Aside from the Pope and the twelve sacred congregations, the Holy See consists of three apostolic tribunals (ecclesiastical courts) and five departmental offices, which exercise legislative, judicial and executive power respectively over Church affairs. The corporate structure of the Holy See can be charted as follows:

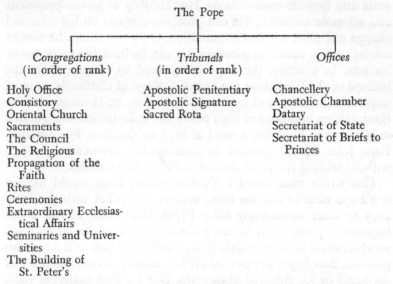

The Pope

Congregations (in order of rank)	Tribunals (in order of rank)	Offices
Holy Office	Apostolic Penitentiary	Chancellery
Consistory	Apostolic Signature	Apostolic Chamber
Oriental Church	Sacred Rota	Datary
Sacraments		Secretariat of State
The Council		Secretariat of Briefs to
The Religious		Princes
Propagation of the Faith		
Rites		
Ceremonies		
Extraordinary Ecclesiastical Affairs		
Seminaries and Universities		
The Building of St. Peter's		

Some would alter this chart by inserting the College of Cardinals between the Pope and the congregations, but actually the cardinals operate as a group only when the Apostolic See is vacant. It therefore exercises no real legislative or executive function, merely furnishing personnel to the other organisms. (See Chapter IX.) Each of the congregations, tribunals, and offices is normally headed by a cardinal except for the Sacred Rota, which is usually headed by a prelate of lesser rank.

The sacred congregations, which are more important than the tribunals or offices, are in effect a series of interlocking directorates. The system of congregations dates from the late sixteenth century, although from time to time it has been revised. Most Curia cardinals sit in four or five congregations; some may sit in as many as nine. Many cardinals and bishops of sees far removed from Rome are listed as members of the various congregations, although they can seldom attend meetings. Cardinal Francis Spellman, Archbishop of New York, for example, is on the Sacred Congregation of the Consistory. Thus inevitably the real power over the congregations devolves on the Curia cardinals who can attend meetings regularly.

A sacred congregation at the Vatican is headed by a cleric, normally a cardinal, called the prefect. His chief executive officer, called the secretary, normally has the rank of monsignor. Exceptions are found, however, in the first three congregations, where the Pope himself has retained the post of prefect. In these cases the office of secretary is held by a cardinal, whose chief executive officer is an assessor. The secretary, or the assessor, as the case may be, is generally in line for promotion to the Sacred College of Cardinals.

The prefect or (in the first three congregations) the secretary generally has on his staff a committee of cardinals who meet regularly and decide by vote on questions brought before them. Each congregation contains a group of consultants of lesser rank, who also meet regularly and vote on matters to be passed up to the cardinals. Other personnel varies with the congregation. The Holy Office, for example, has a group called "qualifiers." The Sacred Congregation for the Propagation of the Faith has numerous special committees. In general, each congregation has working for it a number of clerics who specialize in narrow fields. One may be an authority on sin, another on baptism, a third on lay-clerical relations, a fourth on Mary the Virgin. Congregations differ greatly in size. The Congregation of the Religious, one of the biggest, has something like 250 clerics on its staff; the work of the Congregation of Ceremonies, on the other hand, is practically all done by two people, supervised by a cardinal.

The three most important congregations—those of which the Pope is the prefect—are the Holy Office, the Consistorial Congregation, and the Congregation for the Oriental Church. Of these the Holy Office far outranks the others. Known originally as the

Board of the Inquisition, it was founded in 1542 by Pope Paul III, on the heels of the Reformation, as the Catholic agency to combat and stamp out the Protestant heresy. It is the oldest, most of the others having been established in 1588.

The Holy Office guards Catholic doctrine, decides cases of faith and morals, protects dogma, examines and condemns movements and ideas dangerous to the faith, and judges some reading matter. The Holy Office also, together with the Pontifical Biblical Committee, interprets the Holy Scriptures or at least determines how not to interpret them. (In this field the Holy Office's pronouncements are far from clear; there is apparently no accepted Catholic interpretation of the Old Testament.) Recent pronouncements issuing from the Holy Office include a warning against the use of psychoanalytical examinations for candidates to the priesthood. Another has to do with the secrecy of the confession. "Not even the Pope," the Holy Office decreed, "with his high authority, is in a position to free the confessor of his strict obligation to keep absolute secrecy."

The Holy Office is by its nature the pillar of Catholic conservatism, and resistant to change. Its chief—in this case, the cardinal-secretary, not the cardinal-prefect—is almost invariably a member, if not the leader, of the "conservative" wing of the Vatican. Nevertheless, the Holy Office has undergone certain changes in attitude in recent decades, perhaps because its strictures no longer have the effect they once had. Burning at the stake is out of fashion. Interdiction, the dread instrument of the Middle Ages that closed all churches in certain areas, is no longer tried. Formal excommunication is infrequently attempted and not always effective.

In 1949 the Holy Office decreed that Communists could no longer receive the sacraments, but this has been practically unenforcible at the village level in Italy, for which country it was primarily intended. Numerous parish priests have virtually ignored it, with or without the connivance of their bishops. Who is to say for certain who is a Communist and who is not? Furthermore, if a known Communist wants to have his children baptized or married in the Church, isn't it better to maintain contact rather than break off relations entirely? As for heresies, the last time the Holy Office pronounced against one was at the turn of the century, when modernism was read out of the Church. Since then the word "heretic" has come to be used less and less. The new, less opprobrious term, favored by John XXIII, is "separated brother."

The famous Index of prohibited books has also by and large lost its effect. One small office could not possibly review the vast number of books now published in all languages of the world, let alone decide which should be deemed dangerous for the soul. The Index section of the Holy Office now seems most concerned with condemning books that some Catholics might assume were approved, but that actually contain error. Thus, *La Vie de Jésus*, a little-known recent work by Jean Steinmann, a French author, was recently put on the Index with the explanation that while certain parts of it undoubtedly came from Catholic sources, the whole of it constituted an "adventurous interpretation."

The Index, it has been suggested, may either be changed or possibly even dropped as one result of the ecumenical council. In these days of mass entertainment media such as the cinema and television, it is infinitely more important to place a watch over these means of communication than over books.

The Consistorial Congregation is essentially the personnel branch of the Church. It constitutes new dioceses and church provinces, proposes bishops and apostolic administrators, and receives and examines the periodic reports of the bishops. Again, however, certain exceptions must be noted. For example, bishops in mission territory are nominated and consecrated by the Congregation for the Propagation of the Faith, while bishops for the Oriental rites are named (always with the consent of the Pope) by the Congregation for the Oriental Church. In certain special cases, too, the Secretariat of State can name bishops.

The Congregation for the Oriental Church, the third body headed by the Pope, is the newest, dating only from 1917. This is the governing body for the nine million or more communicants of the Oriental rites, most of whom are in the Middle East. It not only handles relations between the Latin and Eastern rites but operates independently of the other congregations in the matter of naming Eastern rite bishops, instituting Eastern dioceses, running Eastern rite seminaries, and supervising Eastern orders. The Congregation for the Oriental Church has lately assumed greater importance by virtue of John XXIII's special interest in the Near East. Should any part of the Orthodox Church join Catholic ranks it would be even more important.

The Sacred Congregation of the Religious has jurisdiction over the Church's 180 male and 1,150 female orders, with their 160,000 and 370,000 members respectively. The heads of the Church's religious orders have less hierarchical rank or administrative power than the prelates of the Curia, and thus, from the standpoint of Church government, are less important. Members of the orders can rise to exalted rank, but ordinarily do not. However, under the present Pope some six prelates who were monks have been appointed to the Sacred College. A Jesuit, a Benedictine, a Franciscan, a Dominican, a Salesian, and a member of one of the lesser Oriental Church's orders have all received red hats. A few Popes were originally monks (Gregory the Great was a Benedictine), but the present tendency is to raise to the Papacy only those who were members of the secular clergy.

Many but not all of the orders maintain headquarters in Rome, although not in the Vatican; and a few of the orders' superiors, including the general of the Jesuits, have the right to see the Pope at infrequent but stated intervals. The orders furnish much personnel, all of it free, for the Holy See. The Jesuits, for example, man the Vatican Radio. The Dominicans, whose specialty is preaching, always furnish the chief theologian of the Sacred Palace.

The Congregation of Rites functions mainly as the organism which judges the validity of claims to beatification and canonization. Much energy and time are consumed before a saint is proclaimed and the name inscribed in the official hagiography of the

Church. Even before the case reaches Rome, the diocese in which the proposed saint was born, lived, and died must consider the matter. The average time between the introduction of a cause at Rome and its conclusion is estimated to be around forty years.[3] Some causes move relatively fast, others remain in the files for decades, sometimes for centuries. These trials are all secret; in fact, only after one hundred years have elapsed can some details of them be disclosed. Nevertheless frequent communiqués of the activities of the Congregation of Rites are released, as for example:

Yesterday, in the Apostolic Palace of the Vatican the Congregation of Rites met to discuss the heroic nature of the virtues of the Servant of God Maria Fortunata Viti, a nun of the Order of St. Benedict. She was born at Vereli, Italy, on February 10, 1827. She lost her mother at the age of fifteen and had to take charge of a numerous family. To keep them she had to do all kinds of work, and was also a servant to an honest family in that place. In 1851 she entered the Benedictine convent of Vereli as a convert, and the sanctity of her life was well known. Some years later, when running after some thieves who had entered the convent and had made off with loot, she was struck down by heart and liver disease, from which she had suffered all her life, although she had concealed her sufferings in the deep humility with which she dedicated herself to her tasks. She died on November 19, 1922.

The Congregation of Rites also maintains a section devoted to liturgical studies.

To the Congregation for the Propagation of the Faith, another of the bigger ministries of the Holy See, is entrusted the exclusive care of all mission territory. Thus a missionary bishop reports to the prefect of this congregation rather than to the chief of the Consistorial Congregation. Mission territory now covers a large part of Asia and most of Africa, but is constantly shrinking as local churches in the underdeveloped areas show signs of wanting to stand on their own feet and be treated in the same manner as the older Catholic communities. The Congregation for the Propaga-

---

[3] The process of proclaiming saints is further discussed in Chapter VII.

tion of the Faith, often called by its Latin name of "Propaganda Fide," is thus roughly in the same position as the British Colonial Office; with the disappearance of empire it will also disappear. Even so, the Catholic population of the mission territory grew from thirty million in 1950 to forty-five million in 1960.

It is Propaganda Fide which has had to meet and deal with the troublesome problem of colonialism. The Church's original mission territory was largely in what, until only a few years ago, were colonies of various European nations. With the retreat of colonialism, the Church embarked on a policy of increasing emphasis on native participation. Native religious art was promoted, and the creation of a native priesthood was encouraged.

Here Propaganda Fide ran into difficulties: Catholic powers like Portugal and France, with close relations to the Vatican, frowned on the idea of too many native priests and bishops. Even so, notable progress has been made. The seminaries of mission territory are more and more in the hands of the native hierarchy. Between 1930 and 1957 (the latest year for which such statistics are available) the number of native-born priests in Asia, Africa, and the South Seas increased by around six thousand, while the number of European priests in these territories dropped by one third. In Asia now about half the Catholic priests are native born; in Africa, 16 percent are native born and the percentage is rising every year. In 1921 there was only one native bishop in all Asia and Africa; now there are 113, of whom 38 are in Africa, 75 in Asia. Such countries as Vietnam and Indonesia, not to mention Japan and the Philippines, now have their own hierarchy, and thus are no longer mission territory. Most of India was long ago taken from mission territory. All the African nations which were once French colonies now have their native hierarchy. One African and four Asians—an Indian, a Japanese, a Philippine, and a Chinese—are now members of the Sacred College of Cardinals.

Among the lesser congregations is that of Seminaries and Universities, which is in charge of education for the priesthood and supervises all universities directed by the secular clergy or by religious orders. Under this congregation come 128 centers of high studies, including 45 full-fledged universities. One recent decision of this body ordered the teaching of sociology in all seminaries. At the same time, the rule was laid down that all seminarians must study a language foreign to their own during summer vacation.

The Congregation of Sacraments, one of the biggest from the standpoint of personnel, has jurisdiction over the seven sacraments as administered in the Latin rite. Its work, to a layman, seems mainly technical. Among its recent decisions, for example, was one allowing certain dioceses suffering from a shortage of priests to use the services of young seminarians not otherwise fully qualified. This congregation also has a large commission dealing with marriages that, for one reason or another, were never consummated. The commission investigated in 1961 some five hundred such instances, passing on its findings to another branch of the Holy See, the Sacred Rota.

The Congregation of the Council was originally set up to enforce the elaborate and then novel provisions of the Council of Trent in the sixteenth century. It is mainly concerned with the discipline, behavior, and pastoral activity of the clergy. It also lays down rules for the management of Church finances and the administration of religious properties. There is some talk that this congregation may be discontinued after Vatican Council II. In its stead there would presumably be instituted another congregation to enforce the decisions of the new council, which in many ways will probably supersede the decisions of Trent.

Three congregations of the Holy See deal with matters far removed from religious or spiritual questions. One is the Congregation of Extraordinary Ecclesiastical Affairs. Its main function is to supervise negotiations between the Church and foreign powers. During the reigns of Pius XI (1922–1939) and Pius XII, many treaties were negotiated and concordats signed. But by and large these have proved unnecessary in those parts of the world where freedom of religion is fully recognized. The last negotiated concordat of the Holy See was that signed with Spain in 1954.

The Congregation of Extraordinary Ecclesiastical Affairs also frequently negotiates with foreign powers in questions of naming bishops. In nominating the heads of dioceses in Catholic countries like Spain, Portugal, France, and Italy, the Holy See must first obtain the concurrence of the government in the country concerned. In most cases, although not all, this consent is automatic.

The Congregation of Ceremonies, the smallest of the twelve, may seem relatively unimportant to outsiders, but its decisions and pronouncements are nevertheless anxiously watched not only by the Vatican prelates but by the diplomats accredited to the Holy See. The Congregation of Ceremonies determines such questions as precedence among the cardinals and other prelates. It decides who follows whom in processions, and who sits nearest or farthest from the Holy Father at solemn functions.

In the case of an ambassador arriving to present his credentials, the Congregation of Ceremonies also stipulates who is to meet and accompany His Excellency and how and where he will be received by the Supreme Pontiff. In some cases it is determined in advance exactly what each will say and what gifts will be exchanged.

When it comes to receiving the head of a state the Congregation of Ceremonies works overtime. If the visitor is Catholic the question arises whether he will genuflect and kiss the Pope's ring; and if he does, will photographs of this act be permitted? In the case of the late King of Italy, Vittorio Emanuele III, who paid two official visits to the Vatican, there was no genuflection. The Savoys were old political rivals of the Popes, whom they regarded as their earthly equals, and besides they were Masons. Nor was there genuflection when President Luigi Einaudi, also sturdily anticlerical, paid a visit to Pope Pius XII. But President Giovanni Gronchi, Einaudi's successor, a leftist but also a devout Catholic, not only went down on his knees before the Pope but was photographed so doing.

In the case of such Protestants as President Eisenhower or Queen Elizabeth, as well as all the Moslems that pass through Rome, the question of kneeling does not, of course, arise. The

President, in his call on John XXIII, wanted the ceremony simplified as much as possible, and so the protocol makers of both sides classified the visit as "unofficial."

The exact opposite took place when Elizabeth II came to Rome. Every detail of the Queen's visit was carefully decided in advance. For weeks before the event, protocol experts on both sides met to discuss particulars. The final result, issued in advance, was a detailed fifteen hundred word communiqué.

Seven Vatican cars would call on Her Majesty and His Royal Highness the Duke of Edinburgh and their suite at the appointed hour and transport them to the Vatican. They would be accompanied by a total of seven Secret Chamberlains of the Sword and Cloak as well as by Prince Leone Massimo, ranking member of Rome's Papal nobility and general superintendent of the Vatican Post Office, who would wear a full-dress uniform.

At the "border" between Italy and the Vatican the group would be met by, among others, Prince Carlo Pacelli, nephew of the former Pope Pius XII and Councilor General of the Vatican; a double guard of honor of the Swiss Guards; a company of the Palatine Guards; and a platoon of the Papal Gendarmery. Prince Pacelli would approach the royal car and greet Her Majesty, after which the royal procession would proceed through the Arch of the Bells and then around St. Peter's Basilica to San Damaso Court.

Here they would be greeted by the Majordomo to His Holiness and numerous other personages of the Papal court, including the Furrier of the Apostolic Palace, various bearers of the prized decoration the Golden Rose, the commanders of the Guards units, and numerous *bussolanti* and *sediari* ("throne bearers"). This ceremony would be accompanied by the sound of trumpets and band music.

At the entrance to the Papal apartments, which is the Clementine Hall, others, including the Pope's Master of the Chamber and the Secret Almoner of His Holiness, would greet the royal party. The suite of Her Majesty would then proceed down the long chain of anterooms to the Hall of the Noble Guard. From here the Queen and her consort would proceed to the Throne Room, there

to be formally presented to the Pontiff. The chair in which His
Holiness would sit and the chairs prepared for Her Majesty and
His Royal Highness were stipulated in the communiqué. The
speeches and the exchange of gifts completed, the Queen would
depart. The leave-taking from the Vatican would be almost as
complicated as the arrival; it, too, was fully covered.

The twelfth sacred congregation is called in Italian the *Reverenda Fabbrica di San Pietro*. Literally translated, this is the
"revered factory of St. Peter's." The Basilica of St. Peter's is something of an oddity among ecclesiastical edifices. It is not, for example, the parish church of the Vatican; the Church of St. Anna
serves that purpose. Nor is it the cathedral church of Rome; that
honor belongs to St. John Lateran. Nor is it the Pope's special
church or cathedral. Actually, the Popes have used St. Peter's
relatively seldom. Pius XII, for instance, descended into St. Peter's
only on special occasions; he almost never celebrated mass there
in his later years. On the other hand, John XXIII has appeared
there more frequently. In 1960 he assisted at the celebration of
mass at the high altar eight times. He took part in one of the forty
stations-of-the-cross ceremonies during Holy Week at St. Peter's,
to be followed on Easter Sunday by a pontifical high mass at which
he was the celebrant. He also presides at ceremonies inside the
basilica on the eve of the Feast of St. Peter and St. Paul, which
falls on June 29. On this occasion the Pope, accompanied by the
Swiss Guards, enters St. Peter's after dark and goes to the tomb
of the Apostle, where he blesses the palliums, circular bands of
white wool that the Holy Father gives to bishops as a visible sign
that he shares with them the supreme pastoral power.

In one year, John XXIII used the great nave of St. Peter's thirty-seven times for his mass audiences; there is no other place in the
Vatican where so many thousands can be accommodated. Canonizations are, of course, held in St. Peter's, as are the public consistories, which confer red hats upon the cardinals. St. Peter's is
also used for great Church occasions, such as the coronation and
the funeral of a Pope. St. Peter's will be the meeting place, too,

of the second Vatican Council. In substance, St. Peter's is a special basilica for the special use of the Holy See on high, solemn, and official occasions. It belongs neither to the diocese of Rome nor really to Vatican State; instead, it can be said to belong to the Church at large.

The chief prelate of St. Peter's is called the archpriest of the basilica, and he is assisted by a cathedral chapter of canons of various nationalities, including an American, Monsignor William A. Hemmick. Recent archpriests of St. Peter's have been Cardinal Eugenio Pacelli (later Pius XII), Cardinal Federico Tedeschini, and Cardinal Domenico Tardini. The present occupant of this high post is Cardinal Paolo Marella, a little-known prelate who is also assigned to the Secretariat of State.

The Congregation for the Revered Building of St. Peter's functions as a sort of overseer of the physical health of this great and historic edifice. As such the members of the congregation have much to worry about. As might be expected, most of the employees are laymen, experts in engineering and construction. This, in fact, is the only congregation of the Holy See in which laymen predominate.

The crowds of faithful and curious who now enter St. Peter's in the course of a year are many times greater than the crowds of any past period. The old edifice, built for the ages as it was, was still never meant to undergo such constant use. Moreover, great solemn functions now occur so frequently that the intervals between them are all too short for necessary repairs. Even so, during 1961 and 1962 considerable improvements were effected. For one thing, a new lighting system was installed. Most of the priceless art treasures of the basilica can now be seen in all their splendor. Cupolas, domes, statues, tombs, friezes, and other decorations,[4] once so hard

[4] The question of modesty in statuary and painting at the Vatican has disturbed various Popes, not to mention other less important dignitaries, and as a result "clean-up campaigns" have been waged from time to time. The most notable of these took place in the sixteenth century during the four-year reign of Paul IV, a Neapolitan Pope. He hired Daniele da Volterra, a well-known sculptor and painter, to paint over certain parts of the nude figures in

to make out, are now well illuminated. A new lighting system has also been prepared for great Papal functions. The figure of the Pope, both at the altar and on the throne, will now be outlined more clearly by floodlights, as will the cardinals who normally assist him at solemn functions.

St. Peter's now has replaced the organ in use for the past two centuries. Another improvement is a new elevator to take sightseers to the cupola. The great Chapel of the Confession, in the center of the crossing, from which arises the central altar with Bernini's bronze baldacchino over it, will also have a new seating arrangement. For the first time since 1888 the pavement of the atrium is to be replaced. The great bronze middle door of "Filarete," put up in 1433, will be cleaned, repaired, and outfitted with ball bearings so that it may be opened more easily. All in all, St. Peter's promises to have a new look for Vatican Council II. Besides caring for the basilica, the Congregation for the Revered Building of St. Peter's has one other chore: it operates a mosaic studio in the Vatican gardens.

Of the three tribunals of the Holy See the best known is the Sacred Rota, which is a court of first instance. This body sits as a regular law court, with the judges, called *uditori,* or "listeners," serving in rotation by threes. The Sacred Rota judges matters that the diocesan bishops are not competent to decide. Although in theory many cases may come before it, in actuality it now deals almost exclusively with requests for annulments. The participants in an annulment case are almost never allowed to appear in person before the Sacred Rota, whose sessions are always secret. Presumably long before the case has reached Rome the two parties have made their sworn declarations and been questioned. The cost

---

Michelangelo's frescoes of "The Last Judgment" in the Sistine Chapel. Two centuries later Clement XII, still not satisfied, ordered further clothing to be painted on Michelangelo's figures. Fig leaves were long ago placed on most of the Greek and Roman statuary in the Vatican museums. St. Peter's has also felt from time to time the effects of these campaigns.

of carrying a case to the Sacred Rota can be prohibitive, but the tribunal now has a "poor man's fund" with which it can assign lawyers to plead cases for those who otherwise could not afford it.

The Supreme Tribunal of the Apostolic Signature is a court of cardinals, which can be convened to support or reject the decisions of the Sacred Rota. In certain cases it can even review matters previously handled by the Holy Office. The third tribunal is the Apostolic Penitentiary, which judges cases of conscience and extraordinary sins. Inevitably there is some overlapping of jurisdiction, particularly in questions concerning marriage. The Holy Office, the Congregation of Sacraments, and the Sacred Rota all deal with one phase or another of marriage.

Of the five offices of the Holy See the Apostolic Chancellery is the oldest. In fact, before the system of congregations was set up the Chancellery was the place where all those questions now handled by the congregations were treated. In those days the Chancellery filled the vast square Renaissance palace off Corso Vittorio Emanuele, partly built by Bramante. But now the Chancellery's mission has been reduced to guarding the Church's official seal, and to distributing apostolic letters, Papal bulls, and the like. Most of the space in the old *palazzo* is now occupied by other Papal offices. Both the Apostolic Chamber and the Datary were important branches of the Papal government when the Pope enjoyed temporal rule, but now they have only minor importance. The same can be said for the Secretariat of Briefs to Princes, which is now mainly a special office devoted to the study of Latin.

The largest and only really active office of the Holy See today is the State Secretariat, which operates not merely as the Pontiff's foreign ministry but also as his executive office. The cardinal-Secretary of State sees the Holy Father normally at least once a day and may talk to him over the telephone another half-dozen times daily. As John XXIII has said, the Secretary of State is "my closest collaborator."

The Secretary frequently represents the Pope on official occasions. In the case of a visit by the head of a state, it is the Secretary of State who invariably repays the call.[5] The Secretary of State normally sits on all important congregations. In addition, he is usually a member of the pontifical committee for the government of Vatican State and the cardinals' committee overseeing the finances of the Holy See. He is also, of course, the Vatican's chief negotiator. The Secretary of State is often a ranking candidate for election to St. Peter's Throne. Next to the Pope himself, he is the most important personage of the Holy See.

To the outsider the Holy See's maze of congregations, tribunals, and offices would seem to be cumbersome. Many Catholics think that some streamlining is in order. However, this complicated labyrinth of interlocking congregations has an important purpose: it serves as a system of checks and balances on the executive power. No Pope could consistently ignore the recommendations of the congregations and still hope to have an efficient rule over the Church.

[5] The Pope never makes an official call, although John XXIII has made several pastoral calls on sick friends and officials. The one time in recent history that this precedent has been broken was early in the pontificate of Pius XII. Vittorio Emanuele III had just made a state visit to the Vatican. The clouds of war were darkening, and Benito Mussolini was threatening to bring Italy into it. It was known that the King of Italy was against any declaration of war. Probably with the idea of strengthening the King's hand, Pius XII returned his call by going personally to the Quirinale.

IV

THE LIFE AND WAYS
OF POPE PIUS XII

There can be an enormous difference between Popes. One Pope may be warm and *simpatico*, while another is cold and aloof. This Pope may be mainly interested in people and their sins, while that Pope's chief interest is in high-level dogma and doctrine. There have been Popes who counted every lira the Vatican spent, and others so open-handed and generous they left the Vatican coffers empty. The Church has known Pontiffs who were weak in administration and strong in theology, and vice versa.

One Papal reign tends to complement another; the deficiencies of one pontificate are often compensated for in the strong points of the succeeding regime. Thus a "political" Pope may follow a "religious" Pope, a poor administrator may be succeeded by a Pontiff with a rich experience in the administration of parishes and dioceses, and a good theorist in St. Peter's Chair may well come after a great pastor.

So saying, it is clear that no understanding of the present pontificate of John XXIII is possible without a backward glance at that of his predecessor, Pius XII. In some respects the present Pope is doing what the late Pope failed to do. It might be said that the

Sacred College chose Angelo Giuseppe Roncalli with the idea that
he would fill some of the gaps left by Pius XII.

Some Protestant writers believe that Eugenio Pacelli will go
go down in history as the outstanding figure to occupy St. Peter's
Throne in several centuries. Indeed, Pius XII had an undeniable
appeal for the non-Catholic world. This was perhaps because his
general approach to most problems seemed less partisan, less
doctrinal, more universal, than that of his predecessors. Not only
did he steer the Church safely through a disastrous war to greater
prestige than ever in modern times, but he later rose magnificently
to the postwar Communist challenge.

Moreover, he was remarkably modern, in little as well as big
things. He was the first Pope to fly in an airplane, the first to use a
typewriter normally and easily, the first to use an electric razor.
He used the telephone often, even calling minor officials. Vatican
officials never became really accustomed to picking up the receiver
and hearing a voice on the other end announce, "Pacelli speaking."
Their usual flustered reply was "Sì, sì, Santissimo Padre." ("Yes,
yes, Holy Father.") He was the first to appear on television, and
he did not hesitate to use make-up for these appearances.

Pius XII took the first few steps toward modernizing the dress
of men and women in religious orders. He ordered both heating
and plumbing to be installed in Italy's medieval monasteries and
abbeys. Among his more popular innovations was his decision to
allow mass to be said routinely during the afternoon and early
evening, as well as in the morning, and to allow water to be drunk
before Holy Communion. These provisions have enormously increased attendance at mass. In fact, in the big European cities
evening mass now has a better attendance than morning mass.

Pius XII's pronouncements, although by no means uniform in
quality, at least reflected the concerns of the twentieth century.
Above all, the Pope was a product of the scientific age. He appeared to trust the new techniques. Although an aristocrat, in his
memorable speech of the Christmas of 1944, when Nazi Germany
was not yet defeated, he put the Catholic Church on the side of

democracy. Leo XIII, a half century before, had reluctantly admitted that the Church and democracy might be reconciled, but Pius XII was the first to accomplish the reconciliation.

In another speech Pius XII spoke out for religious tolerance in a way few Popes have done before him. In still another pronouncement he acknowledged the population problem, and made at least a tentative move to re-examine the Church's stand on birth control. The old Pope showed an understanding both of psychiatry and of nuclear physics; he was plainly worried about the implications of explorations of outer space for a religious system which to many seems terrestrial.

The literary production of Pius XII was formidable. In the course of his pontificate he reviewed almost the whole of Catholic doctrine. All in all, he issued thirty-six encyclicals, a few of which, like *Humani generis*, of 1950, were particularly responsive to the perplexities of the times. He also produced seven apostolic exaltations and twelve pontifical letters. His speeches, all of them written out, ran into the hundreds; it took twenty large volumes to print them.

The pontificate of Pius XII was rather long as pontificates go, lasting for almost twenty years and thus approaching the classic twenty-five years of St. Peter's reign. The basic outline of both his life and his reign has been told and retold, and it would be superfluous to repeat it here. But a few pertinent facts are in order.

Pacelli was born and reared in Rome, where he came naturally by his sophisticated, slightly cynical attitude toward men and events. Pius XII had great respect for humanity but little trust in individual people. He did not like the elaborate trappings of the Papal Court, with its incurable obsequiousness. Although he felt he must dutifully meet the crowds that came to see him, he had few friends, and the few he did have were laymen. The suspicion grew in his late years that he felt uncomfortable in the company of the clergy. The cardinals of the Curia, who by tradition are the Pope's closest advisers, felt isolated and cut off from contact with him.

Pius XII was a man of less than average height who never weighed more than 150 pounds. His outward appearance was that of a distinguished Roman. His nose was prominent, and his profile strong. He rarely smiled, and often when meeting people he seemed to be thinking of faraway things.

Pacelli is one of the few Popes never to have been a parish priest and never to have filled a bishopric. He was also one of the few who never lived at a seminary. He took his classes at a seminary, but his father, an official at the Vatican, arranged that the boy would meanwhile continue to live at home—an unusual procedure.

Almost immediately upon graduating from the Gregorian University young Pacelli, although offered a post teaching canon law, chose instead to enter the Vatican Secretariat of State. There he remained, first as a *minutante* (secretary-researcher), then as a Papal Nuncio, and finally as Secretary of State, until elected Pope in 1939. It is almost as if a man were to join the diplomatic service of the United States, work his way up through the ranks of the State Department to Secretary of State, and end by being elected President of the country.

In many ways Pacelli revealed all his life the bureaucratic habits of the civil servant. With him there could be no undue hurrying. He insisted that matters go through their proper channels. There must be a meticulous crossing of the t's and dotting of the i's. He was fastidious even when it came to signing a letter, wanting to be sure that the ink was dry before passing the letter on. He had a purist's horror of hybrid words and especially disliked those many Italian expressions adapted from the French. On one occasion he supplied the Secretariat of State with a small dictionary of Frenchified expressions to be avoided. The Pope in the early part of his pontificate had a Secretary of State, but he found the Secretary's work so disorderly that upon his death His Holiness thenceforth decided to be his own Secretary of State, depending only on the services of two vice-secretaries.

In one capacity or another, during his secretariat career, Pacelli traveled over the entire Occident, including North and South

America. He spent many particularly fruitful years as Papal Nuncio to Germany, which he came to admire almost as much as he loved his native Italy. Life first in Munich and then in Berlin greatly enlarged his range of interests and experience. He became fond of many phases of German culture. Pacelli's most fluent language, outside of Italian, was German; he spoke it rather than Italian in his own household. (He also spoke good French, acceptable English, rather inferior Spanish and Portuguese.) His favorite composers were Bach, Wagner, and Mendelssohn, in that order. Nothing delighted him more than a concert of all-German music played by the various orchestras from Germany and Austria, which sometimes in their visits to Rome would give a concert at the Vatican. The records Pius XII kept near his gramophone, and usually played before going to bed, were almost all German classics.

Pacelli liked to discuss German politics, and perhaps because of this it was sometimes whispered, without justification, that he was pro-German during World War II. Lending some substance to this charge was the undeniable fact that it was Pacelli, as the Pope's representative in Germany, who had negotiated with the Nazis the first Vatican-German concordat. This concordat was soon, however, to be violated by the Nazis.

Much has been written by anticlerical and anti-Catholic writers about the allegedly too friendly relations between the Vatican and the Mussolini regime. Ernesto Rossi, the able and well-known anticlerical Italian author, has written an entire book about the negotiations for the Lateran Treaty in which he has recalled some of the friendly references made by Vatican spokesmen to the Fascist government during those years. Undoubtedly in their eagerness to obtain a final settlement of the Roman question Vatican prelates were at one period prepared to overlook some of the more brutal features of the Mussolini dictatorship and even to utter flattering references to the Duce. But little of this can be attributed to Pius XII. Cardinal Pietro Gasparri, and not Cardinal Pacelli, conducted the Lateran Treaty negotiations. There was a Pacelli among the negotiators, but he was Francesco, the brother of

Eugenio. About the only thing that can be said is that during the period of Pacelli's secretariat the Vatican looked with obvious favor on both the Fascist-Nazi intervention in the Spanish Civil War and on Mussolini's conquest of Ethiopia. The Duce even gave as one reason for this latter adventure the fact that the Ethiopians had been guilty of heresy toward the Roman Church. The heresy was that of the Monophysites, dating from the fifth century. Not much later the Duce was declaring himself the "Protector of Islam."

As the clouds of war became darker, Pius XII foresaw many difficulties for the Church and tried to persuade the Mussolini government not to bring Italy into the struggle. He went out of his way to be friendly to the Italian royal family. He spoke frequently of peace. Some plain speaking took place, too, between the Pope's Secretary of State and the Italian representative to the Holy See. But it was all, in the end, in vain. The Duce was to have his war and to lose his life as a result.

At the outbreak of the Russian-German-Italian war both Hitler and Mussolini hoped to persuade the Pope to declare a holy crusade again Communism, but Pius XII did not oblige. The Vatican by now had become thoroughly disillusioned with the dictatorships and was determined to steer a neutral course. The Pope's constant urging for peace, even when the Germans were winning great victories in the East, enraged the Nazis.

The Pope's declaration of neutrality was perhaps the determining factor in limiting to two the Allied bombardments of Rome, then serving as an important railroad center for Axis arms. During much of the war the Vatican ran what was virtually an underground, saving many of the persecuted and hunted of Europe from being summarily executed. During the Nazi occupation of Rome, in the winter of 1943–44, when the Germans were hunting down anti-Fascist Italians, the Vatican authorities gave sanctuary to many prominent men, among them a number of Socialists. Such leftists as Giuseppe Saragat and Pietro Nenni, both of whom were later to play a prominent political role in the Italian Republic, were housed in the extraterritorial Palace of St. John Lateran. German soldiers gave the Vatican a wide berth during the war, but once the Allies had taken over the Eternal City, the Vatican threw open its arms to tens of thousands of uniformed men of the Allied nations. On Christmas, 1944, Pius XII presided at an unprecedented midnight mass at St. Petcr's in the presence of thousands of Allied soldiers and Axis diplomats.

All the while the Pope's private household remained more German than Italian. He had no private sccretary as such, but he did employ two German Jesuit researchers from the Vatican library. One of these, Father Robert Leiber, came to be well-known. Probably because of the fact that hc was accessible to the press, Father Leiber's influence at the Vatican was exaggerated. He never wrote the Pope's speeches and contributed little to them. He did not live in thc Apostolic Palace and did not see the Pope regularly. He could never have brought a matter before the Pope. He was a researcher and little else.

The Pope's confessor was another German Jesuit, Father Augustin Bea, the Vatican's ranking Biblical scholar. His special talents appear to have been more appreciated by Pius XII's successor, John XXIII, who elevated him to cardinal. The Pope's best friend of the war years was still another German, the late Monsignor Ludwig Kaas. He had once been a Catholic Center leader in the Weimar Republic, but had then left Nazi Germany for Rome, where he became in due time the secretary for the Congregation of the Revered Building of St. Peter's.

The nuns who attended the Holy Father were also Germans. These three or four sisters—their number varied from time to time —did a prodigious amount of work. Admittedly there was not much cooking to do, but a nineteen-room apartment had to be kept spotlessly clean. And besides attending to every need of the Holy Father these nuns were able to knit something like twenty sweaters a month for the use of the country priests in Italy.

A separate chapter could be written about the head nun of the Papal household, the famous Sister (now Mother) Pasqualina

Lehnert. Here the conscientious writer runs into touchy and delicate matters. The Pius XII–Sister Pasqualina relationship is difficult to define, if only because it was so shrouded in secrecy. Almost ten years had passed after the election of Eugenio Pacelli to the highest dignity before people in the Vatican learned of her existence. Even prelates whose business took them repeatedly before the Pope never laid eyes on her. Cardinal Eugene Tisserant, the dean of the College of Cardinals, was to meet her for the first time after Pius XII's death. The press corps covering the Vatican became aware of her presence only about 1950. Only one picture, taken with a telescopic lens, was ever made of Sister Pasqualina.

Why such secrecy? One reason doubtless stemmed from the fact that it was unusual, if not irregular, for a Pope to have women in the Papal apartment. Lesser prelates of the Vatican normally have housekeepers or nuns, always older women, to take care of their quarters. But in the case of Popes it has been an unwritten rule for centuries that their households should be run exclusively by men. For example, when Cardinal Achille Ratti became Pius XI, he reluctantly left his old housekeeper, who had been with him for years, behind in Milan. While he was Cardinal-Patriarch of Venice, Pius X's household had long been run by his two sisters, but when he became Pope the sisters were not permitted to live in the Vatican, but instead werc put up in a modest Rome apartment.[1]

Monsignor Eugenio Pacelli, Nuncio to Germany, first met Sister Pasqualina, of Bavarian peasant stock, when he was in the Swiss Mountains convalescing from a chest ailment, during World War I. Somewhat later she was invited to take up service in the Nuncio's residence at Munich. Here again was an unusual situation. Generally speaking, young women are not permitted to work and live in the households of priests and prelates. Church discipline stipulates that the women of such households be of "canonical age," which is generally assumed to mean beyond the age of

[1] Pope John XXIII, like Pius XII, has also chosen not to observe the tradition; he brought with him to Rome the nuns who had served him in Venice.

physical attractiveness. But Sister Pasqualina, when she first entered the Pacelli household, could have been barely past her twentieth year.

Sister Pasqualina remained with Pacelli uninterruptedly, except when he was traveling, for about forty years. By special dispensation of the College of Cardinals she was even allowed to stay at Cardinal Pacelli's side and look after his always delicate health inside the otherwise restricted conclave area in 1939, during the Papal election that elevated Pacelli to the Throne of St. Peter.

In time Sister Pasqualina became more than a mere housekeeper. She combined the management of the Papal apartments with secretarial, nursing, and even administrative activities. During one period, when the Pope was suffering from arthritis, she took down notes for his diary in longhand. She saw to it that the Holy Father followed to the letter the regime prescribed by the Papal doctor.[2] Sometimes she would interrupt audiences to tell him that it was time to do this or that. She did not hesitate to scold an official who kept the Pope waiting in an unheated elevator. On another occasion she interrupted a conversation between Pius XII and John Foster Dulles to tell the Holy Father that the soup was on the table.

In time Sister Pasqualina assumed administration of the Pontiff's private charity, although by tradition this function is assigned to a cleric and, indeed, has been so assigned in the succeeding pontificate. The funds for the Pope's private charity flow in from many sources. For example, a bishop making his periodic report to the Holy Father will generally present a cash gift to the Pope. This can differ greatly according to the wealth of the bishop's diocese. American bishops generally give checks of $1,000; Cardinal Francis Spellman of New York, who rules over perhaps the richest diocese in the world, was said to have habitually given $5,000. Pilgrims from all over the world also bring gifts, not always in cash. The

---

[2] The Papal doctor has a title in Italian of *archiatro*, roughly equivalent to the word "archiater," an archaic English expression of Greek origin meaning physician to an emperor.

Fiat workers of Turin, for example, may present a car. The wine growers of Tuscany may bring down a hundred cases of Chianti. The textile workers of Milan may present clothes for the poor and needy. Whatever the gifts, Sister Pasqualina took charge of them all. The checks were deposited in the Vatican's banks; the more tangible presents she stored, temporarily, in the several large vacant rooms of the Apostolic Palace. Later she would distribute the goods and money to needy parishes.

How much real influence did Sister Pasqualina have? She undoubtedly had the Papal ear. In later years she was able to bring to the Pope's attention some matters that were screened from him by other officials, including questions that some prelates were afraid to raise. She was even able on occasions to arrange an interview with the Pope.

The fact that all sorts of people tried to court her favor would indicate that she was not without power. She had her favorites and she played them. One of them was Dr. Riccardo Galeazzi-Lisi, the Pope's *archiatro* during most of his reign. Others included the Rev. Riccardo Lombardi and the Rev. Virgilio Rotondi, founders of the "Movement for a Better World." But whether all this added up to any substantial power is difficult for an outsider to determine. An editor of *L'Osservatore Romano* who knows Sister Pasqualina once told this writer:

"Sister Pasqualina's great value to Pius XII was that she knew what her field was and kept strictly to it. She occasionally would interest herself in matters touching charity, but she knew nothing about doctrinal problems or even Church government. She simply could not have known what to advise in such cases. The Pope would not have dreamed of consulting her in any serious matter. I heard her once say that she never read the newspaper; she had only the vaguest idea of what was going on outside the Papal apartment."

On the other hand, contrary opinion from reliable sources can also be cited. For example, the late Silvio Negro, head of the Rome office of Milan's *Corriere della Sera* and acknowledged as one of the best lay experts on the Vatican, believed that Sister Pasqualina had a decided influence on the Pope's widely publicized devotion to Mary the Virgin. The Vatican press corps believed that Monsignor Paul-Emile Leger, rector of the Canadian College at Rome, owed his appointment as Cardinal-Archbishop of Montreal in 1950 to Sister Pasqualina. Monsignor Leger had contributed regularly and heavily to the Pope's private charity. Certainly the elevation of Leger was unusual, since the rectors of the various colleges are not generally in line for the Sacred College. Moreover, in the case of Canada, the red hat traditionally went to the Archbishop of Quebec, and not of Montreal.

Rumor to the contrary, Sister Pasqualina was treated quite generously at the death of the man who had been her master and her charge for four decades. At the death of a Pope the Papal apartment is immediately sealed against all comers. Only the new Pope, who is elected two or three weeks later, can break these seals. This precaution originated because in the past there have been some unseemly scrambles for the personal effects of the newly deceased Pontiff. Thus Sister Pasqualina found herself at first barred from the apartment which she had cared for and where she had lived for almost twenty years. But within a few days the rules were relaxed, and Cardinal Tisserant, nominally in charge of the vacant Apostolic See, invited her to return and put her warehouse of goods for charity in order. The conclave over, the new Pope received her and thanked her for her long service with his predecessor.

Sister Pasqualina was for a time transferred back to her convent, that of the Sisters of the Holy Cross in Switzerland. From time to time there would be stories that she was finding it hard to adjust in those surroundings. Then friends rescued her. She was soon called back to Rome to take the job of mother superior of the nuns who run the bustling new American seminary near the Vatican. There her recognized administrative ability, plus her knowledge of Rome, was bound to be useful. There, too, on the Janiculum Hill, she is only a few steps from St. Peter's and the last resting place of Pius

XII. It is Sister Pasqualina who keeps the tomb of the old Pope continually supplied with flowers.

Pius XII was extremely conscientious, with an exalted sense of duty. He feared losing time above all. Unlike most Italians, he regarded punctuality as a cardinal virtue and was annoyed if circumstances forced him to keep people waiting even for five minutes.

The Pope hated waste in any form. The lavish surroundings in which he lived seemed to make him all the more austere in his habits. He cut down on his staff. The Vatican payroll was sliced to the bone. In later years, Pius XII gave orders that envelopes containing messages or memoranda from one Vatican office to another should not be sealed tightly; in that way they could be opened without tearing, and used again. The late Pope's will, which left everything to the See of Peter and nothing to the Pacelli family, was written on the back of a used envelope.

Pius XII also practiced strict economy in the matter of electrical current, occasionally making the rounds of the Papal apartment to turn off lights. He refused to sanction even simple improvements at the Vatican and often did not want to spend money for necessary repairs. Frequently he would answer a request for approval of expenditures by saying, "But I cannot be extravagant with the funds of the Holy See."

In line with his sense of economy was the Pope's dislike of ceremony. He was not liturgically-minded. Before he came to the Throne, canonization ceremonies often lasted from 8 A.M. until around 2 P.M. He cut the time in half. In his later years he abolished various Holy Week ceremonies at the Sistine Chapel. His most celebrated ceremonial economy, however, had to do with the trains that cardinals attach to their vestments on special occasions. By tradition these were exactly seven meters in length, having been used originally not only to cover the horse of a cardinal but to trail after horse and rider. They were so unwieldy and heavy that each cardinal had to have a trainbearer, or *caudatario*. In 1952

Pius XII, without warning, ordered the cardinals' trains cut to half the usual length.[3]

In matters of charity the Pope was generous. During the last war, the Vatican spent millions for the relief of the oppressed of Europe. By one estimate, a total of $2,000,000 was spent in helping the Jews of Rome escape the Nazi-Fascist terror. On a lesser scale, too, Pius XII was benevolent. Like all Popes, he kept a drawerful of Italian banknotes which he liked to pass out to needy priests who came to see him. One year, however, the Italian government called in all the old notes, specifying a deadline. But Pius XII, not a very careful newspaper reader, let the date pass without changing the money. He was pained to realize later that his negligence had cost Catholic charities the equivalent of several thousand dollars.

After a lifetime of diplomacy Pacelli as Pope remained a diplomat. In fact, he was criticized for putting far too much faith in diplomatic methods. Pacelli's predecessor, Pius XI, was an uncompromising Pontiff who, during the last days of his pontificate, had been given to vigorous denunciations, *urbi et orbi*. Pius XII, on the other hand, preferred the inoffensive note in chancellery, with words chosen for their moderation. The Pope would haggle for hours with his collaborators to find the right word.

Other heads of Roman Catholicism might well have been tempted to lead the Church into an active, heroic martyrdom in a postwar Eastern Europe overrun by Communism. Pacelli believed that the Church's primary mission was to facilitate religious practice for the weak, who were in a majority, rather than create an atmosphere for heroes, who would be in a minority. Other policies might have greatly increased the persecution of Catholics in Communist countries, whereas Pius XII, who always thought in terms of the limits of possible action, was willing to wait for a favorable turn of events, meanwhile succoring the faithful and easing their days of trial.

[3] John XXIII let this order lapse, and the trains are now back at more or less their old length.

The outstanding characteristic of the Pacelli pontificate was, without any doubt, the Pope's proclivity for audiences. Audience-giving with Pacelli was not just a necessary formality; it was a policy, an end in itself. These papal audiences came, indeed, to have something of the quality of the *darshana* in India; the worshipers were supposed to profit merely by setting eyes on a man who, although not a deity, was an exalted personage.

The Pope did not enjoy the give and take of social conversation; yet so strong was his sense of duty that he allowed nothing except serious illness to interfere with his audiences. Known sinners were welcomed along with the saints, and religious preference was not considered. Strangely enough, he often neglected his own clergy. If there was a question of whether His Holiness could see the shoemakers of Lyons or have a conference with the newly arrived Bishop of Santiago, the shoemakers invariably were given the preference.

Under this system the number and variety of audiences grew over the years, until during the last year of his reign Pius XII received an estimated 120,000 persons. This was quite apart from the hundreds of thousands who flocked into St. Peter's Square to receive the apostolic blessing. The Pope also granted in an average year around four thousand special audiences of twenty persons and up, plus six or seven hundred private audiences of from one to six persons, plus three or four hundred audiences for special groups such as doctors, scientists, and lawyers. At the same time the Pope received, in one of the last years of his reign, more than forty heads of states or ministers of outlying countries. No foreign dignitary who stopped at Rome, whether Moslem or Buddhist or Christian, would omit a visit to the Pope. An audience with Pius XII became the climactic point of conventions in Rome. The official Italian tourist bureau was witness to the fact that many conventions were attracted to Rome in the first place by the promise of a Papal audience.

A corollary to the audience was the speech which Pius XII delivered to virtually every group. The Pope took these speeches seriously, some said too seriously. During the later years he neglected his administrative and pastoral duties and devoted the greater part of his time and energy to writing these talks. Moreover, he refused to have others make even first drafts for him; the Pacelli speeches were from first to last the work of the Pope himself.

Observers in Rome were of two minds about these speeches. One critic said they were "too frequent, too uniform, too diluted." The point was sometimes obscure, the manner of expression always indirect. This school would have preferred that the Holy Father limit his pronouncements to the traditional Christmas message, an occasional encyclical, and perhaps a speech or so a year on auspicious occasions. They would have reduced the audience to a personal appearance, a greeting, and a benediction, which is what, in fact, it had previously been.

On the other hand, there were those (among them this correspondent) who held that this is an age of words, and one must speak out. Failure to talk as often and as emphatically as possible is to leave the field to others. Granted that not each speech of Pius XII could be an important document, still the cumulative effect of talking seriously to so many representative groups from all over the world was bound to be good.

This is obviously not the place to review the twenty volumes in which the speeches of Pius XII are printed, but some hint of their content can nevertheless be given. The range of subjects was wide —from nuclear energy to civil law, from birth control to archaeology, from the groans of modern agriculture to the problems of urban growth. The display of learning was impressive.

Canon law was the Pope's specialty, and his annual speeches before the *uditori* of the Sacred Rota are among his best. But he was equally fascinated by the new scientific and engineering age, and seems to have entertained no fears that new scientific discoveries could shake the foundations of the Roman faith. He became a regular subscriber to numerous scientific journals, and was assiduous in reading and digesting papers of the seminars of scientific conventions. On several occasions he asked scientific libraries to lend him specific volumes.

Nuclear physics was one of the Pope's favorite subjects; several non-Catholic scientists have testified that Pius XII's understanding here was remarkable. Medicine was still another of his interests; he must have addressed in his time a hundred or more medical societies. At times he surprised listeners by his knowledge. At one convention of heart specialists His Holiness referred, almost in an aside, to a rather obscure paper read at the previous convention on the subject of false coronary attacks. A murmur of wonder went through the audience.

The speeches of Pius XII can never make popular reading, but in their entirety they may come to represent a sort of *summa* of Catholic thought in the mid-1900's. The great contribution of Eugenio Pacelli may well be that he put the Church abreast of modern times.

During the nineteen and a half years of his reign Pius XII presided at ceremonies at which twenty-one saints were proclaimed. During the same period there were twenty-three beatifications for a total of seventy-five new Blessed. At one of these latter ceremonies twenty-nine martyrs of the Boxer Rebellion in China were beatified, while at another twenty-five martyrs killed in Vietnam, all of them Dominican monks, were made Blessed. For the Holy Year of 1950 alone the Pope presided at seven canonizations. All during the late forties the old palace of the Congregation of Rites in Trastevere, a few blocks down the river from the Vatican, hummed with the activity of the various trials in process.

The most unusual canonization was that of Maria Goretti. She was born near the Adriatic coast of Italy in 1890, the daughter of poor but devout peasants. They soon moved to the west coast of Italy and settled in the Pontine Marshes at Nettuno, near Rome. At the age of twelve and a half she took her first communion. Only about a month later she was attacked and brutally wounded by a youth of twenty. She died in the hospital the next day, after having pardoned her killer. He would later stand trial and be imprisoned, after which, a greatly changed man, he would find work as an employee of a monastery, where he remains to this day.

The cause for Maria Goretti's beatification was introduced thirty-six years later, in 1938, during the reign of Pius XI. In 1945 her martyrdom was recognized by Pius XII, and in 1947 she was proclaimed a Blessed at St. Peter's. Later that year the cause for her canonization was introduced. It was said that the Pope himself spurred the Congregation of Rites to move in this case more rapidly than usual. In any event, the Pope looked upon Maria Goretti as an example of the purity of womanhood. Her canonization, he thought, would be fitting in the same year that the Dogma of the Assumption was proclaimed. Maria Goretti's sainthood was proclaimed in 1950. The signal feature of the ceremony at St. Peter's was that for perhaps the first time in the long history of the Church the new saint's mother, the aging and paralytic Assunta Goretti, watched as the name of her child was inscribed in the official hagiography.

The most important canonization during the Pacelli reign, however, was that of Pius X, the Venetian peasant boy who rose through ecclesiastical ranks to be elected to the highest dignity in 1903. The habit of canonizing Popes had all but died out since the Middle Ages; the last Pope to be proclaimed a saint was Pius V, whose cause reached its conclusive phase some 250 years ago. The Romans were now glad to see this practice resumed.

The ceremony took place on a beautiful May afternoon in 1955 in a St. Peter's Square jammed with the devout, some of whom could remember the days when Papa Sarto lived. As the large portrait of the new saint was unveiled and as Pius XII, surrounded by more than a hundred bishops, ordered the old Pope's name entered in the official list of saints of the Church, thunderous applause swept over the piazza.

The Romans, ever sensitive in such matters, detected a tendency of Pius XII to become much more introspective and inwardly religious as he passed the eighty-year mark. A photograph published in *L'Osservatore Romano* during one Holy Week showed Pius XII in an attitude of deep grief and suffering, leaning against a life-size crucifix. Members of the former Pope's household saw other indications of the gradual transformation from Pacelli, the worldly-wise and subtle diplomat, to Pius XII, the aloof, ascetic religious teacher willing to suffer for sinful humanity. Many at the Vatican testify that as time went on the late Pope became convinced that man was virtually incapable of solving the problems of this century. In the deepest sense of the word, he became a pessimist.

Pius XII's two announced visions constitute further evidence of his intense religious feeling in late years. The first vision took place in the Vatican gardens in the early afternoon, at about the time of the proclamation of the Dogma of the Assumption of November 1, 1950. The Holy Father saw a revolving sun touch the horizon, and as he looked into the sun without being blinded he saw in it a picture of the Virgin surrounded by bright rays. The sun then shook and changed quickly into a picture of paradise.

The second vision was simpler. The Pope was seriously ill in 1954 and fears were great that he would not recover. But while he was reciting a prayer in bed he suddenly saw Christ at his bedside and heard Him tell Pacelli that his hour had not yet come.

A mild uproar was caused by the announcement of these two visions. Some old Vatican hands, including many Jesuits, were aghast that a Pope should have had a vision, or having had one that he should say so. With their legalistic ways, the Jesuits insisted that it was for Popes to judge the validity of other men's visions, not to have them themselves.

The old Pope was distressed by all this publicity and quickly confessed to his staff that he had made a mistake in divulging the visions. The fact was that he had not originally intended them to reach public print at all. The first vision he had confided to Cardinal Federico Tedeschini, the only member of the Sacred College to call His Holiness "tu."[4] Quite on his own His Eminence, presiding at the concluding ceremonies of the Holy Year of 1950, held by special dispensation at Fatima, in Portugal, instead of Rome, included a description of the vision in his prepared speech.

The second vision was confided to Monsignori Tardini and Dell'Aqua, of the Secretariat of State, and to Sister Pasqualina. Tardini and Dell'Acqua kept silent, but Sister Pasqualina mentioned it to the Rev. Virgilio Rotondi. Rotondi persuaded the Pope to let him sell the story to the popular Italian magazine *Oggi*, the proceeds to go toward supporting the Movement for a Better World.

Publication in *Oggi* was not the end of the matter. The question of whether to publish the vision in *L'Osservatore Romano* was heatedly debated at the Vatican. The Pope by this time wanted nothing more said about it anywhere. He was finally won around to the view, however, that not to print it in a Vatican newspaper was tantamount to denying that it took place. At long last, almost a month after the story had been originally published, a short piece affirming only in the barest of outlines the Papal vision was allowed to appear in *L'Osservatore Romano*.

Connected in an undefined way with the visions was the late Pope's Mariology. It is difficult for an outsider to determine whether Pius XII's intense devotion to Mary caused his visions or whether the visions he had resulted in increased Marian piety. Both the Pope's visions and his Mariology, however, were certainly related to the miraculous visions which three farm children were supposed to have witnessed in the fields near the village of Fatima,

---

[4] Italian (as well as French, Spanish, German, Russian, etc.) has two forms of expressing the word "you." The familiar form of "tu" is normally used among children, members of the same family, and intimate friends. Two priests educated in the same seminary would use "tu" to each other. No cardinal addresses the present Pope as "tu."

in eastern Portugal, on May 13, 1917. This was the day, it so happened, that Eugenio Pacelli was being consecrated a bishop in Rome; the late Pope considered this no coincidence but an act of benevolent dispensation from above.

The Fatima visions were to be repeated four times over the succeeding years. With each vision the Madonna appeared, holding the rosary in her hand, and each time pronouncements, commands, and even prophecies were uttered by Mary herself. Two of the children who saw the original visions soon died, but the third child, Lucia dos Santos, who has since become a Carmelite nun, is still living, and it is on her memory that the Fatima miracles must rest.

Many Protestants and even some Catholic writers have questioned the Fatima stories. The Madonna's "prophecies," or at least that part of them which has been published, have not been fulfilled—certainly not the prediction that Russia would "soon" be converted to Catholicism. Moreover, the commands of Mary on these occasions, as related by Lucia, seem too egocentric to come from a religious figure. The Virgin insists that churches be built to her memory, that prayers be said for her satisfaction, that nations be dedicated to her forever greater glory. (This has been done in the case of Portugal and Germany, among others.)

Nevertheless, under the guidance of Pius XII, the cult of Mary inside the Catholic Church grew strong. Consecratory prayers to Mary were introduced by the Pope himself. In one such she was called the "Victrix in all battles of God" and it was suggested that she was especially efficacious in defeating heresy. A vast sanctuary to Mary was built at Fatima and a costly crown, made of diamonds, pearls, emeralds, sapphires, rubies, turquoises, and amethysts, was placed on the Madonna's statue. At the coronation in 1946, Pius XII declared that Mary's kingdom was now equal to her Son's and that Mary had been raised to "hypostatic union with the Blessed Trinity."

Just as the appearance of the Virgin at Lourdes, in France, in

1858 had been regarded at Rome as an aftereffect of the definition of the dogma of the Immaculate Conception in 1854, so the series of popular visions of the Virgin at Fatima, as well as the Pope's vision in the Vatican gardens, were interpreted as advance tidings of the proclamation in 1950 of the Dogma of the Assumption.

This was easily the most important theological event of Pius XII's reign. According to this dogma, as it appears in the Papal bull, the "Immaculate Mother of God, the ever Virgin Mary, having completed the course of her earthly life, was assumed body and soul into heavenly glory." All manner of arguments were marshaled to justify the dogma. Granted that no scriptural support could be found, the Pope still contended that it was "contained in the deposit of Christian faith entrusted to the Church." Numerous Fathers and Doctors of the Church were cited as witnesses to the truth of the dogma. As in the case of all such definitions, the bishops of the Church were polled, and they were "almost unanimous" in their approval. The only cardinal at the Vatican to vote against was Eugene Tisserant, the dean of the Sacred College. But he had long been virtually estranged from the Pope, and his opinion held little weight.

Once the dogma was defined and approved, there could be no further open opposition within the Church, but before that happened numerous writers tried to forestall its adoption. Many inveighed against what they called a threat to the uniqueness of Christ, charging that Roman Catholicism was in danger of degenerating into a Marian sect. But these voices were not heard clearly at Rome. In 1953 Pius XII issued his encyclical *Fulgens corona* on the subject of Mary, at the same time proclaiming 1954 a Marian year. The major feature of this year was a series of pilgrimages to shrines and churches dedicated to the Virgin, together with continuing consecrations to Mary. To match the Feast of Christ the King, Pius XII now created the Feast of Mary of Heaven and Earth. An image of the Madonna and Child was crowned by the Pope at St. Peter's. While Pius XII in other ways

did much to lessen the hostility between Catholicism and Protestantism his fervent advocacy of what amounts to virtual divinity
for Mary probably deepened the division of Christendom.

The men of influence behind the Throne of St. Peter during
Pius XII's pontificate were not typical. Generally the Pope's closest collaborators are the cardinals of the Roman Curia, those members of the Sacred College who act as the Sovereign's ministers in
the general administration of the Church. But Pius XII, after
giving the various cardinals their assignments, left them by and
large on their own. For a time Cardinal Nicola Canali, the Pope's
viceroy for Vatican State, was fairly close to the Pope, but as the
two men grew older they also grew apart. The cardinal who probably felt closest to Pius XII was the Archbishop of New York,
Francis Spellman.

Nearer to the Pope were the two priests, of no special ecclesiastical rank, Father Riccardo Lombardi and Father Virgilio Rotondi, who had founded the Movement for a Better World. This
organization, incidentally, had its headquarters in the Alban Hills,
across the lake and within sight of the Papal Villa at Castel Gandolfo.

The ideas of Fathers Lombardi and Rotondi apparently appealed to the Holy Father. They shared his disregard of ceremony
and his mistrust of the ancient traditions of the Curia. Fathers
Lombardi and Rotondi believed, and Pius XII concurred to a
certain extent, that Catholic Church administration, especially
in Italy, was old-fashioned and inefficient, and that this had an
inevitable effect on the Church's mission. Father Lombardi,
highly critical of the Curia, thought that no prelate should stay
long at Rome without participating in pastoral work, and favored
increasing participation of the laity in Church policy. He thought
that the Church's training methods should be refashioned, and to
this end he was allowed by Pius XII to conduct a pilot program
for bishops in how to deal with the faithful in modern times. Not
only did these two Jesuit fathers conduct courses for the heads
of dioceses but the bishops themselves were encouraged to in-

vite the two priests to their sees to streamline the individual dioceses.[5]

Fathers Lombardi and Rotondi represented a sort of advance party in Jesuit thinking. Formerly the Jesuits specialized in contacts with the more prominent members of society, convinced that this was the best approach to ultimate influence. One of their big jobs was to run schools for the children of the elite. But the strategy of concentrating on the elite has by now been virtually abandoned. Instead, Jesuit priests are assigned to the labor unions and the great mass Catholic parties. The Jesuits, alone of the orders, have placed a careful watch over such mass media as the movies, the press, television. They cater to popular actors, radio commentators, television stars. Clearly Pius XII's predilection for mass spectacles and mass audiences, and his readiness to receive anybody who had influence with the masses, stemmed largely from this theory, represented so ably at the Apostolic Palace by Father Lombardi.

Of the laymen of influence around Pius XII first perhaps should be listed the Pope's three nephews, Princes Carlo, Giulio, and Marcantonio Pacelli, sons of Francesco Pacelli. The Pacellis had long been petty Vatican nobility, but only after the conclusion of the Lateran Treaty of 1929, in which Francesco took a part, did the Kingdom of Italy recognize the family's noble status. The title of Prince was conferred on Francesco Pacelli (and his heirs) by the late Vittorio Emanuele III upon recommendation of his Prime Minister, Benito Mussolini, in 1941, thus making the Pacelli family Italian nobility but not a part of the famous "black nobility" created by the Popes themselves.[6] This act, according to Vatican officials, was not only unsolicited but unwelcomed by Pius

[5] It is said that among the "pupils" for a series of Lombardi lectures was the former Patriarch of Venice, Cardinal Angelo Giuseppe Roncalli, now John XXIII. What he thought may be gauged from the fact that in the first few months of his reign he quietly downgraded the Movement for a Better World.

[6] While the Popes retain the right to create nobility, as a matter of practice they have rarely exercised it in recent times. Pius XI created two Papal duchesses. Pius XII created none. The present Pope, John XXIII, has told his staff he has no intention of adding to the great number of titled people in Italy.

XII, who felt that Mussolini was in this way trying to curry favor for his war aims. Nevertheless, the three Pacelli nephews have never hesitated to use their titles.

Prince Carlo, the eldest son, was important in the legal and financial circles both of the Vatican and of Italy. Pius XII evidently regarded him highly and saw him frequently. He held the post of legal consultant for many of the sacred congregations; he was (and still is) general counselor for the powerful Pontifical Commission for the government of Vatican State; and he acted as chief legal adviser to the organization which administered the properties of the Holy See, the value of which ran into many millions of dollars. He sat—and still sits—on the boards of many companies in which the Vatican is known to have a financial interest. Some indication of Carlo's importance in the scheme of Vatican things can be seen from the fact that he has eleven separate listings in recent editions of the *Annuario Pontificio*, or *Pontifical Yearbook*.

By comparison with Prince Carlo, Princes Giulio and Marcantonio were of minor importance. Giulio was general attorney for the Sacred Congregation for the Propagation of the Faith and a director of the Banco di Roma, in which the Vatican has a substantial interest. He also acted (and still acts) as Ambassador Extraordinary and Plenipotentiary of Costa Rica to the Holy See, which post gives him diplomatic privileges and immunity, and exempts him from payment of certain Italian taxes. Marcantonio Pacelli, besides holding the post of colonel in the Noble Guard, was for a time director of the Italian air lines, but later turned his energies to real estate.

It has been suggested that the Pope's nephews have profited enormously from these various business connections. Questions about their tax payments were asked in the Italian House of Deputies, with the Minister of Finance himself replying. But not much concrete information regarding the Pacelli brothers' exact income can be gained from this Parliamentary exchange. Papal nephews, incidentally, have been a recurring concern at the Vatican, dating back to pre-Renaissance days when successive Popes habitually gave red hats to the sons of their brothers or sisters.

Dr. Luigi Gedda, a physician and expert on twins (appropriate for a Rome founded by Romulus and Remus), was head of the important Catholic Action during the postwar years when Pius XII was directing an all-out effort to win the Italian election for the Catholic party. He brought out the votes for the Church at a crucial moment. Gedda, however, was mainly a technician. His genius lay in organization rather than in political theory, and when he tried to pledge Catholic Action support for Rightist movements he quickly lost his influence. The late Pope had no political adviser as such.

The layman closest to the Holy Father during those years was Count Enrico Galeazzi, the Vatican's chief architect and building expert, a man with an exceptional administrative ability combined with the most scrupulous uprightness (see Chapter II). He was also the half-brother of Dr. Riccardo Galeazzi-Lisi.

Galeazzi owed almost his entire career to Cardinal Francis J. Spellman, of New York, who was a close friend when this prelate was stationed in Rome. Spellman first chose him as the representative of the Knights of Columbus in Rome. Later he introduced him to Pacelli, then Secretary of State. The two became friends and Galeazzi accompanied Cardinal Pacelli on his holidays and on the various pontifical missions entrusted to him. He went to Buenos Aires in 1934, to Lourdes in 1935, to Paris and Budapest several years later, and finally to New York and Washington. Galeazzi organized the cardinal-secretary's travels, arranged his program, largely set his routine.

After Pacelli was elected Pope, Galeazzi became Director General of Technical and Economic Services of Vatican City. He also continued to act as the Pope's unofficial factotum. Occasionally Count Galeazzi, with Prince Pacelli, would be invited to have an after-dinner coffee or *camomilla* with the Pontiff, an unusual occurrence. Pius XII always ate alone, however, just as have all Popes in recent times up to John XXIII.

All this while Count Galeazzi, who speaks good English, maintained his link with Spellman, and frequently, upon Spellman's
request, took charge of the business of entertaining and looking
after American businessmen and high-ranking laymen visiting the
Eternal City. He arranged for many private audiences with the
Pope. Among those who became his friends were the Joseph
Kennedys, of Boston, whom he presented to the Holy Father.
Meanwhile, Galeazzi's continued and easy access to the Papal
apartments gave Cardinal Spellman an entree at the court not
enjoyed by any other prelate. Spellman averaged three or four
visits a year to Rome during the postwar years, and each time
unfailingly saw His Holiness. He was several times invited to tea
at the Apostolic Palace.

Because of the outbreak of World War II so soon after his
assumption of the Tiara, Pius XII created no cardinals during the
first seven years of his reign. The membership of the Sacred College was down to thirty-eight at the end of the war; and so in
1946 the Pope held a consistory at which he created a total of
thirty-two new cardinals. Never in the history of the Church had
so many cardinals been created at one time. With these additions
to the Sacred College the Italian majority was wiped out and for
the first time since the Great Schism of the fourteenth century there
was a considerable non-Italian majority. In all probability the
Sacred College will never again be half Italian. Seven years later,
in 1953, a second consistory created twenty-eight more cardinals.

Death inevitably takes its toll, however, and it was not long before people were urging the Pope to hold yet another consistory.
By the mid-fifties the Roman Curia was depleted, with only twelve
cardinals left in it. Some of the congregations of the Holy See
limped along with two or three Curia cardinals to supervise their
work. The vacancies in the Sacred College soon numbered fifteen,
with important sees in many parts of the world unfilled. Competent young assistants were, of course, always on hand; even so,
Vatican administration was not vigorous during the last years of

the old Pope. People who knew Pius XII said that his dread of
making difficult choices among rival candidates delayed the calling
of a new consistory until it was too late.

Any summing up of the pontificate of Pius XII must inevitably deal with the Pontiff's choice of doctors. For many years
Vatican oldtimers wondered just how Dr. Riccardo Galeazzi-Lisi,
an eye doctor, had managed to obtain the post of general physician
to His Holiness. Actually, the two first met when Cardinal Pacelli,
then Secretary of State, stopped in one day at the doctor's office
in downtown Rome to get a new prescription for his glasses. Then,
on the very day of Pacelli's election to the Papacy, in March of
1939, an unusual incident took place. In the hour or so between
the end of the conclave and the announcement of the new Pope's
name, the party of conclavists, including the new Pope, moved
from the Sistine Chapel into the adjoining Ducal Hall. Now the
Ducal Hall is divided into two levels by a series of three steps.
As the new Pope talked to various cardinals he unconsciously
backed into these steps and fell down. His elbow slightly bruised,
the Pope quickly summoned Dr. Galeazzi-Lisi, who from that
day on was his physician, despite the obvious fact that his professional standing hardly seemed to warrant such an exalted post.

Dr. Galeazzi-Lisi remained in attendance on the Pope until the
Pontiff's serious illness of 1954–1955. During those months the
Secretariat of State, together with virtually every news office in
Rome, became aware that Dr. Galeazzi-Lisi also had literary am-
bitions and was trying to peddle a sort of "Pope and I" memoirs,
to be written and delivered immediately after the Pope's death.
The asking price was $12,000. Even seasoned journalists were
shocked. The Holy Father, when he recovered, was also chagrined
and quietly changed doctors, choosing Dr. Antonio Gasbarrini,
of Bologna. In order not to create a scandal, however, Dr. Galeazzi-
Lisi's name was kept on the rolls as director of the Vatican's sani-
tation department. Finally, at the Pope's death in 1958 the incorrigible doctor did, in fact, publish a series of articles in which he

described in detail the hardly edifying features of the death agony. A public clamor arose. The College of Cardinals, then running the vacant Holy See, quickly expelled the doctor. The Italian Medical Association barred him from practice. Either the Pacelli family or the Secretariat of State could have made things even tougher for Galeazzi-Lisi by signing a statement of charges against him, but here the inevitable hesitation to wash one's dirty linen in public entered the picture.

During the last several years of his life Pius XII also experimented with a controversial rejuvenating treatment advocated by the Swiss Protestant physician, Dr. Paul Niehans, a descendant of the Hohenzollerns. The Niehans treatment involves the injecting of living tissue from freshly slaughtered animals into the buttocks of the patient, from where its rejuvenating substances are believed by Dr. Niehans to be carried by the blood stream to ailing organs. Varying opinions of the Niehans treatment are held, with majority medical opinion in the United States being dead set against it. Suffice it to say, however, that Pius XII took the treatment twice and even believed that his latter-day spryness came as a result. The Pope showed his esteem for Dr. Niehans by naming him to fill the vacancy in the Pontifical Academy of Sciences left by Dr. Alexander Fleming, the discoverer of penicillin.

Several times during his last years Pius XII said to members of his household: "When my time comes I hope the Good Lord will give me twenty-four hours' warning and then let me go quickly."

On the morning of October 5, 1958, when the Pope was still at his summer villa at Castel Gandolfo, he developed a severe case of hiccups, which for him was a sign of fatigue. The real cause of the hiccups was, however, a small hernia in the esophagus. He rested more than was normal that day, and felt able to be present the next morning at a scheduled audience for notaries. Those about him, however, noticed that he read through his speech only with the greatest difficulty, and that he could scarcely lift his arms for the usual benediction. An alarmed Monsignor Dell'Acqua, of the

Secretariat of State, gave orders to summon Dr. Antonio Gasbarrini, of Bologna, who had replaced Dr. Galcazzi-Lisi as the Pope's regular physician. Dr. Gasbarrini, however, was then attending a convention of Swiss and Italian physicians at Venice. Thereupon, the Secretariat of State called the Patriarch of Venice, then Cardinal Roncalli, and asked him to find the doctor and send him on his way.

Dr. Gasbarrini took the late afternoon *rapido* to Rome, arriving at around 10 P.M. From the station he called the Papal Villa, only to be told by Sister Pasqualina that the Holy Father was much improved. She suggested that the doctor wait until the next morning to come out. This wait proved fatal. During the night the Pope's condition turned worse. Stricken by a cerebral hemorrhage, the Pontiff quickly lapsed into unconsciousness. Extreme unction was administered by the Jesuit Father Wilhelm Hentrich, consultant of the Holy Office.

But the end was not yet. By next morning the Holy Father had regained consciousness; he was now to have the twenty-four hours he had asked for. He was well enough the last day of his life to recite a few prayers and even to listen to music by Beethoven. Slowly, however, he slipped again into unconsciousness. At 3:52 A.M. on October 6, at the age of eighty-two years, seven months, and seven days, and after a pontificate lasting nineteen years, seven months and seven days, Eugenio Pacelli breathed his last.

Definitive historical judgments are impossible at this close range, and it is doubly hard to measure the stature of the late Pope because of the many contradictory elements of his pontificate. Although by his attitude of courtesy and tolerance Pius XII did much to reduce Protestant antipathy toward Catholicism, on the other hand his advocacy of Marianism widened the breach between the two great branches of Christendom. The Pontiff evidently sensed that the Church's thinking on many questions must be adjusted to the realities of a nuclear age, but he never quite had the courage to come out and say so.

The contribution of Pius XII to the temporary setback of Communism in Western Europe cannot be denied, although it must be qualified by the observation that the biggest Communist parties remain in Catholic countries. There are those who believe that an authoritarian political regime cannot be effectively combatted by an avowedly authoritarian religion.

V

THE ELECTION
OF A POPE

The obsequies for Pius XII demonstrated the newly found popularity of the Church. The governments of virtually all the free nations of the world, whether Christian, Moslem, Buddhist, or even pagan, sent special representatives to the funeral. The common people, too, flocked to St. Peter's in extraordinary numbers, with the devout talking of eventual sainthood for the departed. The journalistic coverage was unprecedented.

The mortal remains of the deceased Pope were first exposed in the Swiss Salon of the villa at Castel Gandolfo, where the members of the Papal Court, the Roman hierarchy, and the diplomatic corps accredited to the Holy See came to pay respects. The body was then transferred by car to St. John Lateran, the titular basilica of the Bishop of Rome, where it was again exposed for a few hours in the Chapel of the Confession, at the center of the cathedral crossing. From St. John Lateran the funeral cortege proceeded by foot through the historic streets of ancient Rome to St. Peter's. It passed the Colosseum and wound its way down the Street of the Imperial Forums, reaching St. Peter's as the last feeble rays of a late autumn sun fell over the Bernini colonnades.

87

The bell of St. Peter's tolled plaintively and incessantly during the days of mourning, while worshipers by the tens of thousands waited their turn in the piazza to enter the basilica. The first six of the nine prescribed ceremonies took place in the Sistine Chapel; St. Peter's was jammed for the last three. The members of Rome's black nobility, dressed in mourning, were striking figures in their special stand, while the thousands of seminarians and clerics on hand served as an austere black background for an impressive spectacle. The body of the late Pope was at length placed in a small crypt below the Clementine Chapel; later a monument would be executed in his honor in the Chapel of St. Sebastian.

Once the obsequies were over, all thoughts turned to who should succeed Pius XII. Cardinal Eugene Tisserant, the French dean of the College of Cardinals, became the chief executive officer of the Vatican during the period of vacancy of the Holy See. He presided at daily meetings of cardinals at which were decided all questions of the moment. The date for the opening of the conclave was set for October 25.

Meanwhile, members of the Sacred College continued to arrive daily. Some of the Princes of the Church were old indeed. The late Cardinal José Maria Caro Rodriguez, ninety-two-year-old prelate of Santiago, Chile, could hardly walk down the stairs of his airplane. Cardinal Georges Grente, the eighty-six-year-old Archbishop of Le Mans, came accompanied by two nurses. The one Chinese representative in the Sacred College, Cardinal Thomas Tien Ken-sin, had been in an automobile accident in Germany shortly before, and arrived with his arm in a cast. Cardinal Edward Mooney, of Detroit, was one of the last to arrive in Rome. He had been suffering from heart trouble; doctors advised him to take a ship rather than a plane. He died of an attack in the American Seminary at Rome only an hour before the conclave was to open.

All in all, fifty-one cardinals, of whom seventeen were Italians and thirty-four were foreigners, took part in the conclave. Little thrones were set up in the Sistine Chapel, including two for Cardinal Josef Mindszenty of Hungary and the late Cardinal Alojzije Stepinac of Yugoslavia; but apparently their governments forbade them to leave their countries. On the other hand, no obstacle was placed in the way of Cardinal Stefan Wyszynski of Warsaw, who was even permitted to bring along the chief of the Catholic opposition to the Polish Communist regime.

As the opening of the conclave approached, speculation concerning the *papabili*, meaning those worthy of being elected Pope, grew in intensity. There was talk about the necessity of having a political Pope, a pastoral Pope, a traditional Pope, a transitional Pope, an administrative Pope, an Italian Pope, a non-Italian Pope.

The name of Cardinal Gregory Peter XV Agagianian, Patriarch of the Armenians, was often repeated as the right choice to bridge the gap between East and West. Had not Agagianian and Stalin attended the same seminary at Tiflis, in Georgia, in their respective youths? The Armenian prelate not only had had much experience in the field, but he knew his way about the Roman Curia. He was thoroughly "Italianized," it was said. Moreover, as a sign of his "universality" he read and spoke eight modern languages fluently, both of East and West, not to mention Greek and Latin.

But somehow the moment did not seem ripe for a non-Italian Pope. For one thing, for better or for worse, the Papacy had become deeply involved in Italian politics and was likely to stay involved for some time. Papal intervention might be excused as long as the Pope was Italian, but how would the Italians feel if the Pope were a foreigner, and especially an Armenian? The last time Rome had had a foreign Pontiff was in the early sixteenth century, when a Dutchman, Hadrian VI, was sandwiched in between two Medicis. Since that time the Papacy had become virtually an Italian prerogative.

Cardinal Eugene Tisserant, too, had to be reluctantly discarded as a possibility. The dean of the College of Cardinals, once a French Army artillery captain, had long been regarded a clerical *enfant terrible*. Brilliant but impetuous, witty but caustic, Tisserant was too militantly Gallic to fill the role of universal pastor.

Four or five years before, Cardinal Giacomo Lercaro, the Archbishop of Bologna, had been regarded as perhaps the leading candidate for the Tiara. He was personable, aggressive, liberal-minded. People had great hopes for what he might do when he was first transferred from sleepy Ravenna, on the Adriatic Coast, to the Red stronghold of Bologna. The archbishop's plan to challenge Communism by adopting a fighting program of improving the lot of the working masses seemed admirable. But in the incumbent Mayor of Bologna, Lercaro came up against one of Italian Communism's ablest, most astute administrators. The archbishop-cardinal's candidates for City Hall went down regularly to defeat before the Red onslaught. The Church, like all other institutions, mistrusts those who incautiously court defeat.

Still another incident affected Lercaro's chances of gaining the Throne of St. Peter. This involved the case of the Bishop of Prato, which stirred up considerable anticlerical heat in Italy during the year 1957. Briefly, the pertinent facts were as follows: A young woman of Prato, theretofore a practicing Catholic, was persuaded by her Communist fiancé to marry him in a civil ceremony and to dispense with the usual Church wedding. The Bishop of Prato not only condemned this and similar acts in the regularly published diocesan bulletin but went on to name the young woman and to point out that she must be considered as henceforth living in a state of "concubinage." The couple brought suit, and the Italian court, displaying a remarkable freedom from clerical pressure, found the Bishop guilty of slander.[1]

The result was an uproar at the Vatican. *L'Osservatore Romano* went into official mourning. Pius XII canceled his appearances, and called off celebrations of the anniversary of his coronation. Numerous prelates protested that the Italian courts were making it impossible for them to fulfill their pastoral obligations. Cardinal Lercaro ordered complete mourning in his diocese, with bells tolling every half hour.

To most Italians, the Church's actions on this occasion were mis-

[1] Later on this verdict was to be reversed.

guided. The bishops seemed to be arguing that they had a God-given right to vilify as they pleased. Cardinal Lercaro's sense of judgment, not only because of this but also because of other acts, was called into question. His pastoral zeal was beyond reproach, but he seemed to lack the necessary balance, the required prudence, for the highest dignity. Thus he was eliminated as a serious contender in the 1958 conclave.

Another possible candidate, Cardinal Giuseppe Siri of Genoa, had succeeded where Lercaro had failed. Under Siri's supervision, the Catholics had won back the city government of Genoa from the Communists and had kept it ever since. But Siri, renowned as he was as a theologian, had one drawback. He was then only fifty years old. Cardinal electors in their seventies could not be expected to be enthusiastic about a man who might, if elected, given the present tendency to longevity, retain power through A.D. 2000.

Cardinal Ernesto Ruffini, of Palermo, who had once been considered *papabile*, had damaged his chances in several curious small ways. His Eminence had taken a trip to Spain and returned enthusiastic about the Franco regime. In one published interview he even hinted that he approved of the Spanish government's hardly liberal attitude toward its religious minorities. On another occasion Cardinal Ruffini overtly criticized the generally lauded work among the poor in Sicily by Danilo Dolci. One of the complaints, in fact, of anticlerical leaders is that the Church in Sicily under Ruffini's backing has virtually ignored the island's once all-pervading poverty. Politically, Cardinal Ruffini was generally regarded as a reactionary.

The same word could be used in describing Cardinal Alfredo Ottaviani, the chief theorist of the Holy Office, who had been reproved by the late Pope himself for declaring that, in his opinion, Protestants should not have equal rights in a Catholic country. This was an attitude not generally appreciated by those influential cardinals, such as the Americans, who came from countries with Catholic minorities. Ottaviani's honesty and vigor were beyond question, but in an age of religious and racial tolerance his appeal in the Papacy would be limited.

For a decade or more Giovanni Battista Montini, as Pro-Secretary of State for Ordinary Affairs, had been the late Pope's closest aide, in the absence of a Secretary of State. During this same period Monsignor Domenico Tardini had been Montini's opposite number as Pro-Secretary of State for Extraordinary Affairs, but Tardini had been constantly eclipsed by the younger, more active and more favored Montini. The rivalry between the two was deep-seated.

There was talk around the Vatican that Pope Pius XII was grooming Montini to be his successor, just as Pacelli himself had been groomed to succeed Pius XI. Certainly Montini had built a reputation as a liberal, forward-looking, thoroughly wise prelate who would make the kind of Pope the Vatican needed for this quickly changing world.

But Montini reckoned without Tardini's opposition. When the late Pope began thinking of creating new cardinals he announced his intention of raising both Montini and Tardini to the purple. Tardini, however, declined the honor, thus making it difficult for the old Pope to give either of his vice-secretaries the red hat. Vatican insiders concluded that Tardini had reasoned that with the red hat Montini would be named Secretary of State, and thus would become the leading candidate in the next conclave. Tardini knew that with his own generally conservative outlook he had little chance of the Tiara. (Later on, Tardini as well as Montini was to receive the red hat.)

Matters worked out the way Tardini apparently foresaw. After a few more years in the Secretariat, Montini was named Archbishop of Milan. This is the Church's biggest diocese in the world, but it is four hundred miles away from the center of things in Rome. At the late Pope's death Montini was still archbishop and had not yet been elevated to the Sacred College. Theoretically, even as archbishop, Montini could have been elected Pope, but in practice the cardinal electors of a conclave choose only from their own ranks. (The last time the College of Cardinals chose an outsider for Pope was in 1378, when Urban VI was elected.) Quite probably failure to receive the red hat in 1950 cost Montini the Tiara in 1958.[2]

All in all, no really ideal candidate presented himself for the 1958 conclave. On the day before the opening of the conclave, *Il Corriere della Sera* of Milan, noted for the good sense and accuracy of its Vatican reporting, reduced its list of probables to three Italians, plus Agagianian, the only foreign possibility. First of the three Italians was Cardinal Valerio Valeri, who had long served in the Vatican's diplomatic corps, lately at Paris, after which he had returned to Rome to become a prominent member of the Curia. Prefect of the Congregation of the Religious, Valeri was also a member of some six other congregations and was a protector of numerous orders. His major defect was that he had never had his own see. Second on the newspaper's list was Cardinal Marcello Mimmi, who had occupied several sees in the south of Italy, including the important one of Naples, and had also served in the Curia as Secretary of the Sacred Consistorial Congregation. He sat on seven other congregations, including the important one of the Holy Office. The third possibility was Angelo Giuseppe Roncalli, known mostly as a Vatican diplomat who had held posts in the Near East and France, but who had also for the past few years filled with distinction the historic patriarchal see of Venice. Valeri was seventy-five years old, Mimmi was seventy-six, and Roncalli seventy-seven. Although mentioning Agagianian, *Il Corriere della Sera* hazarded the opinion that the time had not yet arrived for a non-Italian Pope.

Cardinal Tisserant celebrated the customary mass of the Holy Ghost, to the accompaniment of the traditional Palestrina music, before the high altar of St. Peter's on the day of the opening of the conclave. All fifty-two participating cardinals, including Cardi-

[2] Cardinals Agagianian, Tisserant, Ottaviani, Lercaro and Montini are further discussed in Chapter IX.

nal Mooney, who was to die a few hours later, were present. The sermon came from the lips of Monsignor (now Cardinal) Antonio Bacci, the Vatican's ranking Latinist, who also held the venerable title of Secretary of Briefs to the Princes. Monsignor Bacci's words, pronounced in elegant Latin, had the fitting title "*De elegendo Pontifice.*" He spoke of the ideal Pope, saying that it was not enough to have a good administrator or a good theologian as Supreme Pontiff. The Pope should, of course, be an example of high virtues both as priest and as a man, but he should be even more. The modern Papacy was such that it required virtually a saint to fill the job.

The cardinals began entering the conclave area at three o'clock in the afternoon, a good half hour before the doors and entrances were to be shut. The first to arrive, curiously enough, was Cardinal Roncalli.

First order of business, even before the conclave area was closed, was the reading of the constitution of Pius XII dealing with the vacancy of the Holy See and the election of a new Pope, followed by the oath taking. This was the latest series of regulations on how to elect the Supreme Pontiff. After that, the participating cardinals separated to settle down in their assigned apartments. The governor within the conclave was Monsignor Callori di Vignale, Majordomo to the last two Popes; at the designated hour, after the ringing of three bells, he handed over the keys of the area to the conclave marshal, Prince Sigismondo Chigi, dressed in Renaissance finery and aided by a cortege of assistants and pages also dressed in colorful ruffles, who guarded from without.

News correspondents taking the Vatican's conducted tour of the area on the day before the start of the conclave could hardly fail to notice the improvised nature of the accommodations. The area, about an eighth of the Vatican proper, was centered around the courtyards of San Damaso and Pappagallo, a beautiful part of the Vatican but one generally lacking in comfortable bedrooms and adequate bathrooms. Many of Their Eminences had cots instead of proper beds to sleep in, and even the beds were of the old-fashioned iron-frame types. The strong and healthy among the cardinal electors naturally gave way to the aged and infirm. For example, Cardinal Tisserant was content to sleep in the Borgia Armory. Their Eminences' dining room was nearby, in a large anteroom of the Borgia apartments.

For practical reasons, virtually all observers forecast a short conclave. As a matter of fact, all recent conclaves have been on the short side. The one which elected Pius XI lasted three days, that for Leo XIII two days, that for Pius XII only one day. The longest of modern conclaves was the one which took five days to elect Pius X in 1903. Nothing even approaching the famous and scandalous Viterbo conclave of 1271, which ended after two years of voting with the election of Gregory X, has occurred in recent centuries.

The voting started on Sunday, October 26, 1958, with the College of Cardinals casting four ballots without arriving at a final choice. The day itself was typical of the Roman *ottobrata*, a sort of Indian summer, radiantly beautiful, with the temperature hovering in the low seventies. Generally on such a day the Romans would have repaired en masse to the Alban Hills, but on this day most of them chose to crowd into the huge open square between the two arms of Bernini's colonnades and watch for the white puff of smoke from the chimney of the Sistine Chapel that would announce the election of a new Pope.

At eight minutes before noon smoke began to filter out of the narrow pipe and a great shout went up from the crowd. At first the smoke was pale, and the brilliant sun made it seem white. But within seconds it began to darken, and soon there was no doubt that it was black. The two morning ballots had been inconclusive.[3]

Even more spectators came to the piazza that afternoon. By five o'clock, a good 200,000 persons had massed before the basilica. At exactly six o'clock, another great roar went up from the crowd

[3] The black smoke is supposed to be caused by putting soaked newspapers in with the ballots and burning both. The white smoke is caused when dry straw is used along with the ballots.

as a thin film of smoke was seen escaping from the chimney. This time it seemed undoubtedly white, and instantly shouts of "Long live the Pope!" were heard. But minutes later dense clouds of black smoke began to be seen, and again it was evident that there had been no choice. This time, however, virtually all the correspondents and even the Vatican Radio had been fooled and had announced that the election had taken place.

At eleven o'clock on Monday, and still again at half past five in the afternoon, other black clouds of smoke emerged. The same thing was repeated just before noon on Tuesday. Then on Tuesday evening at eight minutes before six, the long-awaited white smoke appeared. This time a crowd schooled in patience waited almost another hour to be sure that no mistake had been made, the numbers swelling by the minute until the sea of spectators reached far beyond the piazza and spilled out into the Via della Riconciliazione. At long last the lights behind the darkened windows of the loggia of St. Peter's were lit, and Cardinal Nicola Canali, senior of the cardinal-deacons, appeared flanked by other cardinals and the new Pope to read into the microphone the historic *"habemus Papam"* formula which, translated to English reads:

"I announce to you a great joy. We have a Pope. He is my most eminent and most reverend lord, Angelo Giuseppi Roncalli, Patriarch of Venice. He has chosen to reign under the name of John XXIII."

Thus was Cardinal Roncalli chosen as the 263rd successor to St. Peter on the eleventh ballot of the eighty-fifth conclave in the history of the Roman Catholic Church. What divisions took place on the first ten ballots before Roncalli received the necessary two-thirds plus one vote for election, or in this case thirty-five votes in all, remains a secret, to be divulged only when some future Pope decides to open the Vatican archives. Counting cardinals, their conclavists, and the few officials of the conclave, around one hundred persons had been inside the Sistine Chapel during the balloting and therefore knew what was happening; but they all respected their oaths of secrecy.

Wide World Photos

ortant Vatican ceremonies display the dignity and splendor of time-honored tradition. At a
mony held in St. Peter's Basilica in 1956, Pius XII blessed the relics of Innocent XI and called
on the faithful to venerate the newly beatified seventeenth-century Pontiff.

Sam Waage

An unusual photograph taken from the dome of St. Peter's shows the maze of buildings that the Apostolic Palace. Immediately behind the plaque commemorating the reign of Pius IX the barely visible spire of the Sistine Chapel.

Flame and smoke billow from a pyre in the atrium of St. Peter's during the blessing of the fire, a Holy Week observance.

One of the Swiss Guard recruits being sworn in at ceremonies in the Belvedere Court raises his right arm, his three outstretched fingers symbolic of the Trinity, and holds the banner of the Guards in the ancient pledge of loyalty. Today the ceremonies are held in the Court of San Damaso.

Wide World Photos

Photo McClure

Atop the imposing Vatican railroad station is the coat-of-arms of Pius XI, who erected the depot after the Lateran Pact of 1929 recognized Vatican City as a sovereign state. The station is now used only for storage.

The Ducal Hall of the Vatican, famous for its ornate ceiling and stucco drapery, leads to the Pauline and Sistine Chapels.

Wide World Photos

Ordination of 54 graduates of the North American College class of 1961 took place for the first time in St. Peter's; previously the ceremony was held in the college chapel.

The dedication of the North American Pontifical College in 1953 signified the growing importance of the American Church in the Roman Catholic world.

Wide World Photos

Members of an American pilgrimage are greeted during a general audience by Pius XII, who received more visitors than any Pontiff in Vatican history.

The Pope's private library in Vatican Palace as it appeared during the reign of Pius XII; it ha since been redecorated by John XXIII.

Pius XII in a photograph taken for the Holy Year of 1950.

The Papal Throne in the Sistine Chapel is empty during a solemn mass celebrated by Cardinal Aloisi Masella.

Seated in St. Peter's Basilica at a service following the death of Pius XII are the following cardinals (left to right): Ernesto Ruffini, Francis Spellman, Gregory Peter XV Agagianian, Elia dalla Costa, Pietro Fumasoni-Biondi, Marcello Mimmi, Federico Tedeschini, Benedetto Aloisi Masella, Giuseppe Pizzardo, and Eugene Tisserant.

Photo McClure

Photo McClure

The humble farm house at Sotto il Monte near Bergamo, Italy, where John XXIII was born on November 25, 1881. The Roncalli family lived on the second floor.

Angelo Giuseppe Roncalli, flanked by two fellow students, was a young seminarian at Rome in 1901.

Archbishop Roncalli when he was the Apostolic Delegate to Bulgaria, where he served from 1925 to 1934

Father Roncalli in the uniform of a sergeant of the Italian Medical Corps during World War I. An outstanding soldier, he still recalls his military career with pleasure, frequently referring to himself as "Sergeant Roncalli."

ın XXIII being carried in the *sedia gestatoria* at the papal coronation in November, 1958.

Photo McClure

John XXIII greeted by seminarians from the United States on a visit to the North American Pontifical College in 1959. He is accompanied by Monsignor Enrico Dante, the Vatican's Master of Ceremonies.

Throngs of the faithful gather beneath the balcony of St. Peter's Basilica as John XXIII imparts his traditional "Urbi et Orbi" blessing at Easter, 1961.

Photo McClure

hn XXIII receives homage from Monsignor John Bucko, titular Archbishop of Leucade, after celebrating a Byzantine-rite mass attended by prelates of both the Latin and Eastern Rites

Monsignor Angelo Dell'Acqua, young and vigorous deputy Secretary of State, holds a key position at the Vatican.

Monsignor Louis Capovilla, recently assigne to several important Vatican posts, is th private secretary and closest daily associa of Pope John.

Cardinal Tisserant of France is Dean of the Sacred College of Cardinals.

Cardinal Amleto Cicognani, Secretary of State of the Holy See, was formerly Apostolic Delegate to the United States.

Cardinal Gregory Peter XV Agagianian is Patriarch of the Armenian Church and prefect of the Sacred Congregation for the Propagation of the Faith. A scholar who speaks thirteen languages, he is believed to have been a strong candidate for the Papal Throne in 1958.

Cardinal Alfredo Ottaviani is Secretary of the Supreme Congregation of the Holy Office, which handles doctrinal and disciplinary matters. He is considered one of the most conservative members of the Vatican Curia.

Cardinal Augustin Bea, a German Jesuit and a renowned Biblical scholar, is Secretary of a new body established by John XXIII in preparation for the ecumenical council of 1962: the Secretariat for Christian Unity.

A recent portrait of Pope John XXIII.

What caused the assembled cardinals finally to choose Roncalli as the next Pope instead of Agagianian or Mimmi or Valeri? Three years or so later a few Vatican oldtimers began to pick up hints that in the initial phase of the voting Cardinal Agagianian had led. They also heard that the successful movement for Cardinal Roncalli had been organized by the late Cardinal Gaetano Cicognani, a veteran Vatican diplomat, former Nuncio to Spain, whom the new Pope was to reward later with several prominent posts. These bits of information hardly explained the course of the conclave; but all evidence would seem to indicate that Roncalli's selection represented a compromise between contending factions in the College.

The new Pope chose November 4 for his coronation. This is an Italian national holiday which commemorates the surrender of the Austro-Hungarian Empire to Italy at the close of World War I, but the date was not chosen for that reason. The new Pontiff decided to be crowned on November 4 because this is also the feast day of St. Charles Borromeo, the great figure of the Counter Reformation, who is one of Pope Roncalli's ecclesiastical heroes. It was in the Roman church dedicated to St. Charles Borromeo that Roncalli had been consecrated as bishop thirty-four years previously.

The coronation ceremonies lasted nearly five hours. Throughout the elaborate rites the voice of the seventy-seven-year-old Pope was sonorous and full. During the entire time he drank only one glass of water.

Fifty-one nations were officially represented at the coronation. Almost one half of the membership of the Italian Chamber of Deputies was there. President Eamon De Valera of Eire represented his government while the Duke of Norfolk came to represent the Queen of England. Representatives for President Eisenhower were Secretary of Labor James Mitchell, the Under Secretary of State Robert Murphy, and the former Ambassador to Italy, Clare Boothe Luce.

Many representatives of now deposed royalty were present. The former Empress of Austro-Hungary, Zita, was on hand; so were the Archdukes Robert and Hubert of Austria, and the former Queen Giovanna of Bulgaria. Princess Irene of Greece, Prince Juan of Bourbon, the Duke of Aosta, and various members of the once ruling houses of Bavaria also sat in favored places. Naturally, too, Papal nobility turned up in full strength, in all its bejeweled finery. A coronation is the one occasion on which jewelry can be properly and lavishly displayed in church.

The Pope's three farmer brothers—Alfredo, Zaverio, and Giuseppe—came down from Bergamo, and His Holiness received them and their many children on coronation eve. They were put up, however, not in the guest apartment of the Apostolic Palace, but in a modest religious hostel called Domus Maria, which was to be used months later as a press hostel for the Olympic Games.

The ceremonies were brilliant. Presiding over them was Monsignor Enrico Dante, Prefect of Pontifical Ceremonies. Monsignor Dante has devoted a lifetime to studying liturgy and is the world's ranking expert on how to conduct such long and complicated functions as a pontifical mass, a consistory either secret or semipublic, a beatification or a canonization, all the various ceremonies for the forty days of the Lenten season, and such other rare functions as a requiem mass for a departed Pope and a coronation for a new Pope.[4] He possesses what is probably the world's greatest liturgical library. During the proceedings the prefect, together with his second in command, stayed close by the Pontiff, giving him constant directions. Monsignor Dante's other aides, six in number, were posted at other strategic places, such as the high altar and the cardinals' stalls.

The morning began at eight o'clock when the cardinals, wearing their great crimson capes, gathered in the Hall of the Congrega-

[4] These ceremonies, including the pontifical high mass with the Pope actually celebrating, are so rare even in Rome that the average cardinal or bishop, let alone the Pope, although knowing the general course of the functions, does not know the details and must be helped.

tions, in the Apostolic Palace. After having removed their mantel-
letas and mezettas, they donned their red silk capes with ermine
trimming, and soon adjourned to the Hall of the Paramenti to
await His Holiness. At the appointed hour Pope John XXIII, accompanied by the Nobles of the Antechamber, entered and donned
the sacred vestments (the chasuble, the stole, the Papal cone with
its jeweled embroidery, and the mitre). The cortege now moved
through the Ducal Hall and into the great Sala Regia (Royal
Hall) adjoining the Sistine Chapel. In the Sistine Chapel the
Pope mounted the *sedia gestatoria;* the assembled prelates took
lighted candles and burst into singing the *Ave Maria Stella.* With
the procession thus formed, the cortege now descended the *Scala
Regia,* or Royal Stairway, and moved past the heroic statue of
Constantine the Great and into the atrium of St. Peter's.

First came two sergeants of the Swiss Guards, to be followed by
the procurators of the Sacred College. After them came the Apostolic Preacher, the Confessor of the Papal Household, the procurators of the religious orders, various bearers, and then the Assistant
to the Papal Wardrobe bearing the Tiara on a velvet cushion. Now
came the common chaplains, the secret clerics, various chamberlains of honor dressed in red capes, the lawyers of the Consistorial
Congregation, the members of the Apostolic Signature, various
clerics of the Apostolic Chamber, and the *uditori,* or judges of the
Sacred Rota. Now followed the Master of the Sacred Apostolic
Palace, the Vatican's chief theologian, who was in turn followed
by two secret chamberlains bearing the mitre that the Holy Father
would wear during the ceremony, and still another judge of the
Sacred Rota carrying the Papal cross and walking between a group
of functionaries called "master doorkeepers" carrying red wands.

After this came the Sacred College of Cardinals, forty-four
members in all, marching two by two. Seven cardinals were too
feeble to participate. Then came Monsignor Dante, preceding by
only a few paces the *sedia gestatoria,* on which the Pope was
sitting. The portable Throne, borne by eight men, was flanked by
bearers of the two great ostrich and peacock feather fans known

as the "flabellums," and surrounding them were the mace bearers with their silver weapons and other Swiss Guards in helmets and cuirasses carrying the pikes that symbolize the Swiss cantons. Also next to the Throne walked the commander of the Noble Guards, Prince Mario del Drago, the commander of the Swiss Guards, and the commanders of the Palatine Guard of Honor and the Gendarmery. Following His Holiness came still two other judges of the Sacred Rota and after them various patriarchs, archbishops, and bishops. The procession ended with the abbots and generals of the religious orders, all brought up by another detachment of Swiss Guards.

On the Pope's entrance into St. Peter's the choir burst into "*Tu es Petrus*" (Thou art Peter), and the Holy Father tirelessly blessed the cheering throng. The actual ceremony took place in several parts of the magnificent basilica. The Pope stopped first in the atrium or entrance of the edifice, halfway between the statues of Charlemagne and Constantine the Great. Here he seated himself on a special throne, and received the homage of the basilica chapter, allowing the eighteen canons to kiss both his slipper and knee, and other clergy to kiss only his slipper. The dean of the basilica chapter presented felicitations and best wishes for a happy reign, after which His Holiness again mounted the *sedia gestatoria* for his solemn entry into the temple.

At the Chapel of the Most Holy Trinity the Pope again descended from the portable throne, this time to kneel in silent adoration a few minutes before the Blessed Sacrament. From there he proceeded to the throne at the far end of the apse and there, as usual at every public appearance of the Pope, he received the homage of the cardinals, the archbishops, the bishops, the abbots and the penitencers, upon whom he in turn bestowed the Apostolic benediction. This act of obedience was to be repeated twice during the morning's ceremonies.

The Holy Father himself intoned the canonical hour of Tierce, during which he removed his cape and put on the many vestments needed for the celebration of a solemn high mass. The cardinal serving as deacon assisted His Holiness in vesting, while the members of the Apostolic Signature handed the vestments to His Holiness. Meanwhile, the Master of the Chamber poured water for the ablutions. At the same time the cardinals in their stalls put on vestments proper to their order.[5] The cardinal-bishops wore embroidered copes and damask mitres, and the cardinal-deacons the dalmatic and the mitre. Other prelates changed their vestments in the nearby Chapel of the Choir.

The Tierce intoned, the procession moved toward the high altar. Three times as it moved its majestic way, the Pontifical Master of Ceremonies halted the cortege, took a tuft of hemp from a silver basin, lighted it and burned it in a flash before the Pope, at the same time intoning as he knelt: "Holy Father, *sic transit gloria mundi.*"

Reaching the altar but not ascending it, the Pope embraced the lowest ranking of two cardinal-priests, then took off his mitre and recited the Confiteor, the prayer of confession. The indulgence followed, while the three eldest cardinal-bishops present recited, one by one, a Latin prayer called "Super Pontificem." When this was over the first of the cardinal-deacons placed the pallium over the Pope's shoulders, fastening it over the stole with three gem-studded golden pins. Now the Pope mounted the altar, while the choir sang the introit for the coronation mass.

The Holy Father himself read the special Introit of the Mass of the Chair of St. Peter and chanted the Gloria. Meanwhile, the first cardinal-deacon, preceded by Swiss Guards and the judges of the Sacred Rota, plus other personages, descended to the tomb of St. Peter and there sang the lauds of the coronation. The epistle was sung both in Latin and in Greek by sub-deacons, while students of the Greek seminary answered the motets of the liturgy in their own language. The Holy Father himself chanted the Credo.

[5] There are three classifications of cardinals—bishops, priests, and deacons, in that order. Virtually all the non-Curia cardinals belong to the priestly order. See Chapter IX.

During this period the officiating cardinal-deacon was at the high altar preparing the chalice, the paten, the purifications, the golden spoon, and the crusts. Having again ascended the high altar, the Holy Father sang the Preface, while members of the Signature with lighted torches took their places around the altar. At the solemn moment of the elevation, when the Supreme Pontiff lifted the Host on high, the silver trumpets far up in Michelangelo's great dome sent triumphant echoes flying through the great hush of the basilica.

A picturesque note ended the coronation mass. The dean of the basilica chapter, accompanied by two sacristans, offered His Holiness a purse of white silk embroidered in gold containing twenty-five coins. This constituted the traditional payment at St. Peter's for a "mass well sung." The Pontiff gracefully accepted the purse, passing it on to the cardinal-deacon.

The coronation proper quickly followed. The procession reformed and passed through the great nave, out through the atrium and then up the Scala Regia to the Hall of Benedictions facing the outer loggia of St. Peter's. There, to the accompaniment of wild cheers of "Viva il Papa!" the Holy Father took his place on the gilded throne of carved wood above which stretched a canopy of red velvet. The great standard of the Holy Roman Catholic Church was held close by.

The cardinal-deacon Cardinal Canali now took the triple crown representing the Pope's sovereignty and put it on the Pope's head, at the same time pronouncing the ancient formula in Latin: *"Accipe thiarum tribus coronis ornatam et scias Te esse patrem principum et regum rectorem orbis in terra, Vicarium Salvatoris Nostri Jesu Christi cui est honor et gloria in saecula saeculorum. Amen."* [6] With this, John XXIII raised his right hand, recited the customary formula for absolution and imparted the *urbi et orbi* benediction to the half-million faithful watching below. Soon after

[6] "Accept this Tiara decorated with three crowns and know that you are the Father and the Leader of princes and kings, and the Vicar on earth of our Savior Jesus Christ to whom honor and glory are due forever."

the benediction there was published a brief note in which the Pope granted a plenary indulgence to all present.

An unusual feature of the coronation was the short homily delivered by the new Pope. The major part of this was a repetition of thoughts that John XXIII had expressed only a few days before to both an assembly of cardinals and a group of journalists:

"There are those who expect the Pontiff to be a man of state, a diplomat, a scientist, an organizer of collective life, or a man whose mind is open to all forms of progress of modern life without any exceptions. Oh, venerable brothers and beloved sons, all these persons are outside the straight path that they should follow, since they have formed a concept of the Supreme Pontiff which is not fully in conformity with the ideal. The fact is that the new Pope, through the happenings of life, is like the son of Jacob who, meeting with his brothers, showed them the tenderness of his heart and, bursting into tears, said, 'I am Joseph, your brother.' The new Pope, let us repeat, realizes first of all himself the splendid image of the Good Shepherd who is described by the Evangelist St. John."

All this had been said before. Now, however, there followed a sentence of less than one hundred words, which, in the general confusion of reporting the dramatic color of the coronation, went generally unrecorded. The new Pontiff said: "In this sheepfold of Jesus no one can enter if not under the guidance of the Supreme Pontiff; and men can be certain to achieve salvation only if they are united to him, since the Roman Pontiff is the Vicar of Christ and represents His Person on earth."

Exactly what did this mean? To the lay mind there could be no doubt. Here was a restatement of the old doctrine of exclusivity of the Church. The Roman Church possesses the fullness of absolute truth. Salvation outside the Church is impossible. Successive Popes from the Middle Ages on had ruled that submission to the Roman Pontiff was necessary to a clear path to paradise. Boniface VIII, in 1302, laid down in one of his bulls: "We declare, say, define and pronounce that it is altogether necessary to salvation for every human being to be subject to the Roman Pontiff." Even Pius XII had warned: "They walk in the path of dangerous error who believe that they can accept Christ as Head of the Church while not adhering loyally to His Vicar on Earth." In other words, here was the highest possible authority declaring that a non-Catholic cannot go to Heaven.

And still, despite the evidence, there seems to be some question whether this statement really represents Catholic dogma, let alone modern Catholic thought. Ask various theologians around the Vatican, and one gets conflicting and cloudy answers. It seems all the more remarkable, then, that in the year 1958 these thoughts and these claims should have been expressed on such an occasion, especially in view of the fact that they were delivered before the invited representatives of fifty-one nations, only a minority of which call themselves Catholic.

But perhaps there is another explanation. These words showed that even in those early days of his reign John XXIII already had on his mind the subject of Christian unity. Only three months later he was to issue his call for an ecumenical council which, he hoped, would further the cause of unity. Perhaps the real meaning of John XXIII's description of the sheepfold of Jesus lay simply in the thought that only if Christians do unite can ultimate salvation be obtained, for Catholics as well as non-Catholics.

VI

THE NEW REIGN

Little was known about the new Pope even in Vatican circles. It was known, of course, that he came from Bergamo, close to Milan in North Italy, and that he had gone to both the Bergamo Seminary and the Lateran University at Rome. A few of the old guard could remember a young Monsignor Roncalli who had been stationed briefly in the Curia, in the Congregation of Propaganda Fide, during the early twenties. A few others recalled that Roncalli the Apostolic Delegate or Apostolic Nuncio to various countries (Bulgaria, Turkey, Greece, France) had periodically visited Rome to report to the Secretary of State, and even occasionally to be received by the reigning Pope. But his visits had been brief.

Nobody knew what Cardinal Roncalli really stood for in the realm of religious doctrine or political theory. Was he a traditionalist or an innovator? Had his long years in the non-Catholic Near East affected his way of life? Would he follow Pius XII in his devotion to Mary? Pius XII's great interest was in canon law; what was John XXIII's? How good a theologian was the new Pope? It was impossible to predict whether the new Pontiff would be a good administrator or a bad one, what his social ideas would be, how he regarded the problem of Communism, what notions he had of the rapidly emerging independence in Africa and Asia. Certainly nobody could have guessed in those early days that John XXIII would call an ecumenical council which would probably become one of the major religious events of the century.

Within minutes after the election announcement the news agencies were busily collecting and supplying the basic facts concerning the life of the new Pope. There were many in Lombardy who could still remember the Pope in his youth. Correspondents at Istanbul, Athens, and Paris were all questioned about the Roncalli career in those cities. Venice turned out to be a mine of information; Cardinal Roncalli had spent an active five years as the patriarch in that city.

The new Pope's peasant background came out in a dozen different ways—in his mode of dress, in his humble manner, in his expressions of sentiment, in his attachment to family and home to a degree that the city-bred Pius XII could never have felt. John XXIII shows often the attitude of a country priest; he is constantly reciting the *de profundis* for the dead.

The Roncallis had for centuries tilled petty acreage on a tenant basis in a tiny hamlet called Sotto il Monte (Beneath the Hill), near Bergamo, a handsome and historic small city nestling in the sub-Alps, about forty miles east of Milan. Its chief claim to fame in modern times had been as the birthplace of Gaetano Donizetti, the opera composer. The Roncallis were poor but not needy. The Pope said his family had never been able to have luxuries but had always been provided with the necessities of life. A look at the photographs of the three living brothers of the new Pontiff is enough to convince anyone that they are simple farmers, undoubtedly of great devotion, but of no pretense whatever.

Angelo Giuseppe himself was the third child of thirteen, of whom nine lived to maturity. He is now the eldest son. Those Roncallis who did not take religious vows were quite prolific. One brother, Giuseppe, is a widower with five sons. The Pope's sister, Assunta, is a widow with four daughters. The Pope's youngest brother, Giovanni, died in 1957 leaving eight children.

The Roncallis are noted for longevity. At ceremonies celebrating his eightieth birthday in 1961 the Pope remarked that his father and mother had lived well into their eighties, that his paternal grandfather had died at the age of eighty-nine, and that his grandfather's four brothers lived until eighty-eight, eighty-seven, eighty-six, and eighty-five years respectively. "The precious substance of this venerable longevity, to which all the living aspire," said the Pope, "is in fact the grace and privilege of but a few. It has its basis in the perfect conformity of man's will with God's will." Talk of John XXIII as a "transition Pope" with a short reign might, indeed, be belied by a glance at the life spans of his ancestors. Plainly, it is quite conceivable that the present reign will be fairly long.

His choice of the name "John" not only came as a surprise but was considered significant. Just why had Cardinal Roncalli gone back to the early fourteenth century for a name under which to reign as Pope? In his first address to the assembled cardinals, His Holiness explained in these graceful words:

"This name [of John] is sweet to us because it is the name of our father. It is dear to us because it is the name of the humble parish in which we received the sacrament of baptism. It is the solemn name of innumerable cathedrals scattered all over the world, and first among them is the sacred Lateran Basilica, our cathedral. It is the name borne by a very long series of Roman Pontiffs, so long that it sets the record number. In fact, there have been twenty-two Supreme Pontiffs of unquestionable legitimacy who have borne this name.[1] We have chosen to cover the littleness of our name beneath the magnificent succession of Roman Pontiffs."

[1] The last legitimate John, twenty-second of the line, was a Frenchman, Jacob d'Euse of Cahors, who ruled from Avignon from 1316 to 1334 during the Great Schism. In the fifteenth century Baldassare Cossa, of Naples, was elected by a conclave held at Bologna and reigned under the name of John XXIII. At that period the Church had three rival Popes. Under threat of being deposed, Cossa was finally persuaded by a council at Florence to abdicate, thus paving the way for the election of a new Pontiff who would once again unite Christendom. The subsequent enthronement of Martin V at Rome ended the schism. For many years this John XXIII, however, appeared in the official Vatican list of Supreme Pontiffs. His grave at Florence is even marked with

But Vatican specialists believed that the new Pope also had other and subtler reasons for his choice. Clearly, they said, the new occupant of St. Peter's Throne wanted to get away from the succession of Piuses that had ruled the Church, with only a few brief interruptions, for the last hundred years or more. Pope John wanted to break with at least part of the immediate past and revert to older and perhaps happier times. The historically minded at the Vatican sensed that a new era was dawning. And they were right.

The very first gestures of the new Pope were graceful and not without significance. He had barely consented to take the high office to which he had been elected when he took the *biretta*, or square red hat, he had worn as a cardinal and placed it on the head of the secretary of the conclave, Monsignor Alberto Di Jorio. He thus automatically made Di Jorio a member of the Sacred College and at the same time revived an old custom. He also showed his awareness of the need to create new cardinals. This accomplished, the new Pope turned to his private secretary, Monsignor Loris Capovilla, whom he had brought down from Venice as his conclavist, and said: "Monsignor, I expect you to stay here at Rome and help me." Monsignor Capovilla would soon become one of

---

the inscription of "Joannes XXIII Pontifex Maximus." But Vatican historians with a passion for legitimacy now list him only as a rival to the legitimate Pope of the time and therefore not of the sequence. One element that the present Pontiff neglected in his mention of the "John" Popes was that his predecessors of the same name included some of the most unworthy occupants of the Throne of St. Peter. John X (914–928), for example, was publicly accused of adultery. John XI (931–935), only twenty-five years old when elected, the son of Pope Sergius II, was of low moral character. This John's grandson, John XII (955–964), became Pope at the age of sixteen and was mainly noted for the orgies staged in the Lateran Palace. Romans rebelled against John XIII (965–972) because of his infamous cruelty. John XIV (983–984) was imprisoned and starved to death in the Castel Sant'Angelo. John XV (985–996) had the distinction of being the father of Papal nepotism. John XVI (997–998) was actually an anti-Pope, but is counted in the sequence. He ended by being murdered in a Castel Sant'Angelo dungeon. John XIX (1024–1032), according to the Catholic historian Hefele, was a "dissolute and aggressive man who did more harm than good to the Church."

the key figures in the new pontificate. John XXIII then turned to
the still assembled cardinals and asked them to remain within the
conclave area for another night. He wanted to have what he called
a series of "family gatherings" with them before they went their
separate ways.

The inevitable confusion of the first days over, the new Pope
served friendly notice that he intended to be in practice as well
as name the Bishop of Rome. This determination had psychological as well as historical overtones. From 1871 to 1929 successive
heads of the Church had considered themselves prisoners of the
Vatican. The Lateran Treaty had finally composed the differences
between Church and State. The event had been popularly labeled
the "Reconciliation"; the date of the signing had become a public
holiday; and the new broad avenue leading from the Tiber to St.
Peter's Square had been named "Via della Riconciliazione." But
the "Reconciliation" had brought little more freedom for the
Pope. True, the treaty had made elaborate provision for the
Popes to move about Rome, specifying that proper notice of any
intended visit be given to the Italian police and motorcycle
escorts be furnished by the Italian government. But here was just
the point; far too much fuss was involved. The result was that in
practice the Pope had remained pretty much confined to the
Vatican. Pius XI had visited Rome only two or three times in all
his pontificate. In the nineteen and a half years of his pontificate
the late Pius XII had gone outside the Vatican on the average of
less than once a year, and almost always on formal occasions.

John XXIII changed all that, and quickly. "The Reconciliation
means reconciliation," the new Pontiff told his staff. So saying, the
Holy Father decided that he would visit not only the historic
churches and the major and minor basilicas of the Eternal City
but also each of the 192 parishes. In his first three years on the
Throne the Pope actually visited around 60 of these parishes.
What interfered with his visiting was his habit of going back to
the same places several times. Thus it early became obvious that
John XXIII's favorite ecclesiastical edifice in Rome was St. Paul's-

Outside-the-Walls, which he visited no less than five times during his first two years on the Throne.

While most of the Pontiff's excursions into Rome were to visit churches, he did other things, too. On one occasion he allowed a circus troupe to perform for him briefly. On another he attended, along with his court, a version in concert form of *Murder in the Cathedral*, based on the life of Thomas à Becket, performed by the Rome Opera. In one trip, in late 1960, he asked to see the new highways that the Italians had built in preparation for the Olympic Games.

There was some difficulty at first. During the first week of his reign the Pope ordered his car and announced he was off for St. Paul's-Outside-the-Walls. That trip meant traversing Italian territory for several miles. It took the assistant Secretary of State to persuade the Holy Father that such an impromptu trip into Italian territory would be, from the standpoint of protocol, lamentable. The trip to St. Paul's was postponed until proper arrangements could be made.

On another occasion the Pope decided to visit a home for aging priests at Monte Mario, about two miles up the Tiber from the Vatican. He wanted to see the ninety-nine-year-old Monsignor Alfonso Carinci, ex-Secretary of Rites, who was an old friend. (Monsignor Carinci was one of those prelates who had long been passed over by Pius XII for promotion to the Sacred College. John XXIII now offered him the red hat, but he pleaded that he was too old.) Although the carabinieri station outside St. Peter's, which maintains liaison with the Vatican on the Pope's movements, was duly notified, the request was made that there be no police escort and that no advance warning be given of the visit. The caretaker who answered the doorbell at the Monte Mario home was surprised to behold His Holiness in person, as was the Monsignor. By the time the visit was finished, however, word had made the rounds of the neighborhood and a crowd had gathered. No fear was felt for the Pope's life—nobody would think of attacking him—but the devout pressed around the Pope's car and his person to the point where there was some trouble in leaving. After that the Holy Father decided that it was preferable, if only for the sake of order, to have the police along with him.

Other trips followed. One day he went up to Castel Gandolfo, which would henceforth be his summer villa, to look it over and get acquainted with the local mayor.[2] On one official trip back from St. John Lateran, cathedral of the Bishop of Rome, the Pope changed the routing at the last minute and had his chauffeur take him up a side street to one of Rome's most interesting minor basilicas, the Church of St. Clement, near the Colosseum, named for the third Pope after St. Peter himself. This church, built on three separate layers, is generally regarded as the oldest place of worship in Rome.

In the second year of his reign the Pope dedicated an entire week to making the rounds of the congregations, the tribunals, and the offices of the Holy See. These were described as "family" visits, and not even reporters of L'Osservatore Romano were allowed to accompany the Pontiff. At the Propaganda Fide Palace at Piazza di Spagna, His Holiness recognized some of the clerics who worked with him there forty years ago. The Holy Father showed the greatest interest, however, in the venerable Holy Office, and in this palace he entered the private apartment of Cardinal Gaetano Cicognani and sat with delight in the chair traditionally reserved for the Pope in all cardinals' apartments. No Pope had done this in the last hundred years. In fact, in most cardinals' quarters this piece of furniture is in bad need of repair as a result of a century of disuse.

Meanwhile, His Holiness began visiting hospitals, seminaries, monasteries. On the day after the Christmas of his first year in office he even appeared at Rome's large jail for men, the Regina Coeli, not far from the Vatican, where he said mass for the imprisoned. In an informal discourse His Holiness recalled that one

---

[2] In the past the Mayor of Castel Gandolfo has sometimes been a Socialist, but in the most recent municipal elections, to the Church's gratification, the voters returned a Christian Democrat.

of his relatives had once been jailed for a month for poaching, thus intimating that even the best of men sometimes land in the wrong place. The Pope especially sees it as his duty to visit the sick; he has called on diplomats, wives of Vatican officials, ailing cardinals.

At Lent, John XXIII revived the old Papal custom, first instituted by Gregory the Great in the late sixth century, of personally walking in the ceremonies of various stations of the cross. Of the forty stations in Rome, John XXIII paid visits, in his first Lenten period in Rome, to three: the Church of the Holy Cross of Jerusalem, by tradition erected by Constantine the Great after he had beheld the cross which signaled his victory over Maxentius; Santa Maria in Cosmedin, a small church in ancient Rome which once served as a pagan temple, then was a grain distribution headquarters, and finally was converted to the Byzantine rite church at Rome; and San Lorenzo-outside-the-walls, at the entrance to Rome's great cemetery, erected in the thirteenth century, on the site where the famous Roman soldier had been grilled alive for his beliefs.

On another occasion the Pope visited the famous Renaissance Church of the Twelve Apostles, in the Colonna Palace, just off the Piazza di Venezia, where he took part in a novena organized by Franciscans. It was here, sixty years before, that the young Father Roncalli had participated in celebrations of the fiftieth anniversary of the proclamation of the Dogma of the Immaculate Conception. Here, too, is the grave of the Greek prelate Cardinal Bessarion, who was a moving spirit in the Council of Florence which, in 1439, brought temporary union between the Greek and Roman churches. The Pope stopped to say a prayer at his tomb.

In other words, John XXIII showed that he liked to move about. In one of his informal chats he expressed great compassion for those of his predecessors who found themselves prisoners in the Vatican, adding that if he had had to stay permanently within the Leonine Walls he would have been unhappy.

Roncalli had acquired the pleasant habit of sightseeing as a young priest. Nothing delighted him more than poking about old churches and monuments, of which there are literally thousands up and down the peninsula. He frequently surprised visiting clerics by telling them more about the history and traditions of churches in their dioceses than they knew themselves.

In his various diplomatic jobs he had also proved to be an inveterate traveler. While in Bulgaria he covered the entire country; in Turkey he toured the storied coast of Asia Minor, the scene of so much of early Christian history; and as the Papal representative to Athens he left no major part of Greece unseen. In 1960, when receiving in audience a group of sports writers who had arrived in Rome for the Olympic Games, the Pope asked how many of the writers present had visited Olympia, where the games originated. None raised his hand. "Well, we have been there," the Pope said quietly.

While Nuncio to Paris, Roncalli visited France province by province. Moreover, he drove the entire North African littoral from Tunis to Morocco, then across Spain and back to France, for a distance of six thousand miles. He infinitely prefers automobile travel over any other.

As John XXIII, he has also ventured outside of Rome. He visited the old Byzantine monastery at Grotta Ferrata. He went to Subiaco, site of the original Benedictine monastery where St. Benedict flagellated himself by wallowing in the thorn bush. The Pope's mood on this occasion was notably unlike St. Benedict's. "It is easy to see," he told the devout who gathered to watch him, "that it has been some time since a Pope came here. All the same, I beg you to be good and orderly, otherwise they will never let me back into the Vatican!"

A much longer trip was the 120-mile jaunt to Roccantica Sabina to visit one of the seminaries where he had studied some sixty years before. This was the longest journey to be undertaken by a reigning Pope since 1851, when Pius IX's horsedrawn carriage took him on a tour of the Papal State. The suspicion is abroad that His Holiness would like to make even more ambitious trips, but so far has not judged the moment opportune. He has spoken of returning to Venice. There was at one time talk that he might fly to Lourdes. In 1960 he even considered the possibility of attending the world Eucharist Congress at Munich, but decided against it when he learned that his going would involve transport and lodging for several hundred other members of the Papal court.

In the first three years in office the Holy Father left the Vatican premises on an average of almost once weekly. By now Romans have become quite used to seeing the big black Mercedes-Benz with the license plate "SCV I" (meaning the Vatican State I) pass by.[3] More than any statistical recapitulation could suggest, Pope Roncalli has regained a freedom of movement for Roman Pontiffs lacking for the last century. But he has accomplished more. By visiting and revisiting the parishes of his own diocese, John XXIII has underlined his concept of the Papacy in a way he could never have done in words alone. He has set an example to be followed by other members of the Roman hierarchy throughout the world.

To John XXIII the Pope is, above all, the "universal pastor." The supreme ruler of Roman Catholicism has many titles, but for the present occupant of St. Peter's Throne the shortest is the best. According to an ancient tradition the Italian word for "Pope" ("Papa") is formed by taking the first syllables of two Latin words, *Pater Pauperum*, "Father of the Poor." [4] Here is the recurring theme of the new reign. Other Pontiffs have been known for their teaching ability (Pius X), or for their advocacy of peace (Pius XII), or perhaps for their brilliantly written encyclicals (Leo XIII); John XXIII wants to go down in history as the "pastoral Pope."

The present Pope expressed this concept early in his pontificate at least three times, once in an address to his cardinals, another

[3] Pius XII always rode in a Cadillac, but John XXIII changed to the German make.

[4] The Pope is Bishop of Rome; Vicar of Jesus Christ; Successor of St. Peter, the Prince of Apostles; Supreme Pontiff of the Universal Church; Patriarch of the West, Primate of Italy; Archbishop and Metropolitan of the Province of Rome; Sovereign of the State of Vatican City.

time in his coronation speech, and still another time to a group of
international journalists who had been covering the conclave. After
noting that he had been staying awake nights thinking of his new
post, His Holiness said:

"They speak of a political Pope, of a gifted Pope, of a diplomatic Pope. Instead, the Pope is the Pope, the good pastor who
forever seeks for the means to reach souls and spread the truth.
All other human qualities—scientific knowledge, diplomatic tact
and skill, organizational qualities—can complement and adorn a
pontifical government, but they cannot in any way replace the
central point."

This concept, as the Pope himself suggested, is an oversimplifi-
cation of a highly complex subject. Quite obviously the occupant
of the Chair of St. Peter must be something more than a glorified
parish priest. The notion of the "universal pastor" is appealing but
insufficient. Indeed, the first three years of the pontificate of John
XXIII have demonstrated that in these days the Roman Pontiff
must above all be a man able to project his personality both on
the Church he heads and on the world at large. And here is where
the present reign has been signally successful. In an age of highly
developed public relations, John XXIII has created in the public
consciousness the picture of a gentle, kind, likable, tolerant,
shrewd, wise, and capable ruler.

Almost everything that the new Pope did in the first months of
his reign seemed in pleasant contrast to the austere practices of the
old Pope. John XXIII, it turned out, was the perfect extrovert as
opposed to the lonely, brooding, introverted Pius XII. John XXIII,
for example, liked to have people about him. Instead of keeping
the vast extension of space on the second and third floors of the
Apostolic Palace half empty, John XXIII quickly filled the various
apartments with new nominees to old posts. At long last the
spacious apartment of the Secretary of State was filled; so was that
of the private secretary to His Holiness. Under Pius XII the windows of the Apostolic Palace were invariably dark; under John

XXIII brilliant light streams out and gives new life to the once quite shadowy St. Peter's Square.

Instead of ordering the Vatican gardens cleared of all personnel when he goes there to walk, John XXIII ordered work to be continued as usual. In the early days the Holy Father had a fondness for striking up casual conversations, especially with the gardeners. (He has since become too busy for such pleasantries.) It was out of one of these chats that the Pontiff became convinced that Vatican employees were woefully underpaid and consequently initiated an inquiry which soon led to important pay rises and allowances in virtually every category. (See Chapter X.)

Instead of dining in solitary splendor, the Holy Father frequently invites people, almost always prelates, to dinner. By now he has had as his guests many cardinals. Not for a century or more has a Pope regularly invited outsiders to dine with him. But early in his reign John XXIII flatly declared that he did not like to eat alone. "It makes me feel like a seminarian being punished," the Pope said. "And I find nothing in canon law which says I cannot eat with other people." The newspaper *L'Osservatore Romano*, in a recent anniversary issue, claimed that His Holiness ate sparingly and drank virtually nothing, but the Pope's generous proportions suggest otherwise. He is certainly no ascetic.[5] Nor, for that matter, are many of the Vatican clerics.

Two nuns, Sisters Paola and Rosa, both members of an order of Bergamo called Little Sisters of the Poor, run the Papal kitchen. They are specialists in the preparation of North Italian dishes known to please the Roncalli palate. The Pope leans toward the simple but rather coarse food of the peasant, but is also qualified to appreciate finer, more elaborate dishes. The Bergamo nuns are good at preparing such concoctions as *risotto alla milanese,* a rice

---

[5] When Cardinal Roncalli was Pius XII's representative at Paris, he was known, even in that capital of gourmets, as an extremely able provider. Not only were his meals excellent but the Nuncio's cellar was also renowned and his choice Havanas were the talk of Paris. The Roncalli cook at Paris has since opened a fancy restaurant.

specialty cooked in the Milanese style, and *polenta*, or corn mush, usually served with either sausages or game such as woodcock and wild hare. Although the Pope now drinks sparingly of wine, for guests he usually has on hand either the red Valpolicella or the white dry Soave, again both from North Italy. From time to time the Archbishop of Bordeaux sends him cases of the finest French wines. When there are no guests to dinner the Pope usually eats with his secretary, Monsignor Capovilla. Pius XII liked to have Sister Pasqualina, among others, read to him while he ate his frugal meals; John XXIII prefers to converse.

The new Pope has proved to be something of an innovator in the matter of Papal dress. He wears the elaborately embroidered red stole, formerly worn only on solemn occasions, at ordinary functions. He called in a special bootmaker and had him design some heavy peasant-type walking shoes in good solid leather which he then had dyed a deep red. These he now wears in place of the velvet shoes normally used by Popes. His headgear has been the despair of the Vatican traditionalists. First he discarded the usual heavy red silk hat in favor of a specially designed white linen or white felt hat. Then one day, in an appearance at St. Peter's, he donned a *camauro*, a red felt cap trimmed in white ermine with big earmuffs. The *camauro* had once been the traditional head-dress of Popes but had not graced the head of a Roman Pontiff since the days of Sixtus V, in the late sixteenth century. One Vatican medal has even been struck showing John XXIII in a *camauro*.

The *sedia gestatoria*,[6] the portable throne on which he is normally carried on ceremonial occasions, bothered the new Pontiff considerably. He not only felt uneasy, but according to one of his staff he complained: "It's too windy up there." He proposed that the use of the *sedia gestatoria* be restricted and that on minor occasions he walk; but the Vatican staff quickly pointed out that this was the only way for the Pope to be seen, and he finally agreed.

Another custom that annoyed John XXIII was the habit of ap-

[6] There are three portable thrones—one for six men to handle, one for eight, and another for twelve.

plauding his entrance in churches. Under his orders loudspeakers at first broadcast the request not to applaud, but when this appeal went unheeded, the Holy Father hit upon a simple device. He ordered the singing of the Credo as he made his entrance. The public would thereupon burst into singing, an act more decorous for a house of God.

John XXIII had difficulty, he said, accustoming "myself to being a universal pastor." Several times during those first few weeks he would fail, even in audiences, to use the imperial or Papal "we" when talking of himself and would lapse into "I." According to the testimony of Monsignor Capovilla, he would sometimes wake up in the middle of the night thinking about a certain problem and would say to himself: "I shall speak to the Pope about it." Then, when he was fully awake, he would say: "But I am the Pope. Very well, I shall speak to Our Lord about it."

The fact that the Holy Father's specialty is the extemporaneous witticism has given rise to many stories about him. Nor is he above an occasional bit of punning. One celebrated pun involved Cardinal Canali (which can mean "canals") of the Curia, and Monsignor Angelo Dell'Acqua (which means "water") of the Secretariat of State. Asked how he found Rome as compared to Venice, His Holiness replied: "Just about the same. At Rome we are still surrounded by Canali and Dell'Acqua."

Many anecdotes revolve around Venice, of which he was very fond. Shortly after he became Pope the question of a coat-of-arms arose. A design, which included among other elements the winged lion of Venice, was submitted to him. He approved everything but the lion's frown. "He looks too fierce," explained the Pope. "Let's change his expression." In talking to a group of Venetians who had come to see their former patriarch, John XXIII said: "Come back again. Unfortunately, you'll always find us here."

On one occasion an ambassador from one of the Arab countries presented his credentials and began to read a long and flowery

speech. At a pause in the reading the Holy Father interrupted to
say: "Your Excellency, let us hand over these formal speeches to
our secretaries, and then we can go inside my library and have a
quiet talk."

The late Pius XII had almost no small talk. The new Pope, on
the other hand, is full of it, and uses casual conversation almost
as a form of recreation.

John XXIII rarely comes out and criticizes anything directly,
but he has been known to lay down judgments about clerics under
his administration. Once, for example, while still Patriarch of
Venice, Cardinal Roncalli said of an overenergetic priest: "He's
the type who would think it necessary to help God Himself create
the world."

Pacelli the aristocrat cut the Papal court to the minimum; Roncalli the peasant has expanded it to the maximum. Starting with
Secretary of State, the new Pope has filled all the traditional jobs
which Pius XII left unfilled, to the point where the present Papal
Court is the most elaborate since the days of Gregory VI, a century
ago. The *sediari* and *palafrenieri* (outriders on the Papal carriage)
are back to full strength. Admittedly these individuals, who in-
herit their jobs, are not often called upon these days to perform
their traditional work. Instead, they now man the cloakrooms of
the Apostolic Palace. The same observation can be made of the
facchini di sala (furniture movers), the *bussolanti*, and the *scopa-
tori segreti* (secret sweepers). The latter have not seen a broom
or cleaning rag for ages, but instead do typing and clerical work
for the Papal household.

Recent Popes have found it unnecessary to have four clerics
called "Privy Chamberlains Participating" to manage their households. For Pius XII one was sufficient, and he was rarely busy.
John XXIII quickly named all four. Pius XII abolished completely
the habit of stationing lay officers called "Privy Chamberlains of
the Sword and Cape Participating" in the Apostolic Palace. John
XXIII, partly because he thinks this group with their Spanish-style

uniforms ornamental and partly because he likes to spread the jobs about, put them back into service.

While John XXIII in general respects the great traditions of the Papacy, he has not always observed the tried practices of the Roman Curia. As just one example, which will be discussed more fully later (see Chapter IX), he has virtually repealed the once sacrosanct rule of seniority among cardinals in the Curia. He has also disregarded the promotion system of the Papal household, or "Pontifical family," as it is technically known, much to the dismay of Vatican traditionalists.

A case in point is Monsignor Capovilla. A dark-haired priest of distinguished presence and short stature, Capovilla looks much younger than his forty-seven years. He comes from a poor family of the Veneto, his father having worked in a sugar factory at Padua. Having gone through the Venice Seminary, Capovilla as a young priest became clerical adviser to the local Catholic Action. During the last war he was a chaplain in the Italian air force. After the war he became chief of ceremonies at St. Mark's. Meanwhile, he also became editor of the diocesan paper and the Venetian correspondent of an old and well-known Catholic paper L'Avvenire d'Italia (The Future of Italy). Later he was connected with the Venice radio in the role of spiritual adviser, in which capacity he delivered a series of impassioned sermons on the New Testament. For reasons not entirely clear, the then Archbishop of Venice did not like these sermons, and they were consequently dropped. Capovilla's future in the Venetian diocese did not at that moment look bright. However, the archbishop, who was to have become a cardinal at Pius XII's consistory of 1953, died before he received the red hat. Roncalli, then the Papal Nuncio at Paris, was elevated to the purple and chosen to fill the Venetian post.

The Capovilla-Roncalli relationship dates from 1953, when the former was sent to Paris to report to the newly nominated Patriarch of Venice. The Capovilla mission on this occasion was the relatively simple one of telling the new cardinal what problems he was likely to find in his new diocese. Apparently the young priest performed his task well. At any rate, upon arrival at Venice, Cardinal Roncalli called him in and asked if he would like to be his private secretary. Capovilla quickly accepted.

In the rarefied atmosphere of clerical Rome, Capovilla has proved to be a brilliant aide to His Holiness. He has also at times been a thorn in the side of some in the Vatican who thought him precocious. In startling contrast to the ever-calm Roncalli, he is a highly strung man, one of whose main jobs has been to do the Pope's worrying about many small matters. The Pope, once asked how he came to choose such a bundle of nerves to be his secretary, quickly replied: "We get along well because we are opposites."

Capovilla also represents for the Holy Father something of a window to the world's youth. The secretary likes speed, wants to go everywhere in an airplane, is an inveterate television watcher and radio listener.

His Holiness, in return, has done well by Monsignor Capovilla, in fact some say entirely too well. The secretary is often allowed to ignore channels in passing down the Holy Father's wishes. He has sometimes been encouraged to usurp the prerogatives of the Papal Master of the Chamber in arranging audiences. The Pope appointed Capovilla a canon of St. Peter's, thus making him a member of the world's most celebrated cathedral chapter. Most important of all, the Pope named Capovilla to the key post of *coppiere* (literally, cupbearer) among the Secret Privy Chamberlains Participating. The Master of the Chamber, Monsignor Mario Nasalli Rocca di Corneliano, objected to this appointment on traditional grounds. He insisted that the eight posts of Secret Privy Chamberlains Participating were reserved to nobility; Nasalli Rocca himself holds the title of prince, whereas Capovilla is a commoner. The Pope was said to have answered bluntly: "I have never much cared for these names that have to have a *di* attached to them," referring to the fact that the Italian nobility puts a *di* (meaning "of") after their names. The *coppiere* among the Secret Privy Chamberlains Participating inevitably leads to bigger jobs.

He is always named Master of the Chamber, and the Master of the Chamber almost always becomes a cardinal. All this augurs well for Capovilla's future, clerically speaking.

The most striking difference between Pius XII and his successor is the way each Pope has conducted his audiences. John XXIII sees far more people but gives many fewer audiences and spends much less time on them than Pius XII. And he usually refuses to be photographed with the visitors. The Papal gendarmery, which keeps track of such matters, computed that in the first year of his reign John XXIII received in audience a grand total of 242,000, which is about twice as many as Pius XII received in the banner Holy Year of 1950.

The great majority of those received were Italians, to whom the Pope could speak in his native tongue. But there were also tens of thousands of foreigners. To some the Holy Father could talk in his fluent but accented French, while with others he had to depend on an interpreter. The Pope speaks halting Bulgarian and Greek and a few words of Russian. He is currently studying English, and was able to say a few words in that language when he received President Eisenhower. But the accent is not good.

The roster of individuals that the Holy Father receives in the course of a year reads like an International Who's Who. During one year the Pontiff received in audience the former King Simeon of Bulgaria, the Queen Mother and Princess Margaret of Britain, King Hussein of Jordan, President Giovanni Gronchi of Italy, Prince Albert of Belgium, President Sukarno of Indonesia, the King and Queen of Greece, President Celal Bayar of Turkey, Prince Rainier and Princess Grace of Monaco, the Prime Minister of Japan, President Bourguiba of Tunisia, the President of Argentina, the British Minister for Air, the President of the Republic of Madagascar and his wife.

Among the diverse groups the Pope received during the same period were the domestic servants of Rome, the policemen of Rome, a group of Catholic journalists, a group of rectors of Italian seminaries, members of the World Blind Congress, the Italian Teachers' Association, the American astronautical research workers, a group of African students and poets, a large group of Japanese pilgrims, an association of Italian farmers, a group of farm machine manufacturers, the diocesan leaders of Catholic Action, and delegates to the World Child Welfare Congress.

At the same time, of course, the Pope was receiving regularly the heads of congregations and superiors general of the major orders. Under Pius XII the bishops on their regular visits to Rome often failed to be received by the Pope. John XXIII would not dream of not seeing a visiting bishop. In 1960, he received in audience a total of 257 visiting bishops from beyond the borders of Italy.

The audiences of John XXIII are informal, almost gay, affairs. Pius XII insisted on writing everything down before he opened his mouth; the present Pope writes nothing down and does not even speak from prepared notes. Instead, he may ramble on amiably about almost anything under the sun. The *Osservatore Romano* man assigned to cover these audiences had such a hard time keeping up with the Holy Father's phraseology that the Pope finally took pity on him and bought him a tape recorder.

The speeches of Pius XII were invariably printed textually in the Vatican organ. John XXIII has directed the editors to print only summaries of those portions of his addresses which could interest the general public. He has never been known, moreover, to object to the reporting of his remarks, although he has directed Capovilla to tone some of them down.

And so the first three years of the pontificate of John XXIII passed quickly. The Pope himself said on the first anniversary of his coronation: "The last year has passed as if it were a week."

What kind of Pope was John XXIII proving himself to be? At the Vatican it is said that three telltale "acts," all taking place in the first two months of his reign, set the tone for all that has followed.

The first came in the coronation, when during the homily the Pope compared himself to Joseph meeting his brethren. Here, it was said, was the true measure of the new Pope's profound sense of humility and his hope for Christian unity.

The second also came in a homily, this one delivered when as Bishop of Rome the Pontiff took possession of his own basilica, St. John Lateran, in an elaborate ceremony dating back centuries and lasting for hours. Coupling "the Book and the Chalice" as the two great manifestations of Christian devotion, His Holiness said:

"The first glory of every pontificate is precise practical obedience to the Gospel command: 'And going forth, teach ye all nations.' This is a great lesson on which there is perfect agreement between the Eastern Fathers and the Latin Fathers. St. John Chrysostom reminded every Pope, every bishop, every priest, of the sacred duty of preaching the heaven-sent doctrine, which is the highest responsibility for each of them.

"And next to the Book, here is the Chalice. The most mysterious and the most sacred part of the liturgy of the Eucharist revolves about the chalice of Jesus, which contains His Precious Blood. Christian life is a sacrifice. . . . The Chalice upon the altar and the venerable rites which join the consecrated bread and wine into one single Sacrament, marking its highest point, represent the sublimity of the union between God and man, the perfection of the Christian profession."

The third "act" was the Pope's visit to prison on St. Stephen's Day. Here was the completion on the part of the Pope of the seven traditional corporal works of mercy.[7] Taken altogether, these three manifestations told the people of the Vatican that under John XXIII the emphasis would be on religious, doctrinal work, with little time left over for other things.

John XXIII, on whom everything depends at the Vatican, has lost only a couple of days of work in his first three years. He is a man of the healthiest sort of irregularity. He eats when he is hun-

---

[7] Feed the hungry, refresh the thirsty, clothe the naked, shelter the homeless, tend the sick, visit the imprisoned, bury the dead.

gry and sleeps when he is sleepy. It goes without saying that he
also works when he wants to work. The Pope often goes to bed
early, in which case he may sleep three or four hours, wake up and
do a couple of hours of work, and then go back to sleep again. He
sometimes rises early, but other times sleeps rather late.

Pius XII took a walk, rain or shine, at three o'clock every afternoon in the same part of the Vatican gardens. John XXIII also
takes walks, but he is as likely to choose the morning as the afternoon and he may wander all over the premises. He never uses the
typewriter, and he touches the telephone only to call the Secretary
of State. He has little time for recreation, although he is interested
in the cinema and has installed a small movie theater in the
Apostolic Palace. The films, which he sees with his private secretary, are mainly documentaries.

There is no set routine for him. He keeps more or less to a
schedule for audiences, but he will also break it if he thinks necessary. He once said: "It really does not matter what they think
and say about me, whether I arrive late or do not arrive at all. I
must remain true to my good intentions at all costs. The main
thing is that I want to be good to all at all times."

In a world of high tensions and serious strains, John XXIII is
calm and assured. He gives the impression that regardless of how
bad things may be now, everything will come out right in the end.
Perhaps it is this self-assurance that is the key to his immense
popularity. In many ways he seems to be the right Pope for the
right period.

John XXIII once said that if anybody wanted to know the chief
characteristic of the new reign he had only to refer to a maxim of
St. John Chrysostom, the early Greek Father who said: "There
would be no more pagans if we behaved like true Christians."

VII

THE BACKGROUND AND
EDUCATION OF A POPE

John XXIII is superbly educated, and demonstrates an intense preparation for his high calling. In him the solidest sort of clerical training has been combined with a thorough schooling in the classics.

The Vatican puts the highest premium on the ability to produce an apt Latin or Greek quotation at the right moment. The present Pope has few peers in this field. Even his extemporaneous speeches are full not only of references to the Scriptures and the writings of the Fathers and Doctors of the Church, which might be expected, but also of quotations from the great literary figures of the pagan world. John XXIII once surprised a group he was talking to, for example, by reciting one of the odes of Horace.

Bedside reading for John XXIII is one or another volume from the 302-volume Migne edition of the Patrology, an exhaustive anthology of the works of the Greek and Latin Fathers which was left in the Papal library by Pius XII. The Pope now has little time to go back over the Greek and Latin classics, but in one reminiscent speech the Holy Father recalled that writers like Aeschylus, Sophocles, Euripides, Xenophon, and Demosthenes "had nur-

tured and delighted our youth," and that he kept these authors
in his personal library, even when moving from place to place.
The visit of King Paul and Queen Frederika of Greece gave His
Holiness an excuse to talk about such theologians as St. Basil and
St. Gregory Nazianzen, "upon whose mighty shoulders rests the
entire later edifice of theology," and to list, apparently from memory, the names of "those early Popes who called Greece their
homeland," such as Evaristus, Telesphorus, Anterus, and Sixtus II.

Roncalli has many ecclesiastical heroes. St. Charles Borromeo is
the obvious favorite, although as a historical figure he cannot be
compared to the great Fathers of the Church. Among the Greeks
the Pope's favorite is undoubtedly St. John Chrysostom, the fourth-
century theologian of Byzantium whose faith led to a particularly
excruciating martyrdom. One of the few times a Pope has walked
into St. Peter's, instead of being carried there, was when John
XXIII went to pray in the chapel in which the relics of this saint
are kept. Still another Greek Father to whom the Pope frequently
refers is St. John of Damascus, the encyclopedist of the eighth
century who authored one of the first attempts at a *summa theo-
logica*.

Of the Latin Fathers, John XXIII has three favorites, all of
them important in the early history of the Church. First is St.
Ambrose, Bishop of Milan in the fourth century, when it was the
capital of the Empire of the West. St. Ambrose was noted more
for his success in dealing with the authorities of the time than for
any special theological contribution. In fact, his most interesting
literary output consisted of letters of Emperors in which he freely
criticized and occasionally commended them. Bertrand Russell, in
his *History of Western Philosophy*, has made this acute observation:

"His [St. Ambrose's] dealings with the imperial court illustrate
a general contrast characteristic of the times: While the state was
feeble, incompetent, governed by unprincipled self-seekers, and
totally without policy beyond that of momentary expedients, the
Church was guided by vigorous, able men, prepared to sacrifice

everything personal in its interests, and with a policy so far-sighted that it brought victory for the next thousand years."

Leo the Great is a second favorite of John XXIII. In history books he has gone down as the Pope who persuaded Attila not to march on Rome, pointing out that Alaric had soon met his Maker after sacking the Eternal City a few years earlier. Attila was convinced, but it did him little good; he died the following year. It was under Leo, also, that the important ecumenical council at Chalcedon took place. This was the council that decided there was both human and divine nature in Christ. This doctrine, incidentally, caused the first great and permanent split in the ranks of Christendom, with the resulting Monophysite heresy, which exists today in the Coptic Church. The characteristic that John XXIII appreciates most in Leo the Great is his preaching ability. The Pope often quotes from his copious sermons, and has produced an encyclical about Leo written on the fifteen hundredth anniversary of his reign.

The third Roncalli hero among the Fathers of the Church is St. Gregory the Great, the Benedictine Pope of the sixth century. More than any other Pontiff of early times he was responsible for the enduring primacy of the Bishop of Rome among all other bishops. He wrote, too, a *Book of Pastoral Rule* intended as a guide for other prelates. Gregory instituted many practices and started many offices which have lasted to this day.

The present Pontiff's intimate knowledge of ecclesiastical history gives him an extra sense of values as he moves through the storied streets of Rome. He knows his way about the Christian monuments of the Eternal City as few guides do. Great figures of the past are buried in many of the older churches, and often John XXIII will stop his car to enter and say a prayer at an ancient tomb. The Pope's easy familiarity, too, with the Church's many saints is remarkable; he recounts incidents of their lives as if he had read about them yesterday. For any conceivable occasion he seems to be able to refer to an appropriate saint. With a group of traffic policemen he speaks of St. Sebastian; with an audience of housemaids he talks about the life of St. Zita of Lucca and how domestic servants in the early Christian centuries often brought the true faith to pagan households; when talking to newspapermen John XXIII invariably brings up St. Paul and St. Francis de Sales.

This deep sense of history is, of course, the result of a long and intense Catholic education that began early. At Bergamo sixty or seventy years ago the family was still intact. A semi-patriarchal society was still the rule. Married sons and their wives and children continued to live under the same roof with their parents. A solid, sensible, unhysterical Catholicism prevailed in that part of Italy's North.

Little Angelo Roncalli was not exceptional in starting to go to mass at the age of six, or in attending catechism every Sunday afternoon. Evenings the entire family, old and young, would gather around the kitchen table in the farmhouse and listen to readings by Uncle Zaverio, the aging bachelor brother of Angelo's maternal grandmother. Sometimes he would read just history, but mostly he selected parts of the Bible or appropriate excerpts from the *Meditations* of Luis Da Ponte, the Spanish author then much in vogue. The present Pontiff, incidentally, remembers Uncle Zaverio with fondness. "How lucky I was to have an uncle in the house with such breadth of learning!" he once recalled.

At just what age Angelo made the decision to enter the priesthood is not clear. But apparently by the time he had reached the age of nine the local priest at Sotto il Monte had taken him in hand and was giving him special lessons in Latin. Life in the Bergamo region in those days centered around the parish church. An authorized biography of John XXIII, by Leone Algisi, published in 1959 with the approval of the Diocese of Bergamo, gives this description of how satisfactorily, from the Church's viewpoint, things were arranged in those days:

"The parish priest was the real chief of the village. He knew every family, its secrets and its history, its hopes and its ideals. The words he spoke from the pulpit, often in dialect, were like manna from heaven. They served as a sort of newspaper, giving details of births, sicknesses and even death. He thus created a feeling of unity in the village. He insisted on a simple, straightforward interpretation of the Gospels, in which he would stress the fundamental virtues, such as honesty, the absence of vanity, the constant presence of God. Young Angelo Roncalli grew up in such surroundings."

At twelve Angelo Roncalli entered the Bergamo Seminary. Soon the young seminarian was deep in the study of the sacred sciences, dogmatic, Biblical, patristic, juridical, moral, and ascetic. He was such a good student that at the age of eighteen he received a scholarship to finish his studies at the Roman Seminary, one of the Eternal City's three great training centers for the priesthood.

One episode recounted by Algisi portrays the young Roncalli as something less than a rebel. It was the period in Church history when the movement called "modernism" was attracting Catholic laymen and clergy. The basis of modernism was that Christ was a historical figure whose words and acts should be considered in the light of the times in which He lived. From this premise the modernist went on to conclude that Church doctrine, instead of consisting of the eternal verities, was subject to constant change, indeed that it must change. The new movement, which struck at the roots of hierarchical authority, was soon to be declared fallacious in Pius X's encyclical *Pascendi gregis* of 1907, but before this happened many younger clergymen and seminarians had embraced it or at least were toying with its tenets.

According to Algisi, classmates of Roncalli surreptitiously passed modernist tracts around and read them during the night. Apparently Roncalli knew about this, but refused to participate. "He distrusted instinctively," writes the biographer, "any teaching which did not perfectly conform to the thinking of the hierarchy, not for lack of courage of his convictions but because he was convinced of the weakness of any theology developed outside the control of the Church."

Roncalli the seminarian saw Leo XIII in an audience, but never formally met him. This Pope, however, was to remain his favorite among modern Pontiffs. Leo XIII died in early 1903; Angelo Roncalli was in St. Peter's Square when white smoke poured out of the Sistine Chapel chimney announcing the election of his successor, Pius X. The following year, on August 10, Roncalli was ordained priest in the Church of Santa Maria in Monte Santo in the Piazza del Popolo, and the following day celebrated his first mass in one of the chapels of St. Peter's. That same day he joined a group of pilgrims seeking an audience with the new Pope. An older priest accompanying Father Roncalli said to the Pope: "Your Holiness, this is a young priest from Bergamo who only this morning celebrated his first mass." Pius X stopped, blessed Roncalli, and asked him when he expected to sing his first mass in Bergamo. "Oh, those bells in Bergamo's churches, how they do ring out!" the Pope, himself born not too far away from Bergamo, said in reminiscence. Roncalli would meet in the course of the years his four immediate predecessors—Pius X (1903–1914), Benedict XV (1914–1922), Pius XI (1922–1939), and Pius XII (1939–1958).

During those years of the Italian monarchy, seminarians and priests in Italy were required to do military service. Roncalli the seminarian volunteered for a year's service in order to avoid a draft which would have lasted three years. According to the official biographer, he also paid a forfeit of 1,000 lire, then equivalent to around $200, to be thus excused. The 73rd Regiment, to which Roncalli was assigned, was stationed at Bergamo, thus permitting him to keep in touch with the seminary and even to continue some of his classes. Much later, in 1915, with the Italian entry into World War I, Father Roncalli again donned khaki, and this time was assigned to the medical corps with the rank of sergeant. A picture of him taken during this period shows the priest in a rough-looking uniform sporting an elegant, almost martial, mustache.

Father Roncalli's first post in the Church was as private secretary to the newly appointed Bishop of Bergamo, Monsignor Giacomo Radini-Tedeschi. This active and devout bishop, who was to influence greatly the young priest's outlook, had chosen Don Angelo,

as he was then called, not especially because he was a Bergamesque
and certainly not because of experience, but rather because he had
found Roncalli "very judicious" and "full of good sense."

The secretary soon became the bishop's shadow, accompanying
him everywhere, doing all sorts of odd jobs about the diocese. For
a time he edited a monthly called *Diocesan Life*; pages upon pages
of copy written by the future Pope appear in this diocesan bulletin,
but the articles were always unsigned and their authorship is thus
now impossible to confirm. During those years, too, Father Roncalli wrote a lengthy, detailed, and not very lively monograph of
the history of religious charitable institutions in Bergamo. At the
same time he conducted some classes in ecclesiastical history at
Bergamo University. Meanwhile, Bishop Radini-Tedeschi died. In
due time Roncalli produced a full-length biography of the deceased
prelate with special attention to his episcopate at Bergamo.

Soon after the war Father Roncalli was called to Rome, where
he worked on the reorganization of the national and international
offices of the Work of the Propagation of the Faith (not to be
confused with the Sacred Congregation for the Propagation of the
Faith). In this capacity he traveled for the first time to France, to
Belgium and Holland, to Germany and Austria. Then came his
first appointment as a Vatican diplomat, Apostolic Nuncio to
Bulgaria, with which country the Holy See had just signed a
concordat. The next thirty years, until his elevation to the purple
and his nomination as Patriarch of Venice, Roncalli spent away
from Rome and Italy in diplomatic work.

The Roncalli career was thus a mixture of pastoral, administrative, journalistic, professorial, and diplomatic duties, with the latter
greatly predominating. There was still time, however, to develop
his own specialties and pursue his particular interest.

A combination of local pride and interest in St. Charles Borromeo started Roncalli on what Algisi called the "distraction of a
lifetime." The present Pope was born in what had once been a
part of the sprawling diocese of Milan, of which Borromeo was

the cardinal-archbishop. The Holy Father believes, and has so said, that it was due to the fervor of this "admirable example of episcopal sanctity" that the northern half of Italy and the southern half of Switzerland did not go Protestant some four hundred years ago. And to this tireless "Master of Bishops, remembered as one of the greatest shepherds of souls in the history of the Church," is also due, according to the Pope, the flourishing spiritual and physical condition of the Diocese of Bergamo today. (See Chapter VIII.)

One day in 1909 Father Roncalli accompanied his bishop on a trip to see the Cardinal of Milan. While the two prelates conferred, the young priest passed the time browsing around the rich archdiocesan archives in the Ambrosian Library. There, high up on the shelves, he caught sight of a series of thirty-nine dust-covered volumes in an old parchment case labeled "*Archivio Spirituale*, Bergamo." He explored further and found to his delight that they contained the reports of the pastoral visits to Bergamo of St. Charles Borromeo.

A half hour of glancing through a few of the decrees, letters, and reports of Borromeo was enough to fascinate Roncalli, the ecclesiastical history teacher. As time went on he conceived the project of arranging, editing, and publishing these data. The moment was ripe for such a work; four years from then would mark the tercentenary of the canonization of Borromeo.

Bishop Radini-Tedeschi quickly fell in with Roncalli's plan. In fact, the bishop was always encouraging his young assistant to branch out. Also encouraging was Monsignor Achille Ratti, the future Pius XI, then prefect of the Ambrosian Library. Ratti gave the young priest permission to photostat the thousands of documents, thus permitting him to work on them at Bergamo as well as at Milan.

Work on the proposed volume (or volumes) did not, however, get under way immediately. In fact, what with one delay after another, the first volume on Borromeo did not appear until 1936, twenty-seven years after the project had been conceived. Roncalli

was then Apostolic Delegate to Turkey and Greece. Volume II
appeared the next year, with the author still at Istanbul, while the
third volume came two years later, on the eve of the outbreak of
the second World War. By the time of the appearance of the
fourth volume, in 1946, Roncalli had been transferred to Paris.

Not until August 5, 1958, scarcely three months before he ascended the Throne of St. Peter's, while he was vacationing with his
brothers at Sotto il Monte, did Roncalli put the finishing touches
to the fifth and last volume. In a gracious dedicatory foreword His
Eminence thanks his collaborators, including stenographers, tran-
scribers, and typographers, with special thanks reserved for his
Florentine publishers. The foreword also contains this note of
apology: "In normal conditions five years of hard work would have
sufficed; it took fifty."

The whole series was published under the title *Gli Atti della
visita apostolica di San Carlo Borromeo a Bergamo*, which may be
translated: "Reports of the Apostolic Visits of St. Charles Borromeo to Bergamo." The price of these books, as might be expected, is rather high. They sell for 10,000 lire (or around $16) a
volume, the set coming to around $80. Since the fifth volume was
published after its author had attained the highest dignity, John
XXIII felt constrained to direct the publisher to make no special
fuss over this singular fact. But, actually, the Pope need not have
worried. These volumes would never be a commercial success.

For the average cleric as well as for most laymen the book is,
in fact, virtually unreadable. It amounts to nearly three thousand
pages in all, most of them devoted to reprints of decrees issued by
the cardinal-archbishop and to reports of what he saw and ordered
on his visits. The first two volumes cover Borromeo's visits to
Bergamo proper; the last three volumes deal with the trips he
made into the province. Most of the time the reports deal with
highly technical or administrative Church matters. There is the
question of a proper altar, or of a better chapel, or of the printing
of the catechism. The Council of Trent has laid down certain
reforms for Church music; some parishes seem slow in adopting

them. The seminary gives constant trouble, not especially because of any unwillingness to do as the council has dictated, but rather because not everybody understands what is wanted. One by one the various parishes are visited. Cardinal Borromeo listens to the parish priests' problems, looks over the churches, orders that inventories be made, makes notes of what is lacking. Occasionally the Milan cardinal-bishop utters a witticism about the characteristics of certain down-to-earth country priests he meets in his archdiocese.

Besides arranging and editing these papers, Roncalli's chief job was to supply copious footnotes. Here, as L'Osservatore Romano suggested in its six-thousand-word review, is the core of the book. Here all the various churches, hospitals, and seminaries are identified, and often their separate histories given. Cross-references to the corresponding decrees of the Council of Trent, which ordered the reforms enforced by St. Charles Borromeo, are supplied.

For the future author of a biography of the great Counter Reformation figure these volumes doubtless present source material of value. A scholar working on a detailed history of the years after Trent would want to look at them. But aside from their contribution to scholarship, the volumes are interesting now mainly because their author sits on the Throne of St. Peter.

To be a specialist on St. Charles Borromeo means also to be something of a student of the Council of Trent, the crucial meeting called in the mid-1500's to deal with the Protestant apostasy. Although Borromeo never actually attended the council, as Secretary of State to his uncle Pope Pius IV he was responsible at one crucial moment for reconvening the council and insisting that it get on with its work.

One of the purposes of the Council of Trent was to define pertinent sections of Catholic doctrine to meet the challenge of the newly born and aggressive Protestantism. A second purpose was to reform Church government and, more particularly, to provide for a properly trained clergy, the lack of which had brought on many of the abuses that led to Martin Luther's successful defiance of Rome. One gathers that the second purpose of Trent interests the present Holy Father more than the first. In fact, John XXIII's absorption with Borromeo and Trent seems to stem from his interest in the welfare, mainly spiritual, of the Catholic clergy.

Here the present Pontiff is in marked contrast with his immediate predecessor. The late Pope, Pius XII, neglected his own clergy to the point where visiting bishops and archbishops often had to be content to be received along with hundreds of laymen in general audience. Obviously the old Pope believed the clergy should be able to take care of themselves, while the plain people badly needed the Holy Father's ministrations. To many this seemed a fair assumption, but not to John XXIII.

Nothing delights the present Pope more than to talk about the priesthood and its problems. Nor does he believe that any topic is more important. To an outsider this preoccupation might appear confining; it is a bit as if a medical man were to be more interested in other doctors than in his patients. But the Pope pursues the subject in many phases of his pontificate.

John XXIII tirelessly exhorts candidates for the priesthood to study and comport themselves well. To a group of young Spanish seminarians he once said: "The Church wants strong and solid men, with well-formed minds and hearts. Belonging to the Church requires an adamantine temper of character and will. It also means a continual struggle against passions and egoism, the overcoming of self with the aid of the Lord." To another class of students the Pope once advised: "Treat temptation like flies; brush it away!"

In one long speech to the rectors of Italian seminaries, the Holy Father warned against the "mania for certain diversions and curiosities." "In lay circles," he said, "there is a widespread impression that some ecclesiastics of our times do not know how to resist the temptations of the present life, temptations which are those of greater and more refined comforts of life, of superficiality in study, opinions, words; of an exaggerated interest in things which make much noise; of discomfort in the face of daily duties which impose abnegation, detachment, patience, mildness. . . . Let us not force the Gospel of Jesus and the teachings of His Church into the narrow limits of personal selfishness and convenience."

The Holy Father insisted that "firm ascetic principles" raised youth from the "state of immaturity, indecision, timidity." The Pope continued: "From his time at the seminary onward the candidate for the priesthood is something sacred, distinct, separate. His very comportment, even in the gladness of recreation, has nothing about it that is dissipated, and certainly nothing vulgar or secular, but denotes someone who is preparing to consecrate himself to God."

Clearly, John XXIII believes that the way to greater influence and power on the part of the Church is through an improved priesthood. "If the priest burns as with fire and therefore gives off a splendid light, pure and ardent, he is beyond price," the Pope has said. "If not, he counts for very little."

The Pope is also worried about the world we live in and its effect on the Catholic clergy. Today, the Pope says, many priests are forced to live in an "atmosphere where excessive liberty and sensuality reign." Often the clergy find themselves "morally alone, misunderstood and but feebly sustained by the faithful to whom they devote themselves." The Pope goes on to say that while self-denial is of course necessary, this should not make the priest withdraw from others. On the contrary, "this chastity should make the priest's heart even more open and ready to meet the needs of his brother." The clergy should be a part of the community they serve.

The Pontiff's advice to the priesthood can sometimes take very direct forms. Once at Venice, after receiving a priest who had neglected to shave, Cardinal Roncalli dispatched an electric razor to the offender. Continually the Pope has urged that Catholic priests learn to avoid what he calls the "two great excesses," authoritarianism and paternalism. In preaching, the Holy Father has said, a priest should be neither didactic nor argumentative, but rather persuasive.

One of the Pope's encyclicals, *Sacerdotii nostri primordia*, deals with this specialized subject. Issued on the hundredth anniversary of the death of the Curé d'Ars, Jean-Marie-Baptiste Vienney, it first recalls in personal terms His Holiness's emotions at both the beatification and canonization ceremonies of the French priest, the "special promoter of pastors throughout the world." Continuing his letter, the Pontiff admits that his heart "turns in a very special way to the priests" and proceeds to call upon all those who engage in pastoral ministry to meditate on this "model of sacerdotal zeal, a model of piety and of Eucharistic devotion."

In the course of this encyclical the Pope also talks about the virtues of poverty, insisting that if priests do legitimately possess a few personal belongings they should not become attached to them. "Today fervent Christians expect much from their priest," the Holy Father concludes. "They would see in him, in a world where the powers of money, the seduction of the senses and the prestige of technical skill reign supreme, a witness to the invisible God, a man of faith forgetful of himself and filled with charity."

Even in canonization proceedings this penchant for the priesthood emerges. For example, two of the four Blessed whom John XXIII has proclaimed saints in the first three years of his reign are men whose great contribution to the Church was their work in the seminaries. One of these, Gregory Barbarigo, was, not at all surprisingly, the Bishop of Bergamo in the period not too long after the Council of Trent, and was responsible for much of the seminary reform in North Italy of that century. As the Cardinal-Archbishop of Padua, he later twice received the offer of the Tiara in conclaves and twice, out of humility, refused. At Padua he founded a printing plant to produce classics and correct versions of the writings of the Church Fathers, and he insisted that the plant be supplied with Greek, Arabic, Syrian, Armenian, and Persian characters, as well as Latin. Barbarigo always kept an alert eye toward the East. In fact, one witness during his trial for beatification said that "if Cardinal Barbarigo had not died so early, the Greek and Latin churches might have been felicitously reunited."

Barbarigo was beatified under Clement XIII in 1761, but after that his case was dropped for two centuries. It had been generally concluded that canonization was not for him, but the present Pope, with his interest in seminaries and the priesthood, not to mention Bergamo, apparently ordered the case to be taken up again. Although three miracles were proved prior to the beatification, the rule laid down by Benedict XIV in 1758 required that two more be proved before proclaiming a saint. Popes, however, can ignore such rules and John XXIII waived them in this case.[1]

Although on paper the rules of admission to sainthood are strict, recent history suggests that the Congregation of Rites will speed up the trials when a reigning sovereign insists on it. The final phase of Barbarigo's case was completed in something less than a year; normally it would have taken five or six.

Altogether six new saints were proclaimed during the first four years of the present pontificate, including Martin de Porres, the sixteenth-century Peruvian mulatto who was canonized in May, 1962. Next to Barbarigo, the most important was Juan de Ribera, Bishop of Badajoz and Archbishop of Seville in the sixteenth century, who also acted for a time as Philip II's viceroy for Valencia. It is interesting that he also belongs to the post-Tridentine period. Beatification for him came in 1796, but it was only in 1925 that the cause for his canonization was taken up. Also named saints were Carlo Da Sezza, a Franciscan friar; Ciocchine Vedruna de Mas, a Spanish nun, and Bertilla Boscardin, an Italian nun. One beatification has also taken place; and St. Lawrence of Brindisi, founder of monasteries in Bohemia and a great debater against Lutheranism, has been officially declared a "Doctor" of the Church.

Generally speaking, beatification and canonization of the same individual rarely take place during the same reign, although there have been some recent exceptions. The process normally starts with

---

[1] A new edifice to St. Gregory Barbarigo, to be known as the "Church of the Priests," is now being planned for Rome as a lasting memorial to the reign of John XXIII.

a minimum of three small diocesan trials, held at the place where the servant of God was born, at the place where he died, and at the place where he lived most of his life. If all three of these trials go well, there follows an apostolic trial at Rome at which the heroic qualities of the prospective Blessed must be tested. He must be proved to have possessed the three theological virtues—faith, hope, and charity—and to have had the four cardinal virtues —justice, fortitude, prudence, and temperance. Of these, prudence is probably now considered the greatest of the virtues; at any rate, it is the quality that John XXIII stresses on many occasions.

The length of the proceedings depends upon the kind of life the future saint led. In the case of young men and women, who lived mostly in one place and whose lives were uninvolved, the process is relatively short. In cases of old men, who led active lives over many decades, the trial is prolonged. If the candidate passes the trials and is pronounced as having the heroic qualities in full measure, a decree signed by the Pope is issued and he becomes Venerable. After that comes another trial to prove the miracles, and only with that proof can the beatification be pronounced.

It is necessary to distinguish between beatification and canonization. To one termed "Blessed," altars can be dedicated but only in stipulated places where the Blessed lived and worked. The Blessed does not yet belong to the Universal Church. Canonization now normally requires proof of three additional miracles. Once canonization has taken place churches can be dedicated to the new saint in any place in the world. The Pope, incidentally, always presides at canonizations but not at those ceremonies involving beatification.

The Congregation of Rites has possibly three hundred causes in various stages of development at this time. Two of these are interesting in that they involve people within the memory of living man. One is Cardinal Merry del Val, an outstanding member of the Curia for twenty-five years, who was Secretary of State under Pius X and secretary of the Holy Office under Pius XII. Report around the Vatican is that while Pius XII was enthusiastic over this trial, the present Pope is less so. If this is true, then Merry del Val faces a long and possibly unsuccessful struggle for sainthood.

The other cause involves Pius IX, familiarly called Pio Nono, the long-reigning Pope of the nineteenth century who issued, among other famous documents, the Syllabus of Errors and the Dogma of Papal Infallibility. He was responsible for the Dogma of the Immaculate Conception, the first dogmatic pronouncement taken by a Pope in the history of the Church without referring the matter to a general council.

John XXIII himself has recently taken an interest in the trial and is pushing it to the point where he has directed the Secretariat of State to advance the funds needed to pursue the cause. He will at least not allow it to drag on for the rest of the century, as well it might in the case of a long and complicated life like Pio Nono's. So far only the words and acts of Giovanni Mastai-Ferretti before his election as Pope have been examined. This means that more than half his life has passed muster; but since the congregation now must go through thirty-two years of his pontificate, much work remains to be done. It is said that in his trial the proving of miracles will be less a problem than the testing of the heroic qualities of his virtues. Estimates at the Vatican are that this trial will consume at least another five years.

If the present Pope approves ultimate beatification and canonization in this case, the Church can expect a loud outcry not only from Protestants but from Italian nationalists. All this decade, up until 1970, lay Italy will be celebrating, on and off, the centenary of its unification. Memories of Garibaldi, Cavour, Mazzini, and Vittorio Emanuele II are already being invoked. But as every Italian schoolboy knows, it was none other than Pio Nono who actively opposed with every means at his disposal the establishment of an Italian nation with its capital at Rome. Granted that recent historians, mostly Catholics, have re-evaluated Pio Nono and his pontificate, especially excusing the issuance of the famous Syllabus, still not all the rewriting of history could make of the old Pope an upholder of Italian nationalism. To applaud the accomplishments of the Risorgimento heroes in one piazza and in another to canonize Pio Nono will certainly be incongruous.

In line with his consuming concern for the clergy the Pope as Bishop of Rome held early in 1960 the first synod in the history of the Diocese of Rome. Again, this was going back to St. Charles Borromeo and to Trent. The council had laid down the rule that each diocese must hold a synod every three years, and Cardinal Borromeo accordingly held six synods in his diocese at properly spaced intervals. But he was one of the few prelates faithfully to observe the law. The successive Bishops of Rome had apparently never thought that the rule applied to them, or that, if it did, they were constrained to obey it. And who was there to call the Bishop of Rome to account?

It was left to John XXIII to summon together all the 190 parish priests of Rome, all the hospital and prison chaplains and the curates, all the rectors and directors of seminaries, all the monsignori and the bishops and even the cardinals. All in all, some twenty-seven different ecclesiastical ranks resident in Rome were represented at impressive opening ceremonies at St. John Lateran in early 1960.

The tangible result of this week-long meeting was a new constitution of 770 articles, written in Latin, which sets forth in precise detail what is expected of both laity and clergy in Rome. Various committees were formed to draw up different parts of the new constitution, but the whole is essentially the Pope's handiwork and is thus destined to serve as a model for other sees. The Pope himself admitted his authorship, and if there ever was any question about it, the pro-Communist Rome newspaper *Paese Sera* cleared up the matter by publishing galley proof corrections made by the Holy Father himself.[2]

[2] How *Paese Sera* got these papers is a fascinating question that has shaken the Papal household, including the Pontiff. This leak, plus the highly informed Vatican reporting of *Paese Sera* in general, seemed to indicate that the Communists had been able to place an agent even inside the Vatican.

Most of the provisions of the new constitution are restatements of regulations long ago issued by the Vicariate of Rome. They deal mainly with ecclesiastical technicalities such as the management of parish finances, the definition of the role of Catholic societies in the life of the devout, the place of the Catholic press in the diocese. The articles ban the use in churches of phonograph records and microphones, the attachment of loudspeakers to bell towers, and the sale of candles, holy cards, statues, charms, or other religious objects inside—though not outside—the churches.

A long list of articles lays down precise rules for the conduct of the clergy. Priests have long been forbidden to attend public spectacles in Rome, and the prohibition is now officially repeated in the new constitution. Article 83 stipulates that "priests and religious are forbidden to be present at film showings or public spectacles of any kind that are not promoted and approved by ecclesiastical authority." Also they are cautioned to use with extreme moderation the radio and television, even in their own residences.[3] In fact, a priest living alone must not have television. According to Article 78, the clergy "should not frequent bars or public places. Should that become unavoidable, they should go there for merely the time necessary and should behave in a manner befitting their dignity." A priest may quench his thirst quickly standing at a bar, according to the rules, but should not sit down in a café to do it. A priest should not travel in a car with one woman only. Priests should avoid attending functions of purely lay character; "priests cannot belong to Rotary Clubs." Priests should not smoke in public.

[3] Coming just before the 1960 Olympic Games in Rome, these regulations caused some confusion and led to some rather elaborate reinterpretation. The young students of the American Seminary at Rome, for example, put in their requests to witness some of the Olympic events; so did numerous priests who accompanied in one capacity or another the various Olympic teams. The Roman Vicariate frowned and finally came up with this modification: visiting priests and American seminarians would be allowed to attend most games and contests but not boxing or wrestling matches and not swimming meets in which women participated.

To many Americans a rule against a priest or monk driving or owning a car or a motor scooter would seem antiquated, but Article 82 is quite specific: "To the lay clergy as well as to monks and nuns, it is forbidden to possess or to drive any mechanical vehicle without previous written authorization from the Vicariate. Even with this authorization, they should limit the use of these vehicles to what is strictly necessary."

The strictures pertaining to lay conduct are less lengthy and less detailed. Catholics are forbidden to read any publication of an "existentialist, atheistic, modernist nature." In Article 238 the Roman Catholics of Rome are reminded not to attend spiritualist séances nor to have anything to do with theosophy (as though the two were on the same level). In the next article the devout are warned away from psychoanalysts. Instructions governing entertainment take up a long section; here, indeed, can be seen the Pope's own thinking. Article 701 says: "Catholics are duty bound to oppose every public spectacle which is contrary to good taste and morals. Directors must choose with great care their actors and actresses, and should even offer them the succor of religion." In Article 704 one reads: "Catholics must not go to motion picture shows without first assuring themselves that the film being shown conforms to the religious and moral principles of the Church." Among the duties of Catholic laymen is to protest to those responsible for radio or television programs "offensive to the principles of morality." Article 720 says: "The art of frenetic dancing invented in our age is a great danger to morals. Christians should not indulge in it nor should they frequent places where it is practiced."

According to an advance announcement from the Roman Vicariate, the Pope's new constitution was to contain severe admonitions against Protestantism. The old canon law strictures against witnessing Protestant ceremonies were to be repeated with force, together with a warning that Protestant houses of worship could only be entered with the consent of the bishop. (There are a few such churches in Rome.) True, one article, No. 240, says that "Catholics are forbidden to enter the churches of non-Catholics and to participate in their services, nor must they discuss sacred matters with them in public"; but, contrary to advance report, Protestants are nowhere named as such and, contrary to past practice, they are not lumped together with Socialists, Communists, atheists, spiritualists, magicians, Masons, and the like.[4] The presumption is that the Bishop of Rome, when he got down to editing the final version, softened somewhat the regulations against the "separated" churches. This is another small instance of the readiness of John XXIII to depart from the heretofore intolerant attitude toward that part of Christendom which does not adhere to the Apostolic See of Rome.

All in all, John XXIII's constitution contains little that is new. Its value lies almost solely in the proof that the Pontiff is determined to leave nothing to a chance misunderstanding and that he wants ecclesiastical government to be one of law and not of improvisation.

A striking example of Roncalli's stubborn commitment to ecclesiastical law concerns the obscure but engrossing question of the iconostasis at St. Mark's, a question raised during his days as a cardinal in Venice.

As a survival from its days as a church of the Byzantine rite, St. Mark's had long had a rood screen which held the giant Evangelistaries but obscured the high altar from public view. During the days of the Serenissima this had hardly mattered. St. Mark's was, in effect, the Doge's chapel; the Doge and his suite could easily get up close and watch the mass, and they cared little whether the public could see or not. Roman Catholic canon law, however, stipulates that the celebration of the mass shall be visible to all the faithful.

When St. Mark's became the patriarchal basilica of Venice in 1807 there no longer remained an excuse to keep the screen, liturgically speaking, in place, and numerous attempts were made

---

[4] The famous Syllabus of 1864 condemned Socialism, Communism, secret societies, Biblical societies and liberal societies all in one stroke.

to remove it. The iconostasis, however, was a masterpiece of art, and every effort to tamper with it was firmly resisted. Roncalli himself was to recall that even the first patriarch, a Hungarian (Venice was still under the Austro-Hungarian Empire), tried to remove the screen but was "providentially prevented from doing so." (He died.)

Roncalli, early in his term at Venice, decided that to continue to allow the screen to block the view of the high altar was lamentable if not exactly, ecclesiastically speaking, illegal. He began by propagandizing all sorts of committees and ministries. He talked with the councilors of the Curia, with the representatives of Catholic Action, with the Mayor of Venice, with the Italian Ministry of Education, with the Pontifical Commission for Sacred Art in Italy, and above all with the Fine Arts Commission, suggesting that they study the problem. To most of these committees, however, this was an old and touchy story, and their feet dragged.

At length Cardinal Roncalli made a concrete proposal. He suggested that the iconostasis, which is made of beautiful marble, be mounted on wheels so that it could be kept in its traditional place most of the time, but could be shifted during the celebration of the mass. Some such solution, according to the cardinal, had been successfully carried out in a similar situation at the cathedral at Pisa.

Soon word got around that the patriarch was trying to disfigure the historic cathedral, and the result was a civic uproar with loud echoes in the press. Nothing excites the Italians as does any attempt to alter a masterpiece. The Fine Arts Commission, on whom the final decision rested, declined the cardinal's suggestion.

As Patriarch of Venice, Roncalli made no further attempt to tamper with the screen. But a few years later, when he became Pope, one of his first acts was to hint that he wanted St. Mark's changed. This time it was done, with a minimum of criticism.

In the first three years of his reign John XXIII issued a total of six encyclicals, a remarkable feat of writing. The first was his programmatic encyclical entitled *Ad Petri Cathedram*, issued on the Feast of St. Peter and St. Paul on June 29, 1959. There followed the *Sacerdotii nostri primordia*, dealing with the priesthood, after which came a third on the reciting of the rosary and a fourth on the subject of missions. The masterpiece of the Roncalli encyclicals so far is *Mater et Magistra*, written for the seventieth anniversary of *Rerum novarum*. This is an important social document, and as such will be discussed in the next chapter. The latest and sixth encyclical, issued on the fifteen hundredth anniversary of the death of Leo the Great, had the political and theological aim of reaffirming the primacy of the Roman Pontiff before the convening of the ecumenical council.

Latin is, of course, the official language of the Vatican, and these encyclicals are all written in that language.[5] If need be, the Pope can converse quite fluently with his subordinates in Latin, but for writing he would normally have the help of the professional Latinists of the Vatican. The working language of the Vatican, on the other hand, is Italian, and it is only in this tongue that the Pope's style can really be judged.

The Italian of John XXIII is excellent, easy to read but deceptively easy to translate badly. Interpreters have a difficult time with him, partly because his pronunciation still retains traces of the Bergamesque dialect, and partly because his speech is tinged with a subtle wit which is dry, rather gentle, and difficult to pin down. It has a sort of old-fashioned quality to it. At times it also has a distinctly northern tone, something approaching the Yankee pungency of the late Calvin Coolidge.

The Roncalli utterances at Venice, in the years before he became Pope, are excellent examples of his style. In that city Cardinal Roncalli moved against the exotic background of one of Europe's most glamorous cities, and he seems fully to have appreciated the surroundings.

In dedicating the new railroad station at Venice, Roncalli built

[5] On special occasions encyclicals can also be written in other languages, as was done on several occasions during the reign of Pius XI.

his speech around the signs "Arrivals" and "Departures," saying that in "this life we are all at one or the other." As for Venice, he said in a neat bit of phrasing, because of stringent geographical reasons she is an earthly symbol of the end of the rails, and thus really a glimpse of paradise.

As Patriarch he developed a special vocabulary which he has carried over into his Papal days. One of his favorite Italian expressions is *talora*, a rather unusual word with a slightly archaic flavor. It means "sometime" or "sometimes," not in the usual sense but rather as the Gershwins used it in the song about a "sometime thing." Whenever Roncalli says *talora*, it is a sign that he does not like whatever he is talking about. Thus mixed camping trips by unmarried youths have received the *talora* treatment. Similarly, tourists were welcome to Venice in particular, and Italy in general, but *talora* they (especially the women) show bad judgment by often dressing indecorously. Roncalli says the press may be dedicated to the truth, but *talora* it leaves its readers bewildered. Television is definitely a *talora* thing. The best example of Roncalli *talora*, however, is to be found in an address to the annual film festival:

"You belong to an intellectual elite accustomed to gathering and interpreting the features and voices of our time. It is an arduous undertaking. *Talora* the subject . . . is so important and delicate that it shakes your sensibilities and leaves you perplexed."

In other words, you cinema people often make bad movies.

Another expression which the Pope sometimes uses, and always with the same hidden meaning, is *disturbare*. To most people this means simply "to disturb," but to the Pope it means "to work for the bad" and can even mean "to be a Communist." Similarly, the Italian word *confuso* or "confused" denotes either a liar or one who believes lies, while *perplesso* or "perplexed" means to be really shocked.

All in all, John XXIII's speeches, unlike those of Pius XII, are not those of a thinker but rather of a sometimes indulgent, sometimes scolding father anxious for his children's welfare. He is worried about the sensuality of the times, and thinks too much stress is laid on technical ability and not enough on moral fortitude, but on many matters he is also remarkably open-minded. For example, although he prefers classical religious art he concedes that "there could well be something to modern art." He has allowed the Vatican Museum to open two rooms showing modern (although not surrealist) paintings. He is equally indulgent about twelve-tone music.

Unfortunately, the Pope's speeches are rarely published in full. Thus the ironically affectionate expressions, the amusing remarks, the measured witticisms almost never see the light of print. The Pontiff's words are heavily edited before publication in *L'Osservatore Romano*. In a way, this is a pity, for it robs these reports of the warmth of feeling that the Pope invariably displays.

VIII

SOCIETY AND POLITICS
IN THE MIND OF
JOHN XXIII

John XXIII is no innovator and no experimenter. As far as the Catholic Church is concerned, he does not think that new times require new methods. Pius XII obviously believed that the Church's machinery was inefficient in many respects. But John XXIII is convinced that the full means of salvation for the world as well as for the individual can still be found in the methods of the Church as they have existed for centuries. "With the passing of the centuries," the Pope recently told an audience, "everything passes, terrestrial power is transformed. Only the ship of St. Peter proceeds calmly on its course. When you hear rumors about the end of the Church just consider that those who say such things will themselves soon come to an end. The Catholic Church will never come to its end; it will continue its voyage to comfort, encourage and direct people's minds on the way to truth and validity."

Quietly the present Pope has discouraged anything that might smack of revivalism. He does not like crash programs. He hates terms like "crusades" and "campaigns" when applied to the

Church; his assistants say he invariably cuts such expressions from his speeches. He believes in the long hard pull, and will tolerate no other approach.

The mass approach to religion, as favored by some Jesuits, has also been discouraged by the new Pope. If the work of the Italian dioceses should be streamlined, then the streamlining should be done by the resident bishops and their staffs and not by outsiders, whether clerical or lay. John XXIII seems innately to mistrust most lay groups; they are perhaps less easily controlled than the clerics. The role even of such an organization as Catholic Action of Italy, with its vast possibilities, has been downgraded in the new pontificate. The former Pope was not afraid of Catholic liberals or radicals; the youth organization of Catholic Action was full of them. But under the new Pontiff, a careful system of rotating the top jobs has been inaugurated. Evidently the Vatican fears that these lay organizations may go astray.

One indication of how the present Pope regards experimentation can be seen in his attitude toward the much-discusssed worker-priest idea of France. This experiment, it should be recalled, was started with the consent and blessing of part of the Catholic hierarchy in France as a means of combating the apostasy of the French working classes. Pius XII may not have been completely sympathetic to the idea, but he was apparently willing to be convinced. Certainly recurring reports from France ought to have been sufficient to show the Vatican that something needed to be done. For example, it has been estimated that only about 5 percent of French laborers attend mass once a week. Less than one-fifth of the babies born to workers in France are baptized.

To counteract the estrangement of the working classes a number of young priests undertook what was called a "practicum" of working in factories and fields during their vacations. The same sort of thing had been tried, on a narrower basis, in several missionary fields. The project soon ran into trouble. Some worker priests became more aggressive than the Marxists in promoting the cause of labor. Some took posts in trade unions that were under Communist influence. A few forsook the ministry and married. In some cases the secular society into which the worker-priests were plunged proved to be stronger than their spiritual fortitude. The Church does not like defection of any kind, but defection of a priest reflects on the Church's training methods.

It was not long before the French experiment was brought before the Congregation of Seminaries, which pronounced strongly against it. Cardinal Giuseppe Pizzardo, the prefect, who was also at that time to all intents and purposes the chief of the Holy Office, soon informed the French hierarchy that "documentary evidence" proved the practicum to have a "negative effect on the training of young priests," and should be discouraged.

Roma locuta est, and that should have been the last of it. But it wasn't. The French bishops tried to save something from the movement. Three French cardinals came to Rome to plead with Pius XII. New regulations were devised. The priests might continue to work at manual labor, but never more than three hours daily. A priest should always be free to exercise his religious duties. Priests might work with labor unions, but they should not accept official posts in them.

Thus the matter stood at the time of the 1958 conclave. French Catholic circles grumbled that once again legalistic Rome had failed to appreciate the special problems of the Church in France. French dissatisfaction over this and other matters was supposed to have manifested itself in the voting for Pope. Some Vatican oldtimers protested that Roncalli, because of his long experience at Paris, had been sympathetic toward the worker-priest experiment. At the least, they said, he thought the French hierarchy should be left alone to work out its own problems.

But all this turned out to be guessing, and bad guessing at that. Within a few months after the conclave the new Pope, as prefect of the Holy Office, signed a new decree which definitely disbanded the worker-priest movement. In due time, John XXIII was to comment not once but twice on the question, leaving little doubt that he had disapproved of the project from the start.

"Every nation has known its storms, and diverse epochs of its history are planted thick with adversity," His Holiness told a group of French clergy and laity. "But the Christian faith, wherever it has held out, will always triumph.

"Not all that is beautiful and useful is new," the Pontiff continued. "That which is sometimes presented as an urgent necessity too often smacks of superficiality and lacks essentials. No one denies that one must take into account changing external circumstances, but when it reaches the point of corroding the foundations of those principles which constitute the essence of a delicate and important activity, then one must have great care and arm oneself with watchful vigilance.

"You are heirs and continuers, both, of the great apostolate of Christian culture, of religious and social activity in your country, which catches the attention of the whole world. May Saints Peter and Paul, in whose power we trust, intercede for us with the Lord. Listen! Listen! Before all else comes the invocation of the power and authority of the Holy Apostles: St. Peter, Prince of Apostles and cornerstone of the Church; St. Paul, the teacher of the nations. . . . And on this foundation—Saints Peter and Paul—stands the Church of Christ, and the gates of hell shall not prevail against her. Twenty centuries have proven the solidarity of this *potestas et auctoritas* of the Church of Rome. Many attempts have been made to crush her, and to weaken her, but they have not succeeded."

John XXIII has never expressed his political philosophy very clearly. He mentions liberty frequently, but mainly in a religious and rarely in a political or economic context. Sometimes, in an aside, His Holiness will indicate that he does not think much of the world as ordered today, but he rarely develops this theme to the point of spelling out his objections. He almost never uses the word "democracy." In his speeches he has been vague about the special problems of mass production, nuclear energy, fast travel, and exploding nationalism. He talks about the family often, and laments its virtual breakup under the pressure of industrialization. He has admitted that women must sometimes go to work, although he obviously would prefer that they stay at home and care for their families. "The family constitutes for woman the principal core of her activity," the Pope has said. "Unfortuately, economic necessity often obliges her to employ herself outside the home." Once or twice he has talked vividly about the special problems created in a fast-expanding metropolis like Rome, but these were more the words of an administrator than of a political figure.

One associate of John XXIII, when asked which kind of political setup the Pope would prefer today, answered: "If you want to know the Holy Father's idea of what constituted as near the perfect community as any place on earth, study the city and province of Bergamo before the turn of the century."

Here, indeed, was an attractive place, alive with vigor and purpose, and still devout. Agriculture was then the main occupation of the Bergamesque and that, the Pope feels, was all to the good. "Work in the fields," His Holiness once told a group of rural social workers, "is one of the most satisfactory of all labors. You have a Pope himself who is the son of a farmer." The young and healthy acted as a sort of insurance against a penniless old age. Instead of building up a savings account, a couple had children. The sick never lacked for care. Occasionally there would be unemployed, but they could always return to the land, where it cost virtually nothing to live.

The early stirrings of Catholic social consciousness, as propounded by Leo XIII, were all felt at Bergamo. The Church was not only patriotic but pro-worker. Many different social schemes were afoot. Small loans with low-interest rates were provided for rural housing. There were cooperatives to insure low prices for necessities. There were community-owned mills and milk stations. One historian of the period counted 124 church-sponsored groups in the province of Bergamo working for the common good.

Bergamo was the most intense Catholic province in all of Italy.

If it had more priests, more seminarians, more members of religious orders in proportion to its population than any other diocese in Italy, it also provided during the Risorgimento more volunteers for Garibaldi's forces than any other spot in the peninsula.

The motto of Bergamo's Catholics was "not words but deeds." As one of the leaders expressed it, "Either we will have Catholicism in action, or we will have Catholicism in a museum." Here ugly Marxism was never allowed a toehold. The Catholics reached the workers long before the Socialists arrived. At a time when Milan and Cremona were the scenes of Marxist inspired disturbances, all was calm and content at Bergamo. Strong Catholic unions which exist to this day grew up early. Father Roncalli's bishop of this period, Radini-Tedeschi, became so imbued with the ideas of *Rerum novarum* that he even took the side of striking workers during that period—a bold act.

It follows, naturally, that at Bergamo the anticlerical parties invariably made a poor showing. When the decree *Non expedit* forbade practicing Catholics either to vote or be elected, Bergamo obeyed the Papal command and boycotted the ballot box by 80 percent of the population. In the first municipal elections after the ban was lifted, however, the Catholics won all the offices. Bergamo was soon to send the country's first Catholic deputy to the Parliament at Rome.

This pattern of electing only good Catholics continues today. In 1948, at the moment of the Communists' greatest challenge, only two of the 380 communities of Bergamo Province failed to return good Catholics to power, and these two backsliding towns belonged, ecclesiastically speaking, to the diocese of Cremona rather than Bergamo.

The outsider is bound to ask how closely the clergy controls local government in such a staunchly Catholic region as Bergamo. The answer is that there is no need for direct control. The faithful know from instinct as well as from training what is expected of them, and obey. The proper lay society is, according to this precept, one which takes its direction from the hierarchy, but this control must never be heavy-handed. The Pope is for law, but for Catholic law. He wants liberty—within the Catholic tradition. He favors freedom of the press—for Catholic newspapers.

Yet John XXIII knows that there are few Bergamos left in the world today. Of all Popes, he has lived and worked longest in non-Catholic countries. His stays in Bulgaria, Greece, and Turkey, not to mention his later service in a far from evangelical France, have conditioned him to deal easily and naturally with non-Catholic societies. Not even Pius XII received as many dissidents and schismatics, not to mention out-and-out infidels, as has John XXIII.

Politics at the Vatican under John XXIII is thus an unemotional affair, differing from country to country according to circumstances. The Vatican has found itself able to maintain relations of a sort with a Communist government of Poland at the same time that it has been continually at odds with one in Yugoslavia. The reactionary Franco of Spain is barely acceptable; the fairly liberal Adenauer government of Germany is favored.

Salazar's Portugal has lately proved something of an embarrassment. This Catholic government had reason to hope for at least moral support from the Vatican in its struggle to maintain its empire. Instead it did not receive a word of sympathy even when Catholic Goa was attacked by the polytheistic Hindus. The Vatican is aware that in the latter half of the twentieth century empire is a losing cause.

Often in the past the Church has been accused of favoring monarchies and dictatorships over democracies, but no longer. In recent years the Vatican has generally sided with popular governments based on universal suffrage, all operating in an economic system of free enterprise. Hence the rise of the Christian Democratic parties in Western Europe.

By and large the Vatican is happier about the United States, with its Protestant majority, than about Latin American countries, with their solid Catholicism. It has been most unhappy about the Cuba of Fidel Castro. To the Vatican, France has long been a special problem; Rome has rarely fathomed the determined secular ways of the French.

For a time it seemed as if under the new pontificate the Church would cease its more active interference, even in Italy. Early in his reign John XXIII ruled that henceforth Italian questions—meaning Italian politics—would be handled by the episcopate and not by the Vatican, as they had been handled since the war. This did not mean, however, the end of intervention. In fact, the hierarchy from the Pope down has insisted that while lay questions should generally be decided by laymen, the bishops have a God-given right to interfere when they consider that a question touches ethics or morals. John XXIII put the matter in this way:

"Catholics in their economic social activities often find themselves in close contact with others who do not share their view of life. In these circumstances, our sons should be very careful that they are consistent and never make compromises on religion and morals . . . let them show themselves animated by a spirit of achieving objects that of their nature are good or at least reducible to good. It is clear, however, that when the hierarchy has made a decision on the point at issue Catholics are bound to obey their directives because the Church has the right and obligation not merely to guard ethical and religious principles but also to *intervene authoritatively in the temporal sphere* when it is a matter of judging the application of these principles to concrete cases."

The publication of a now-famous editorial entitled *"Punti Fermi"* in *L'Osservatore Romano* in May, 1960, is a case in point. This title has been translated both "Firm Points" and "Standard Points," but "Guiding Principles" is perhaps more accurate. Originally the editorial was scheduled for publication in *Il Quotidiano*, the Rome organ of Catholic Action, but as one Vatican official admitted, "In *Quotidiano* the editorial would have made no splash at all. To get our point across we needed *L'Osservatore Romano*."

The article starts with the observation that an "unhealthy theory" current in lay circles has "obfuscated" the basic principles of the Christian doctrine on the structure of the Church as well as on its mission and its magistracy. This has brought about a tendency to restrict the relations of the hierarchy and the laity. The hierarchy is now supposed to operate only in the "sphere of the purely sacred ministry" at the same time that the "autonomy of the believer in the civil sphere" is proclaimed. From all this comes an "absurd schism of conscience between the believer and the citizen." The idea has taken root that religion is something apart, merely an occasional phase in the life of the spirit, and not an "idea which engages and orients the whole existence of man." This "great confusion" has even spread among Catholics and has affected the "relations between Catholic doctrine and the social and political activities of the people" as well as "between the Catholic hierarchy and the lay faithful in the civic field."

From this point the editorial continues to develop its theme:

1. The Church as constituted by Jesus Christ as a perfect society with its own hierarchy has full powers of jurisdiction over the faithful and therefore has the right and the duty of guiding them, and correcting them in their ideas and actions, conforming with the dictums of the Scriptures as far as is necessary for the supreme end of man, which is eternal life. With this aim the Church proposes a truth in which to believe, a law to be observed, and offers divine grace for the exercise of all virtues—individual, domestic, and social. Not only must a Catholic take note of the teachings and directives of the Church, but in every sector of his activity his conduct must be inspired by the laws, orientations, and instructions of the Church.

2. Politico-social problems cannot be separated from religion. This is because they are extremely human problems and as such have at their roots an ethical-religious exigency which cannot be suppressed, just as conscience and the sense of duty, which play a large part in these problems, cannot be suppressed. As a result the Church cannot remain agnostic, particularly when politics touch upon the altar. The Church has the duty and the right to intervene in this field to illuminate and assist people's consciences

according to moral principles and the principles of Christian sociology.

3. As regards politics, the problem of collaboration with those who do not admit religious principles can present itself. It is then up to the ecclesiastical authorities, rather than to any single Catholic, to judge the moral permissibility of such a collaboration, and a conflict between such judgments and the opinion of single Catholics is inconceivable in a truly Christian conscience. Any such case should be resolved through obedience to the Church, which is the custodian of the truth.

4. The irreducible antithesis between the Marxist system and the Christian doctrine is self-evident, if only because the first opposes materialism to spiritualism and atheism to religious faith. Therefore the Church cannot permit Catholics to belong to, assist, or collaborate with those movements which adopt or follow the Marxist ideology and its application. Such support or collaboration would inevitably bring about the compromise or sacrifice of the intangible principles of the faith and Christian morality.

This editorial was printed at a time, incidentally, when Senator John F. Kennedy was protesting, in various United States primary election campaigns, that he would never permit ecclesiastical interference with his duties as an elected official of the United States. American correspondents in Rome filed the "Guiding Principles" article, assuming that what was true for an Italian Catholic, especially when presented in such didactic terms, ought also to be true for the Catholic in America. But they were soon corrected. The editorial was meant only for Italians.

Its immediate cause was one of those countless and by now forgotten political maneuvers on the part of a faction of the Italian Christian Democratic party to form a coalition with the Socialists. The printing of the article in L'Osservatore Romano would hardly have been ordered without encouragement from the Pope himself. The inevitable conclusion is that the perfect society in Italy and that in America are two different things. In politics as well as in some other matters, Rome suffers from parochialism.

The socio-economic thinking of the Pope, unlike his political thinking, has apparently undergone a considerable change during his pontificate. The Holy Father originally patterned his ideas on those of Leo XIII, the Pontiff of his formulate youth. He was consequently vague on some modern issues. For example, in discussing industrial strikes, John XXIII attributed them to the fact that "man has been treated almost exclusively as a machine, a piece of merchandise, a worthless cog in some great machine, a mere productive unit." His concept of just wages came down to one main criterion: they should be adjusted according to the number of dependents.

In his various May 1 pronouncements Pope John XXIII struck admonitory notes, often against the Communists. "Unfortunately, there are mistaken ideologies that laud the most undisciplined license on the one hand and impose the suppression of the individual personality on the other," His Holiness said on May 1, 1960. "These are the people who would snatch away its laurels from labor, who would use the workingman as a tool in their battles and then leave him to shift for himself. They are the people who sow the seeds of discord, who try with all their might to set class against class in the same society. They have even tried to steal the workers away from God. . . . Our heart bleeds when we recall that many of our children, honest and upright though they are, have fallen prey to such evil theories. . . ."

Perhaps the nearest the Holy Father came until recently to a definition of social justice in an industrial society was with these simple words, directed at a Catholic management group: "Capital, management and labor are not and must not become irreconcilable antagonisms. They are co-workers in a common undertaking which requires first of all mutual understanding and a sincere effort to overcome the temptation for each to seek his own advantage at the expense of the other participants. . . ."

These several speeches were all made before the publication, in May, 1961, of the encyclical *Mater et Magistra* (Mother and Teacher), the longest such document of any Pope and the most impressive statement of John XXIII's reign. The publication of *Mater et Magistra* represents the latest attempt to put the Vatican abreast of social developments in a fast-changing world.

The ideas expressed in this encyclical seem curiously modern for the present Holy Father. In fact, this pronouncement was reportedly a collaboration from the start. The first draft, it is said, was written by two Jesuit fathers, both specialists on social questions and both teachers in the Gregorian University of Rome. The final draft, according to indications from the Vatican, was entrusted to the late Cardinal Tardini, who in fact worked evenings on the encyclical even in failing health. The Pope, of course, made suggestions from time to time, and put his signature to the encyclical, thus making it the most authoritative modern opinion of the Church on social questions.

Because of its length (more than twenty thousand words) only a short summary of *Mater et Magistra* can be attempted here.

The last two decades, the encyclical reminds us at the outset, have witnessed "profound transformations" in the internal structure of society:

In the field of science, technology and economics: The discovery of nuclear energy, its application first to the purposes of war and later its increasing employment for peaceful ends; the unlimited possibilities opened up by chemistry in synthetic products; the growth of automation in the sectors of industry and services; the modernization of the agricultural sector; the disappearance of distances through communication effected especially by radio and television; the increased speed in transportation; the initial conquests of interplanetary space.

In the social field: the development of systems for social insurance and, in some more economically advanced political communities, the introduction of social security systems; in labor movements the formation of, and the increased importance attached to, a more responsible attitude toward the greater socio-economic problems; a progressive improvement of basic education; an ever-wider distribution of welfare; an increased social mobility and the resulting decline in the divisions between the classes; the interest in world events on the part of those with an average education. . . .

In the political field: the participation in public life in many political communities of an increasing number of citizens coming from diverse social strata; a more extensive and deeper activity of public authorities in the economic and social field. To these must be added, on the international level, the end of colonial regimes and the attainment of political independence of the peoples of Asia and Africa; the growth of close relationships between the peoples and a deepening of their interdependence; the appearance on the scene and development of an ever-growing network of organizations with a world-wide scope and inspired by supernational criteria; organizations with economic, social, cultural and political ends.

An important section of the encyclical deals with socialization of property, which is in the main endorsed as an "expression of the tendency in human beings to join together to attain objectives which are beyond the capacity and means of single individuals." In a shorter section on private property the Pope makes this acute observation: "Today men strive to acquire professional training rather than become owners of property. . . . They have greater confidence in income deriving from work or rights founded on work than in income deriving from capital or rights founded on capital."

The question of population increase is attacked cautiously. The Pope notes that some people think that in a "few decades the human family will reach a quite high figure, while economic development will proceed at a slower rate. From this they deduce that, if nothing is done in time to check the population growth the lack of balance between the population and the food supply in the not-too-distant future will make itself felt acutely." But the encyclical ventures the opinion that, "at least for the moment and in the near future," the disparity between population increase and economic development "does not seem to create a difficulty; in any case the elements from which one can draw sure conclusions are too uncertain and changeable." At this point the Catholic case against artificial control of birth is restated, but in nondidactic language:

God in His goodness and wisdom has diffused in nature inexhaustible resources and has given to man intelligence and genius to create fit instruments to master it and to turn it to satisfying the needs and demands of life. Hence, the real solution of the problem [of overpopulation] is not to be found in expedients that offend against the moral order established by God, and which injure the very origins of human life, but in a renewed scientific and technical effort on the part of man to deepen and extend his dominion over nature. The progress of science and technology, already realized, opens up in this direction limitless horizons.

What attracted most public attention in *Mater et Magistra* when it was first published was the section dealing with the underdeveloped countries. The most difficult problem of the modern world, the encyclical declares, concerns the relationship between political communities that are economically advanced and those in the process of development. The standard of living in the former is high, while in the latter extreme poverty exists. "The solidarity which binds all men . . . imposes upon political communities enjoying abundance of material goods the obligation not to remain indifferent to those political communities whose citizens suffer from poverty, misery and hunger, and who lack even the elementary rights of the human person." This problem is all the greater because of the growing interdependence of peoples. "It is not possible to preserve lasting peace among peoples if glaring economic and social inequality among them persists," the Pope concludes.

Mater et Magistra is an important document; those wanting to understand the social thinking of the Church should read it in its entirety.

IX

THE SACRED COLLEGE
OF CARDINALS

A Ph.D. thesis could be written on the decline in power, quality, and vigor of the Sacred College of Cardinals. This body of Princes of the Church has at this writing (1962) a total of ninety members, far more than it has ever had before in its long history, and twenty more than the limit of seventy which Sixtus V set in the sixteenth century. But probably never before in history has its collective membership exercised so little power and influence.

Traditionally the cardinals are supposed to be the Pope's closest collaborators. Those who are stationed at Rome and thus form part of the Curia are popularly supposed to be the Pontiff's chief advisers. But the tendency of the past few decades has been to bypass the Church's once venerable Senate. Far from having their opinions asked, the majority of cardinals are often not even informed of what is happening until it is done.

Consistories are now called only on formal occasions, such as canonizations and the naming of new cardinals, when strong tradition demands them. But otherwise the Curia cardinals as a group are expected to be seen quite a bit but seldom heard. They are decorative, with their lovely capes and their long trains, and when a score or more of them are gathered they provide a splendid back-drop for the Pontiff's appearances. But the main functions of the cardinals today are presiding over the obsequies for a dead Pope and electing a new one. The Sacred College has exercised these prerogatives exactly five times during the twentieth century.

The real decline of the College of Cardinals set in with the promulgation of Papal Infallibility at the first Vatican council in 1870. This dogma put the Roman Pontiff on such a high pedestal that the Princes of the Church grew smaller by comparison. It was during this Council that the last open criticisms of the Pope were heard from members of the Church's hierarchy.

Time had been when the Curia cardinals not only discussed matters thoroughly with the Pope but occasionally quarreled with him. Nobody at the Vatican could imagine such things happening today. A rebelling cardinal has today as much chance of enduring at the Vatican as a capitalist has at the Kremlin. The old forms remain; what old form does not remain at the Vatican? But they are meaningless.

When nominating new cardinals, for example, the Pope still summons Their Eminences to the Hall of the Consistory and asks the tried question, "*Quid vobis videtur?*" (How does this seem to you?) To this the cardinals, if they agree on the new nomination, take off their hats and make a small bow. Presumably if they did not agree, they could signify that, too, but it would be of little avail. The list of the cardinals-elect has been published weeks in advance, and the nominees themselves have by now arrived in Rome to receive their red hats formally.

In the case of proposed canonizations, the formula is slightly different. On being asked whether he approves, a prelate rises and says: "*Placet juxta votum a me scriptum et subscriptum,*" which means that his affirmative vote has already been deposited. The key word here is "*placet,*" or "it pleases." Presumably a prelate could answer "*non placet,*" but that combination of words has not been heard in the Hall of the Consistory for decades. In fact, the last time any objection was made in a consistory came in the

1930's, when two cardinals thought there could have been better proof of two miracles attributed to Giovanni Bosco, the newly created saint of Turin.

There are still a few individual cardinals in the Curia who, by operating backstage, are both powerful and influential; but as a Church Senate the Sacred College of Cardinals has virtually ceased to function except during the brief interregnums. The Pope's commanding position, moreover, means that other strong personalities in the Curia have a difficult time expressing themselves; for they are always afraid of saying or doing something that could be construed as against the views of the reigning Pontiff.

Pius XII was said to have become convinced during the later years that the system of maintaining a large number of the Princes of the Church at the headquarters establishment at Rome was unsound. He preferred simple priests with administrative ability at the Vatican, putting the Princes in outlying sees. His refusal to hold a new consistory in the last five years of his life may have stemmed partly from this conviction.[1]

John XXIII has reverted to the practices of old by tripling the number of cardinals in the Curia. At the same time, he has used headquarters at Rome as a sort of old-age home for ailing Princes unable any longer to carry their weight in regular dioceses. At this writing thirty-four cardinals are nominally serving in the Curia, but of these not over ten or twelve could be called active. At least a dozen are more or less permanently bedridden, while others can walk only a few steps by themselves. For even a solemn occasion at St. Peter's, not more than seventeen or eighteen of the cardinals can normally muster up the strength to be present.

Starting a few weeks after his ascension to the Throne, John XXIII has to date held five consistories, at which he has created

[1] The situation of cardinals of the Curia versus cardinals with sees is like that of headquarters service versus command in the field in a peacetime army. Most officers, like most prelates, would rather have their own commands, but on the other hand it is at headquarters that the promotions come regularly and fast.

a total of fifty-five new cardinals.[2] These include three cardinals *in petto* (literally, in the breast), whose names have yet to be announced.[3] One or more of these may be bishops now serving in countries back of the Iron Curtain. The total known membership of the Sacred College at this writing (it varies from month to month, according to the number of deaths) is thus eighty-seven, plus the three unknown, for a total of ninety.

Several features of the consistories of John XXIII should be noted. The new Pope has, first of all, kept the numerical superiority of about two non-Italians for every Italian established by his predecessor. More significant, a total of eleven non-Italians (most of them, alas, quite old) are now in the Curia. To be precise, at Rome there are now two French cardinals, two Spaniards, one Argentine, one Portuguese, one Briton, one Armenian, one Syrian, one Irishman, and one German.

The youngest member of the Sacred College is Cardinal Julius Doepfner, forty-nine years old, former Bishop of Berlin, now the Archbishop of Munich. The oldest is Cardinal Francesco Morano, former secretary of the Apostolic Signature and a life-long friend of Roncalli. He was elevated to the purple at eighty-seven. Statistics on this point are vague, but old hands think that this is the first time a man has become a cardinal at such an advanced age.[4]

The new Pope's quick naming of new cardinals soon after his accession created the impression that John XXIII was injecting fresh blood into the Sacred College. Actually, no such thing has occurred. The average age of the new cardinals is slightly higher than that of the prelates who had been in office for years. Of the eighty-seven known cardinals at this writing a total of fifty are over

[2] As compared to Pius XI, who created twenty-five cardinals in fourteen consistories during a reign of seventeen years, and Pius XII, who created sixty cardinals in two consistories during a reign of nineteen years.

[3] Should the Pope die before making these names public, his successor could accept or refuse to accept these nominations as he wished.

[4] Not so with Popes, however. Pope Agatone, who reigned in the seventh century, was elected to the Tiara at the age of ninety-nine and reigned three years.

seventy years old and more than half are seventy-five or over. Some fourteen cardinals are in their eighties, while only two are in their late forties and seven in the fifties. The habit of appointing older men to the Church's highest posts can doubtless be partly attributed to the medical fact that people stay alive longer nowadays. But the gentle administrative policies of John XXIII also enter the picture. The new Pope has been more than generous in giving red hats to one-time associates and friends, no matter what the state of their health. Twelve or fourteen former diplomats, friends of Roncalli when he himself was one, have thus been elevated to the purple. Here are the Curia cardinals, and their respective ages: [5]

Non-Italian
Gregorio Pietro XV Agagianian—Armenian, 67
Anselmo Albareda—Spanish, 70
Augustin Bea—German, 81
Michael Browne—Irish, 75
Santiago Luis Copello—Argentine, 82
Acacio Coussa—Syrian, 65
William Theodore Heard—Scottish, 78
André Jullien—French, 79
Arcadio Larraona—Spanish, 75
José da Costa Nuñes—Portuguese, 82
Eugene Tisserant—French, 78

Italian

Benedetto Aloisi Masella, 83	Paolo Giobbe, 82
Ildebrando Antoniutti, 64	Paolo Marella, 67
Antonio Bacci, 76	Clemente Micara, 82
Francesco Bracci, 81	Francesco Morano, 90
Fernando Cento, 79	Alfredo Ottaviani, 71
Carlo Chiarlo, 80	Giovanni Panico, 67
Amleto Giovanni Cicognani, 79	Giuseppe Pizzardo, 85
Pietro Ciriaci, 76	Francesco Roberti, 73
Carlo Confalonieri, 69	Gustavo Testa, 76
Alberto Di Jorio, 78	Luigi Traglia, 67
Giuseppe Ferretto, 63	Valerio Valeri, 79
Efrem Forni, 73	

[5] As of early in 1962.

While all the Curia cardinals have been assigned posts on the congregations, only a few can attend sessions regularly. This means that major decisions are often made by a tiny handful of the Princes of the Church, and sometimes by younger prelates without proper rank.

The lack of vigorous cardinals in key positions in the Curia, in fact, has led to what some would call abuses of power. During the extended illness of Pius XII in 1954 the Curia cardinals knew no more than what they read in the papers. Access to the Apostolic Palace in those days was severely controlled by a "committee" composed of Sister Pasqualina Lehnert, Count Pietro Enrico Galeazzi, and Prince Carlo Pacelli. Rumors began to circulate that the Pope was dying; to allay them, these three held a "council of war" and decided to invite Cardinals Eugene Tisserant and Nicola Canali to check on what was being done, medically speaking, for the ailing Pontiff, and to reassure the Curia.

A somewhat similar situation has now developed in the Apostolic Palace under John XXIII, involving the Pope's secretary, Monsignor Capovilla. As long as the hard-working and clear-headed Cardinal Domenico Tardini headed the Secretariat of State, Monsignor Capovilla apparently confined his activities to the four walls of the Pope's office. But after Tardini died in 1961, and the Pope named the aging Cardinal Amleto Cicognani [6] to succeed him, a power vacuum was created in the most important of the Holy See's offices. Monsignor Capovilla, it is said, has moved to fill the vacuum. Cardinal Cicognani is able to devote at best only a couple of hours daily to his work. He limits his appointments to five or six a week.

Capovilla's activities have been the subject of a long, bitter, and detailed attack published in *Il Borghese,* a right-wing intellectual weekly of some standing. Since the *Borghese* article could not have been written without the help of insiders at the Vatican, it shows

[6] He will be remembered as the former Apostolic Delegate to the United States.

to what depths the old guard, including the cardinals, have been shocked by the secretary's assumption of power.[7]

If the question of the secretary has thus disturbed the under-surface tranquillity of the Vatican, the same is true in even greater degree of the Pope's decision, announced in a *motu proprio* of early 1961, to ignore the hitherto sacrosanct seniority system of the cardinals. The Sacred College, it should be remembered, is composed of three orders: bishops, priests or presbyters, and deacons. To the layman there is little difference between one rank and another, but to the cardinals themselves there is a good deal.

The cardinal-deacons are in general prelates of the Curia who do mostly administrative work and are not heads of active sees. The great majority of cardinals, however, belong to the priestly order; they have all headed dioceses, but may now be assigned to the Curia. The cardinal-priests also have titular churches in Rome. The cardinal-bishops, the highest of the orders, are six in number. Besides being members of the Curia they are also bishops of the dioceses nearest to Rome, which are known as "suburbicarian sees": Ostia, Albano, Frascati, Palestrina, Sabina, and Velletri. These are not only historic but also wealthy dioceses, and their possession has long been considered a valued prize.

With the cardinal-deacons and the cardinal-priests, seniority depends on the date at which each received his red hat. But with the cardinal-bishops another system has prevailed from time immemorial. Their seniority dates from the time they take possession of their suburbicarian sees. The cardinal-bishop who took possession of his see the longest time ago becomes dean of the Sacred College of Cardinals, a post of honor and privilege.

But how does a member of the Sacred College become a cardinal-bishop? Until now the succession has been automatic, established by Canon 236, paragraph 3, of the Code of Canon Law.

---

[7] Capovilla's apartment, just above the Pope's, has windows which resemble portholes. The Italian word for portholes is *oblii;* when Vatican officials want to refer to Monsignor Capovilla these days without mentioning his name, they raise their eyebrows and say softly but meaningfully: *"Oblii."*

Upon vacancy of a suburbicarian diocese the highest-ranking cardinal-priest resident at Rome has the option of taking the see in question and thus becoming a cardinal-bishop. It was this system of options which John XXIII decided to change. The upholders of tradition, not to mention canon law, at the Apostolic Palace were shocked. Monsignor Enrico Dante, the Prefect of Ceremonies, is said to have flatly told the Pope: "But, Your Holiness, this is quite impossible!" But the Holy Father did it nevertheless, canon law or not, insisting that times had changed, that the dioceses in question had grown, that as a result "the exercise of pastoral functions has become more arduous" and that the Pontiff must be free to choose whomever he wants.

In terms of their background in the church, the cardinals can be divided into three chief categories. First, there is the cleric who works his way up through the diocese, grade by grade, from parish priest to archbishop to the red hat. He should, of course, know his theology, but perhaps more important today is his administrative ability. And it also never hurts if at some point in his career he learns his way about Rome. The second category comes out of the Holy See's far-flung diplomatic service. They are all experts in canon law and should know international law too. A tradition has grown of promoting to the cardinalate the nuncios to such countries as Italy, France, Spain, Portugal, Brazil, and Belgium. The third category of cardinals is that of the higher administration of the Curia. Once it was tacitly assumed that a monsignor who functioned well and long as the secretary of one of the sacred congregations could look forward one day to elevation to the purple. Nowadays, he is no longer sure.

A fourth and special category of cardinal has risen under the present Pope. Thus the Rev. Augustin Bea was elevated to the Sacred College because he was a well-known Biblical scholar and the Pope had a special assignment for him as head of the new Secretariat for the Union of Christians. Alberto Di Jorio is rated as a brilliant financial expert, while Francesco Roberti is an excellent lawyer. Obviously the coming to independence of large sec-

tions of Africa dictated the naming of the first Negro cardinal of
modern times, Lauriano Rugambwa, of Tanganyika. The need to
stress the universality of the Church as well as the lack of color
line was in all probability, also, the chief factor behind the choice
of the first Japanese prelate to become a member of the Sacred
College, Cardinal Pietro Tatsuo Doi.

The Italians have their own system of dividing the cardinals.
They classify them either as "integrationalists," meaning most
conservative, or "progressives," meaning less conservative. About
ten of the Curia cardinals, including Ottaviani, Micara, and Pizzardo, can be said to be integrationalists. The progressives on the
other hand, include Agagianian, Bea, Cicognani, Ciriaci, Ferretto,
Giobbe, Larraona, Roberti, and Tisserant. A whole group of other
cardinals, including Bacci, Bracci, Copello, Heard, Marella,
Morano, and Testa, are unclassifiable.

Fine doctrinal points cause little heat today, either outside or
inside the Vatican. One simply cannot imagine getting excited
over the question of whether yeast should or should not be used in
communion bread, or just how the Holy Ghost proceeds, whether
from the Father through the Son or from the Father and the Son.
But there are questions of policy about which even the Curia
cardinals sometimes differ. For example, what should the Church
do about the fact that a great segment of the voters in Italy, in
the Vatican's own backyard, has joined the Church's great enemy,
Communism? Plainly, it is embarrassing that despite fifteen years
of amazing prosperity under Church-sponsored governments more
Italians than ever vote the Red ticket.

It is here, in the broad sphere of high politics, that differences
of opinion have appeared within the Vatican. There are those who
believe in taking a "modern" approach to these problems, and thus
advise the Pope, while others insist that the Church must stand
high above such matters. The collective mind of the Holy Office,
the great keeper of the Church's tradition, as personified by its
secretary, Cardinal Ottaviani, insists on combating Communism
on a doctrinaire level. On the other hand, the collective mind of

the Congregation for the Propagation of the Faith, as personified in Cardinal Agagianian, has insisted that methods as well as doctrine are important.

Men like Palermo's Cardinal Ruffini and Genoa's Siri are both rigid upholders of standards and doubtless insist that the "modern" approach ends only in watering down the true faith. They would be charitable to Communists personally but uncompromisingly against Communism. On the other side of the fence would be found the Archbishops of Paris, Cardinal Maurice Feltin, and of Bologna, Cardinal Lercaro; both have presided over heavily red archdioceses, and both have concluded that orthodox methods of getting the workers back into the Church are no longer adequate. Said one of Lercaro's assistants in an interview in 1957:

"The old idea of priests sitting in churches waiting for the communicants to come to them simply won't work any more, especially not in Italy. What happens is that the churches get emptier and emptier. The priests must now get out and go to the people. We are back to the days of the traveling preachers." Lercaro, incidentally, organized teams of wandering monks for his archdiocese. When he asked Rome for approval, the answer came back: "Go ahead and do it, but don't tell anybody that the Vatican is backing it."

Of strong personalities in the Curia, there are now three. The deaths of Cardinals Tardini and Canali removed from the Vatican scene two men who despite everything could still take decisive steps.

Cardinal Tisserant, the French dean of the Sacred College, must be classed as a strong personality, though he is not a favorite of the Pope. According to French sources in Rome, Tisserant made the mistake of calling Roncalli down for untidy attire on the occasion of a cardinal's funeral during the interregnum. As the chief executive of the vacant Holy See at the time, Tisserant had a perfect right to do so; he little guessed that within a week Roncalli would occupy St. Peter's Throne.

Tisserant's important post during the last pontificate had been that of secretary of the Oriental Church. For this job he seemed eminently fitted. He is considered an expert in Hebrew, Syriac, Arabic, Ethiopian, and Assyrian; he has lectured in the United States for the Carnegie Foundation on Semitic languages. Within a few months after the election of Roncalli, however, he was asked to resign this post. He now spends most of his time in the suburbicarian see of Ostia. Year by year he becomes less important in the Vatican scheme of things. He will, however, keep the post of dean of the Sacred College to his death, and in the event of another conclave he would again briefly be in a commanding position.

Cardinal Agagianian, the Armenian-born prefect of the Congregation of Propaganda Fide, which has charge of the Church's still vast mission territory, is another figure of commanding importance. The "Red Pope," as Rome calls him, is currently the most influential non-Italian in the Curia, and seems likely to remain such. One source of his strength is that he came to Rome when a boy and has since spent a good half of his time in the Eternal City. He knows Italy and the Vatican, speaks Italian perfectly, and is still not Italian. Supposed to have been the chief rival of Roncalli at the last conclave, Agagianian and the Pope apparently get along well. He has an audience with His Holiness the first Tuesday of every month.

The strongest personality of the Curia—outside the Pope—is Cardinal Ottaviani, leader of the Vatican conservatives, chief of the Holy Office, the son of a Trastevere baker, with the ready tongue of the Romans. Ottaviani is easily the Vatican's most controversial figure. He has long cultivated the habit of speaking both bluntly and indiscreetly, often on touchy political subjects that other clerics at the Vatican would not dream of discussing. At times he has embarrassed the Secretariat of State. At one delicate moment of interparty negotiations in Italy, when members of the ruling Christian Democratic party were urging a coalition deal with the Socialists, Cardinal Ottaviani came out against what he called the "Leftists of the Sacristy" who, he charged, were willing to betray Christian principles for a temporary advantage. On another occasion Cardinal Ottaviani, on the very day chosen for the departure of President Giovanni Gronchi for a state visit to Russia, made a speech in which he left no doubt that he disapproved of such contacts with the Communists.

Most Curia cardinals refrain from having books published, unless they are works of hagiology or of historic erudition, but Ottaviani is an exception. In 1961 he published a volume under the title of *Il Baluardo* (The Bulwark), which is devoted entirely to current situations. Ottaviani sees the world of today as in an apocalyptic phase. From the pages of his book he seems to leap forward with a flaming sword of faith uplifted in his hand. His dragon is the modern anti-Christ of laicism, in which, according to him, "converge all the most different and diverse concepts of the world, among them that of the liberals, the atheistic Communists, the Masons, the radicals, the Socialists."

He continues: "A kind of madness disguising itself as social redemption, dressed in politics and diplomacy, wearing the yellow gloves of legitimate power and with its following of espionage spread everywhere, is devastating, with impunity, all humanity, destroying civilization, wishing to make this world a fearsome desert." He adds that had not the Church existed to provide a "strong bulwark which can validly resist the upsetting of the moral and social order," the world would have long ago become a "Sahara of the spirit."

The cardinal is a firm upholder of the need for the Church to intervene in political situations to judge "whether those who have public power use it for the good of citizens." He criticizes strongly "those Catholics who have imbibed a little of the lay poison." As for such experiments as worker-priests, he says that a "priest should be a priest, and not plow the fields, work in factories, or participate in class struggles."

Cardinal Ottaviani's favorite historical figure is Pius V, the armed Pope who turned back the Turks at Lepanto. He has named the Roman institute which he founded after this Pontiff, who "never feared to speak the truth, even when it was unpleasant for those who had to hear it." As the Church's chief theologian, Ottaviani has been responsible for most of the Holy Office's celebrated decrees of the past decade or so. He wrote not only the excommunication decree against practicing Communists, but also another famous one which prohibited Catholics from belonging to Rotary without permission of the local bishop. While many in Rome would recognize Cardinal Ottaviani's valor as an upholder of the faith, others believe that he belongs to an earlier century.

Cardinal Ciriaci, prefect of the Congregation of the Council, is a long-time sufferer from a disease of the spine, and his voice is seldom heard nowadays. However, his congregation deals with matters near to the Pope's heart, and were his health better he would perhaps be a key figure of this pontificate. Cardinal Cento, the former Nuncio to France, is similarly little known. He has no fixed appointments with the Pope, but he is a good friend and moves freely in and about the Apostolic Palace. Cardinal Bea, the first Jesuit to be elevated to the purple since 1938, is a respected figure but not an intimate of the Pope. As the head of the Secretariat for the Union of Christians, Cardinal Bea has been in charge of relations with all non-Catholics. In this activity he has had perhaps more mention in the press during the past several years than any other Curia cardinal.

The Pope has two old friends in the Sacred College whom he invites regularly to meals. One is Cardinal Testa, a fellow Bergamesque; another is Cardinal Confalonieri, also born in Lombardy. There is no evidence, however, that serious questions of Vatican policy are discussed with these two.

John XXIII is such an extremely healthy man that at this writing a new conclave seems improbable in the near future. An old Italian proverb says that a man who passes his seventy-seventh birthday will live on and on; His Holiness quoted the saying to friends when he passed that milestone in 1958. Notwithstanding the robustness of the Supreme Pontiff, however, there is always speculation about future candidates for the Papacy.

There seem to be few *papabili* among the recently created cardinals. The one exception is perhaps Montini of Milan. He has an outstanding personality. He has the reputation of veering to the left in his social and political thinking, but not so much as to be dangerous. His past relations with the episcopate abroad were excellent. He might have been elected Pope in 1958 had he entered the conclave. But, thanks to his colleague Tardini's refusal, he was not yet a cardinal. "I have missed the bus," Montini told an intimate friend on that occasion. And it is quite possible that the bus may never stop for him again.

Otherwise, the *papabili* are pretty much what they were in 1958. Few of the newcomers seem to fit a Pope's role. If the times were ripe for the election of a non-Italian, and perhaps they will be the next time, then Agagianian would still be the only practical possibility. But one year's *papabili* are not necessarily the next year's.

X

THE COFFERS
OF THE HOLY SEE

Mystery surrounds the question of Vatican finances. Correspondents knowledgeable on the subject of money have tried from time to time to estimate the wealth of the Church's headquarters at Rome, but nobody has arrived at more than an educated guess.

The prevailing attitude at the Vatican is that its finances are not the business of outsiders. In fact, queries in that general field are likely to be treated as an attack on Catholicism itself. No budget is ever published. The few statements made by the Church spokesmen on the subject are confusing or misleading. Other religious, charitable and educational institutions, not to mention sovereign states, all reveal their receipts and expenses, but not the Vatican.

Nobody—except perhaps a few extremists—has ever entertained the thought that either the Pope or any of his cardinals was bent on personal enrichment. The Holy Father does not have to worry about personal spending money; although he has no fixed salary, he can draw at will from the Vatican's cash and can even, if he likes, sell off the Holy See's priceless treasures. As for the cardinals, most of them live austerely. A few have inherited money, and one or two are said to be millionaires. But gone forever are the Renaissance days when the Princes indulged in lavish entertainment in luxurious palaces.

What worries Italians about the Holy See's finances is not the thought that individual churchmen may be getting rich, but the suspicion that those in charge of finances at the Holy See have become greedy in their attempts to build up an endowment fund for the Vatican. Some Italians go further and say that what the Vatican could not accomplish by open political manipulation in Italy it is now trying to do through penetration of the country's economy.

It is obvious that the Vatican is an institution with little income and large expenditures. Vatican citizens pay no taxes, and about the only direct income comes from sales of stamps and admissions to the Vatican museums. The Vatican newspaper once admitted that stamp sales came to around $400,000 yearly. The museums probably take in less and must, besides, be maintained. The Peter's Pence collections, whereby Catholic churches all over the world are supposed to send to Rome sums collected on one special day of the year, cannot amount to much. There are said to be 450 to 500 million Catholics in the world, but only a fraction would be found at mass on any specific Sunday, and of these only a small percentage would be able to make any significant contribution.

Against this income must be placed some sizable outlays, especially during the past few years. What amounts to a private army must be uniformed and paid. (The Swiss Guards and the Gendarmery alone, consisting of around two hundred men, receive a total of around $260,000 a year.) Huge palaces, not to mention a whole series of office and residential buildings, must be heated, painted regularly, and kept in continuous repair. Spacious gardens must be groomed. A fleet of some sixty cars must be maintained. A powerful radio station must be operated. A sizable diplomatic corps must be supplied with funds. The upkeep of St. Peter's Basilica, not to mention St. Peter's Square, is costly; the daily cleaning bill alone must run into three or four figures.

The late Cardinal Tardini once volunteered the information in an unusual press conference that the Vatican's payroll was around 4½ billion lire, or about $7,250,000 annually. It was assumed that he was talking about both Vatican State and the Holy See. The question remains what percentage of the total outlay is represented in the payroll. Oldtimers at the Vatican press office have tentatively reckoned the total annual expenditure at from $25 to $30 million; this correspondent would estimate it somewhat higher today, if only because John XXIII, essentially a prudent man not given to extravagance, has ordered so many new projects that cost money.

He was in office only a few months before he ordered a general pay rise, affecting cardinals as well as ushers, secretaries of congregations along with the electricians, ranking Latinists as well as throne bearers and curtain pushers. A cardinal of the Curia, for example, now draws $650 monthly base pay, as against the $560 he used to get. Furthermore, a cardinal living outside the low-rent area of the Vatican can now draw an extra housing allowance at $100 monthly; if he also happens to head a congregation he receives another $50. Thus a Prince of the Church can now receive as much as $810 monthly.[1] As Cardinal Tardini explained: "If you consider the expenses of a cardinal, who obviously must maintain an establishment suitable to his rank as Prince of the Church, you can readily see that this is not an excessive sum."

The Pope's instructions, in tune with the principles set forth by Leo XIII in *Rerum novarum*, lay great stress on family allotments. For example, the lowest-grade Vatican usher, with ten years' service, a wife, and four dependent children, now gets $235 monthly as against the $170 he formerly received. A manual laborer who before was paid at the monthly rate of $85 now receives $115 base pay, but if he has a wife and four dependent

---

[1] Actually, many cardinals have at their disposal much greater sums. Some, for example, are protectors of various orders, and in that way receive all manner of donations. The cardinal-bishops can draw money from their suburbicarian dioceses. Furthermore, Curia cardinals are always in demand in Rome for weddings, funerals, and cornerstone layings, for which services they invariably receive generous fees.

children his monthly pay envelope swells to $220. Other Vatican salaries now in force include $120 for a Swiss Guardsman, $335 for the secretary of a congregation, $340 for the editor of *L'Osservatore Romano*. These are still not impressive salaries compared with those that prevail in the United States. But rents are low and taxes are nil, and the pay compares favorably with similar stipends in neighboring Italy. Administratively, the pay rises have been important. In the past, many Vatican employees tried to supplement their wages by part-time work elsewhere; this is now necessary in fewer cases.

The extensive improvements in the Vatican ordered by John XXIII (see Chapter III) are also costly. Perhaps the most expensive work is that undertaken on the Leonine Walls themselves. The biggest of the walls' twenty-four towers, known as the Tower of St. John, has been remodeled into a summer residence for the Pope.[2] A team of carpenters, stone masons, plumbers, and others worked on it for about a year. It is now complete, even to a small elevator and a chapel.

Pope John XXIII has never much liked Castel Gandolfo. Dutifully he goes there every July, but his stays are shorter than those of Pius XII, and he often makes special trips back into town. It is for these short stays in Rome that the Tower of St. John will be used. With the beautiful rose beds now surrounding it, the Tower of St. John should make an enchanting and supremely quiet summer home for His Holiness.

The costs of the ecumenical council which the Holy Father has called will be large. In fact, Vatican officials doubt if Pius XII would ever have called such a council for fear of the expense. Travel expenditures alone for the two thousand delegates will be

---

[2] This tower, sixty-three feet high and about fifty feet in diameter, was built in the ninth century to withstand the Saracen attacks. In those days a small wooden castle stood on its top and served as a lookout for marauders. Centuries later Vatican astronomers established themselves there and it was covered with a metal cupola. The scientists moved to Castel Gandolfo in 1939 and took the cupola with them, leaving the tower roofless. Since then it has deteriorated considerably.

formidable, and these are only the initial costs of running such a large gathering of such long duration. But John XXIII not only thinks money is to be used, but believes he has it to use.

The supposition is that all these expenses are being paid out of income from the Vatican's invested capital. Here again, however, the inquiring correspondent runs into a wall of silence. The late Cardinal Tardini once branded stories of the Vatican's great wealth as a "myth," but this is a matter of definition. His Eminence also once told a small group of journalists that he regretted the original decision to invest most of the Vatican's funds in Italy rather than spreading it about other countries. "We thought we were helping Italy," His Eminence lamented. "Instead, we have been constantly accused of trying to take over the Italian economy."

The Church has long possessed large tracts of real estate in Italy in general and Central Italy in particular, but most of these were the property of specific churches or monasteries of various orders and did not belong to the Holy See as such. The Vatican proper's invested wealth dates from the Lateran Pact of 1929, when the Italian government agreed to hand over to the Vatican, as an indemnity for wiping out the Papal States in 1870, the sum of 1,750,000,000 lire. Of this amount, 750,000,000 lire came in convertible cash and the remaining billion came in the form of notes payable, which the Vatican agreed not to collect immediately.

Modern currencies have all greatly depreciated, and how much this sum represents today is a matter of speculation. One writer on economic affairs has estimated that in 1870 this amount would, at the old rates, have been roughly $100 million [but that as of now it must be calculated at perhaps $400 million]. The official lira-dollar rate in 1929, however, was nineteen to one, which would put the paid indemnity at around $90 million.

It should be remembered, however, that with the Lateran Pact the Vatican's periodic financial embarrassments were at an end. Before then the Holy See had had trouble meeting current expenses. When Benedict XV died in 1922, for example, the *camerlengo* or cardinal in charge found the Vatican cupboard so bare that he floated a loan of around $10,000 to pay the expenses of the ensuing conclave. In 1928 Pius XI borrowed money from American bankers to get the Vatican by a particularly difficult period. Since 1929, the Vatican has been in a liquid position.

An Amministrazione Speciale of the Holy See, with offices just off St. Peter's Square, was set up by Pius XI to handle the Lateran Pact funds. Heading this office for many years was an elusive figure named Bernardino Nogara, former vice-president of the Banca Commerciale of Italy, with a long experience in the Levant. Nogara's specialty was said to be gold, and for some time his dealings for the Vatican were largely limited to arbitrage, the trading of gold bullion for gold coins, or vice versa.

It was Nogara who laid down the rule that neither religious nor political considerations should hamper the Vatican's investment policy. Thus for a time government bonds of Protestant Britain were considered better risks than those of Catholic Spain; nor was there any hesitation, apparently, about going into stock market operations on Wall Street. In fact, hovering in the shadows of the Vatican for years were men known to have close connections with Hambro's Bank in London, J. P. Morgan & Company in New York, and the Crédit Suisse of Geneva.

A committee of three cardinals in theory supervised the workings of the Amministrazione Speciale at first, but in practice Nogara was virtual dictator until his death in the late 1950's. His place has since nominally been taken by the Papal Marquis, Enrico de Maillardoz, formerly of the Credit Suisse, who by now, however, has an able clerical overseer in the person of Cardinal Di Jorio. His Eminence is also in control of the Vatican's bank, the Institute for Works of Religion. Tourists to Rome during the late forties will remember this bank as the one which often gave the best lira-dollar rates.

Just when the Vatican began to invest heavily in Italian industry cannot be determined. Suffice it to say that in the late 1940's and early 1950's many Italians began to be aware of the weight of the Vatican in the financial affairs of their nation. Various utilities were said to be controlled by Vatican money. Men associated with the Vatican now sat on the boards of directors of at least three important Italian banks—the Banca di Roma, the Banca Commerciale, and Il Credito Italiano. They also occupied posts of authority in various water and gas companies, two or three electric power companies, and the important telephone company, known as TETI.

The biggest of Italian real estate companies, known as the Generale Immobiliare, which operates on a vast scale in the fast-expanding Italian capital, was Vatican-controlled if not Vatican-owned. In one year alone the Generale Immobiliare, which in the last ten years has absorbed perhaps ten other large real estate outfits, constructed some two thousand different buildings of one size or another, mainly in Rome but also in the provinces. It has recently embarked on large and costly housing projects, complete with modern shopping centers. It also controls a hotel chain and it has provided about three-quarters of the capital for the construction of a new luxurious four-hundred-room Hotel Hilton in Rome. Total assets of the Generale Immobiliare alone could hardly be less than $100 million.

All these things were known in general terms, but details have been hard to pin down because ownership is not a matter of immediate public record. Also complicating the situation is the existence of a number of agencies not always easily recognizable as of Vatican origin. Besides the Amministrazione Speciale and the Institute for the Works of Religion, there are also such entities as the Pontifical Work of Assistance, the Pius XII Foundation for the Lay Apostolate, the Instituto Centrale Finanziario, and the Società Finanziaria Industriale e Commerciale, all of which can and do own industrial shares.

Of late a few journalistic investigators, mainly from Italy's enterprising left-wing press, have pierced the haze of confusion on this subject and have been able to come up with a certain amount of impressive documentation. For example, one writer had a simple but excellent idea. Unable to establish ownership, he proceeded to compile lists of the boards of directors of the leading holding companies, utilities, and industrial corporations of the peninsula, and compared the names he found there with the names of known Vatican agents.

Thus, whenever Count Enrico Galeazzi's name appears on a board of directors it is a safe assumption that he is there as a watchdog of Vatican interests. The same can be said of the three Pacelli princes. Massimo Spada, a lawyer with the official post of administrative secretary of the Institute for the Works of Religion, is another, as is Dr. Luigi Mennini, who holds down perhaps a half-dozen posts at the Vatican. Other recognizable figures are Dr. Luigi Gedda and Vittorio Veronese, both former presidents of Catholic Action, with many Vatican titles. Antonio Rinaldi, listed as vice-secretary of the Apostolic Chamber, is still another, as is Count Paolo Blumensthil, a Secret Chamberlain of the Sword and Cloak.

The names of all these men—and others almost equally well known—appear time and time again on corporation lists. Count Galeazzi must be a member of at least a score of large Italian companies, starting with the Generale Immobiliare, of which he is vice-president, and continuing down to L'Acqua Pia Antica Marcia di Roma, one of Rome's chief water suppliers. Prince Carlo Pacelli's name appears on almost as many lists. Prince Giulio Pacelli and Spada are on the board of Italgas, a company which has the concession to supply gas for some forty cities in Italy. Prince Marcantonio Pacelli is a member of the board of the Generale Immobiliare. Rinaldi is the president of the Instituto Centrale Finanziario; Mennini is vice-president of the Società Finanziaria Industriale e Commerciale. One of the most important holding companies in Italy is La Centrale, which controls a great part of the electrical energy generated in central Italy. On the boards of the various companies known to be controlled by La Centrale appear again and again the names of Galeazzi, Spada, Blumensthil.

The conclusion is inescapable that the Vatican today has invested funds in electric power companies, gas companies, water supply companies, real estate corporations, a hotel chain, several construction outfits including a big cement company, insurance companies, a string of provincial banks, and at least one shipping line which enjoys a virtual monopoly of the Sicily-to-the-mainland passenger trade. This is not, of course, to say that the Vatican has controlling interest in all these companies. The Generale Immobiliare is certainly mostly owned by the Vatican, but it may well be that the Vatican's interests in most of the other industrial outfits are those of a minority stockholder.

Italy has enjoyed an economic boom of almost unprecedented proportions during the past decade; the value of the properties in which the Vatican has an interest must be several billions of dollars, but exactly what percentage is Vatican-owned remains a secret. Some economic students would put its investments at several hundreds of millions of dollars; others would place them higher.

Nobody doubts that the headquarters of a religious community of 450 million or more souls should have funds, although even Catholics have suggested that some of the expensive pomp and splendor of the Papal court could be eliminated without diminishing the spiritual drive of Roman Catholicism. The only question is whether the Vatican is not overdoing its economic drive. If, as Cardinal Tardini insisted, the stories about the Vatican's great wealth are a myth, they could probably be quieted with an accounting of the facts.

XI

NEWS-GATHERING
AT THE VATICAN

The Vatican is not a satisfactory place for a news correspondent, especially if he is from America. The developments of the Holy See translate badly into the language of modern journalism. There is news in plenty to be found within the Leonine Walls, but it is so special in scope and breadth that it requires very different treatment from that provided by most American newspapers and magazines.

A sense of caution mixed with fear seems to come over American correspondents when they deal with Vatican subjects. The pressure of organized Catholicism in America is so great that many newsmen are afraid to suggest that the men of the Church are of flesh and blood. In fact, an American correspondent at Rome who tries occasionally to hint that the Vatican has other interests besides pure theology, that the Pope's time is not entirely consumed in prayer, that cliques and rivalries and even a few intrigues exist within the Leonine Walls will probably soon find himself in trouble with the home office.

European newsmen have much less difficulty on this score, perhaps because their reading public understands better that the

Pope's infallibility covers only faith and morals, and in any event does not extend to the acts of his subordinates. Undoubtedly the best journalistic coverage of the Vatican is provided by the Italians. Dailies like *Il Corriere della Sera* of Milan and *La Stampa* of Turin have long had excellent Vatican reporters. If familiarity in this case has not bred contempt, it has at least inspired a certain degree of realistic reporting. And the average prelate at the Vatican, far from being offended, highly approves.

In covering Vatican news, American media suffer from an old city-room adage that a good newsman ought to be able to cover any story at any time at any place. The result is that many correspondents assigned to Rome are woefully ignorant of Church government, ecclesiastical history, and Vatican tradition. Many cannot distinguish a rite from a doctrine, a heresy from an error, an ordinary church from a basilica. Some blatant mistakes have been made. One journalistic visitor thought the Holy Office was a shrine. Another was confused on the subject of congregations, which means one thing in Protestant terminology and quite another in the Holy See. A highly paid special writer, this one from Fleet Street, described the people in St. Peter's Square on Easter morning as shouting *"Viva Joannes"* ("Long live John!") in plain defiance of the traditional cry of *"Viva il Papa!"* ("Long live the Pope!")

Of late, with the development of quick travel, news chiefs have begun to assign star reporters to make occasional descents on the Eternal City, stay four or five days or perhaps a week, and "update" the situation at the Vatican. This is another deplorable journalistic tendency. If there is any place in the world which needs continuous watching and not just occasional checking it is the Vatican. Moreover, a correspondent asking to be "updated" at the Vatican would find no one to talk to. No official would have the remotest idea of what he wanted. The usual result of such visits is yet another pen portrait of the reigning Sovereign, written in vivid prose but saying little.

The practice of dispatching the "specials" to the Vatican

reached its zenith in October of 1958 on the death of Pius XII and
the election of John XXIII, when Rome was invaded by no less
than four hundred newsmen from all corners of the earth. John
XXIII, when he received them, called them an "armada." They
often stood five deep at the sizable bar of Rome's Foreign Press
Association. And still their output was unimpressive. Several of
the visitors received prizes for their reporting. Their writing, however, displayed more of a capacity for purple prose than an understanding of the ways of the Vatican.

One of the major difficulties in covering the Vatican is that
everything there moves at a snail's pace. The average correspondent does not have the patience, much less the equipment, to follow
these moves in slow motion.

Not even in seeming emergencies are things done at the Vatican
in a hurry. One example comes quickly to mind. When a few
years ago Cardinal Ottaviani advanced the old theory that non-
Catholics in Catholic countries could hardly expect to have full
freedom to propagate their "errors," Pius XII waited all spring, all
summer, and well into autumn before expressing his disagreement
with the cardinal in a speech before the judges of the Sacred Rota.
By that time, of course, most of the correspondents had forgotten
the original speech, and the Pope's reprimand went virtually unreported.

A second difficulty in writing about the Vatican is the calculated
subtlety of its moves. There must be no vulgar display of authority.
It is better to hint than to issue an order. A minor change in the
liturgy, a word dropped out of an old prayer, a ceremony in the
Byzantine rather than the Latin rite, a Papal audience that lasts a
little beyond the allotted time, an odd sentence inserted in an
otherwise routine speech, an encyclical presumably on one subject
but actually for the purpose of emphasizing another point—these
are the ways normally used to make Vatican policy known.

Examples could be multiplied. A few sentences in a Papal speech
about obstetrics were the chosen medium for hinting to Dr. Vittorio Veronese, then chief of Italy's Catholic Action, that he should

resign and allow a more dynamic man to take over. An even more extraordinary example of this sort of indirection came in an aside during an otherwise innocuous Papal address at an audience for the Knights of Malta. The Pope, in this case Pius XII, admonished his hearers that the past glories of this order "must not be allowed to lull" the members into disregarding the needs of the present. The knowledgeable of the Vatican, whose antennae are always at work, immediately sensed that here was the signal for an investigation of the Sovereign Order. It came—some twelve years later.

The appointment a few years ago of Cardinal Samuel Alphonsus Stritch, of Chicago, as vice-prefect of the Congregation for the Propagation of the Faith and thus the first American cardinal of the Roman Curia, was widely believed at the Vatican to be Pius XII's way of trying to resolve an old quarrel between Cardinal Francis Spellman, of New York, and Bishop Fulton J. Sheen, Auxiliary Bishop of New York and the American head of the Congregation for the Propagation of the Faith. Quarrels between prelates are nothing new in Church history, and normally the Vatican pays little attention to them. But this one looked serious because it could have affected the efficiency of Bishop Sheen (who normally raises over $10 million yearly for the work of the Congregation). The Stritch appointment, by ending the long-established primacy among American prelates of the cardinal-archbishop of New York, was designed to give Bishop Sheen more freedom. Unfortunately Cardinal Stritch died soon after arriving in Rome; the situation reverted; and the Spellman-Sheen quarrel remains unresolved. Almost nothing has appeared about it, however, in the American press. It developed so slowly and undramatically, and in Rome took such a subtle form, that it became virtually impossible to convey its meaning in an ordinary dispatch.

Still another reason why the Vatican remains a relatively unsatisfactory assignment is that the basic concept of gathering and printing information for no other reason than that people ought to know what is going on is neither properly understood nor appreciated within the Leonine Walls.

The Pope may occasionally grant an audience to special press groups, but never holds anything resembling a press conference. Most of the high-ranking ecclesiastics of the Curia turn away when they see newsmen approaching. The heads of the congregations are equally aloof. A few trusted correspondents, perhaps three or four in all, and none of them Americans, occasionally manage to have a talk with the Cardinal-Secretary of State or his second in command, but the conversation is always off the record.

The one recent exception to the rule of silence was the late Secretary of State, Cardinal Tardini. After a lifetime of virtual seclusion within the Secretariat, this cardinal suddenly grew talkative and even informative. He invited correspondents twice to a boys' home he was running, and even submitted to questioning. The result was felicitous. On a third and memorable occasion he invited the press to his own apartment in the Apostolic Palace itself. True, His Eminence called these meetings "talks with the correspondents" rather than "press conferences," but the terminology did not matter. Rome's press corps mourned Cardinal Tardini's death in 1961.

There is no official spokesman at the Vatican to deny, confirm, or explain anything. Correspondents are largely at the mercy of gossip mongers and rumor factories. Even the large Papal audiences are considered off limits to newsmen, who must therefore depend on *L'Osservatore Romano* to find out what the Holy Father has said. This Vatican organ's reporting, however, is often doctored. Many of the Pope's asides, his quick and ready comments, his criticisms go either unprinted or must be reported second-hand.

On one celebrated occasion two news agency men defied the rule of no correspondents at audiences by joining unnoticed a rather large group of scientists being received. It was during the pontificate of Pius XII, at a time when rumors were flying that the former Pope's recovery from a recent illness had been far from complete. The Pontiff gave his speech, and then came five or ten minutes during which he was presented to the various delegates. One of the news correspondents genuflected, kissed the ring, and hoped out loud that His Holiness' health had by now been completely restored. The Pope replied that he had rarely felt better. The correspondents had their quotes and were soon on the wires with the story. However such aggressive journalism might be admired in other quarters, official Vatican was not amused, and precautions were ordered to insure against a repetition of this event.

Secrecy prevails at the Vatican on a large scale. All the proceedings of all the congregations and tribunals are closed, with the dry results of their deliberations being only periodically announced in official bulletins. All personnel of these congregations, from the highest to the lowest, must take oaths not to talk to outsiders. In the case of the Holy Office a special oath is administered, and the person breaking this vow can be absolved only by the Pope himself.

The secrecy reaches its climax at a conclave to elect a new Pope. Doors are locked and barred. Nobody can enter, nobody can leave a conclave area which normally covers about one-sixth of the entire Vatican. Even the food must be scrutinized as it is passed in. No telephones, telegraph lines, radios, television sets, or microphones are allowed inside. Mail must be supervised by a conclave committee before being delivered. The participating cardinals are encouraged to practice disguising their handwriting in the days prior to the conclave so that those counting the vote will not recognize who cast the various ballots. After that, of course, the ballots themselves are burned in the Sistine Chapel stove, a homely affair resembling those our grandfathers used a century or so ago.

This passion for secrecy is a fairly recent development. Up until the eleventh century the Popes of Rome were generally chosen through acclamation by the clergy and the people of the city. Since during those centuries temporal and spiritual power were by and large one and the same, this rough-and-ready method, though admirable in some ways, often caused a political struggle, which sometimes degenerated into bloodshed.

Conclaves as we know them today began with the bull, entitled "In the Name of Our Lord," of Pope Nicholas II in 1059, which stipulated that only cardinals had the right to participate in a secret meeting for the election, usually of one of their number, to the highest dignity. Since Nicholas II's rules were first issued, no less than twenty-eight different sets of regulations have been laid down on this subject by successive Popes. With each set has come a tightening of security. The latest two sets, one issued by Pius X in 1904 and the other issued by Pius XII in 1945, put the greatest premium on secrecy and are most severe for any infraction.

No less than automatic excommunication with absolution possible only from the Pope is now the penalty prescribed for those who even innocently betray a conclave's secret. In fact, these constitutions lay down the principle that details of a conclave must die with the participating cardinals. The bare results of the various ballots are supposedly kept in the Vatican archives, to be unveiled perhaps centuries later. But nothing else can be written down. Cardinals are not only forbidden to talk about a conclave among themselves, either before or after the event; they are also not permitted to keep diaries, take notes or write anything whatsoever about it at any time or place.

Several reasons are advanced for this policy. The Church wants to insure absolute freedom in the balloting for the cardinals. Above all, the Church wants to eliminate political pressure from interested outside governments. For centuries the European powers haggled over the Papacy as if it were one of the most glittering of international prizes. At one period the Spaniards virtually captured the Throne of St. Peter, as witness the rule of the Borgias at Rome in the late fifteenth century. During an earlier period the French considered they owned the Papacy, demonstrating this fact by keeping the Pope at Avignon.

During the Renaissance and after, European governments vied openly with each other in trying to gain the Tiara for their favorite candidates. Pastor's classic *History of the Popes*, which deals with the Roman Pontiffs from Clement V in 1305 to the end of the reign of Pius VI in 1799, is filled with details of bickering and horse trading among the voting cardinals. It was not at all unusual for votes to be bought with either cash or the promises of lucrative jobs. One of Savonarola's repeated charges, hurled from the pulpits of Florence, was that the second Borgia Pope, Alexander VI, had gained the throne by simony.

The most famous conclave was the classic one at Viterbo in the thirteenth century, which lasted a total of two years, nine months and two days. Even so, it was only finished when the angered population of that city, an hour's ride north of Rome, removed the roof of the palace housing the participating cardinals and put Their Eminences on a diet of bread and water. Viterbo started the so-called locked-in conclaves (meaning, literally, "with a key"). From then on, each cardinal was permitted to bring with him into the voting area only two "conclavists." But for a long time this rule was more honored in the breach than in the observance. Pastor relates that for the conclave of 1549 all sorts of agents of secular princes managed to squeeze into the area under one guise or another. The King of France had his secretary there, as did the Duke of Florence and the Viceroy of Naples. Nobles and barons crowded in. Instead of two conclavists, most cardinals had a minimum of four and some as many as eight. There were only forty-seven voting cardinals in the area, but there were some four hundred people in all.

Canon law stipulates that the mode of life within the conclave area should be severe and austere, but this was also long disregarded. Still relating the events of 1549, Pastor comments that the "feasts were of a nature to satisfy a Lucullus, while the cardinals issued invitations to one another, as well as to their conclavists, and both sides sent the most elaborate dishes to their friends." The election of a Pope was supposed to be a spiritual matter, with the Holy Ghost participating, but in centuries past the Sacred College of Cardinals frequently went about it in a nonspiritual way.

Gradually, and especially after the Council of Trent, with its emphasis on reformation, the conclaves became infinitely more proper. All during the late eighteenth and nineteenth centuries, however, there still continued a certain amount of discreet juggling for position among the European nations. Even as late as the conclave of 1903 a behind-the-scenes struggle occurred between France and Austria. It seemed an almost foregone conclusion that Cardinal Mariano Rampolla del Tindaro, the late Pope's Secretary of State, would succeed Leo XIII. But Cardinal Puzyna of Cracow, Poland, vetoed his candidature in the name of Franz Joseph I of Austria, who claimed this traditional right as the lineal heir of the old Emperors of the Holy Roman Empire. The voting cardinals accepted the veto and proceeded to elect Cardinal Giuseppe Sarto, Patriarch of Venice, as the new Pope. He, as Pius X, then abolished the veto once and for all.

There has been, therefore, even in the recent past some reason for keeping a conclave's proceedings secret. What cannot be so easily explained, however, from a journalistic standpoint, is the secretiveness after the event. This, in fact, is a development of this century. Almost nothing is known of the four conclaves held at the Vatican since 1903. None of the down-to-earth reporting that distinguishes the Pastor history is possible when writing of them. The regulations against keeping diaries or taking notes have been followed rigorously, except in the case of two French cardinals who participated in the conclave of 1922, which elevated Achille Ratti (Pius XI) to St. Peter's Throne. Relatives of these cardinals, after their deaths, threatened to publish their notes unless the Vatican bought them. Pius XI refused to be thus blackmailed. The notes were sold elsewhere, but in the end stirred hardly a ripple of excitement. Present-day conclaves, it would seem, have little to conceal. The real reason for the current secrecy appears to be not that there is anything special to hide, but that the men of the Vatican have a fixed principle against allowing outsiders even a furtive glance backstage. As the efficiency of news communications has increased, so has the Vatican's passion for secrecy.

In an audience for foreign and Italian journalists shortly after ascending the Throne, John XXIII admitted he had been doing some midnight reading of various writeups of the conclave that had just elected him. He was both appalled and amused by what he read. Most of the journalists had, quite naturally, tried to guess what happened inside the conclave area. A few insisted that theirs was the true story. One Italian magazine even gave what it said were the ballot-by-ballot results. His Holiness was able to boast that the conclave's secrets had been so well kept that he had found "no two lines that correspond to the truth." The press is powerful, the new Pope commented, but the "secret kept by the College of Cardinals is more powerful still." Pointing the inevitable moral, the Pope went on to say that silence would have been preferable to all this bad guessing.

There can be no escaping the conclusion that John XXIII feels uncomfortable about the press. He has even suggested to the Prime Minister of Italy that it be curbed. The Pope comes back time and again to this subject, and almost always in the same admonishing tone.

At Venice, Cardinal Roncalli used to preside at annual gatherings of the press on the feast day of St. Francis de Sales, the patron saint of journalists. The reporters were invariably reminded that denial of truth was a sin against the Holy Ghost for which there could be no redemption. The cardinal inveighed frequently against "that perfidious and insidious press which today is master of the piazza and for which any action seems permissible. It spreads false-hoods, makes up stories out of whole cloth, misleads and confuses people." He once complained that when the press asked for freedom. It was not "freedom to offend, invent, calumniate, and trample underfoot what our fathers held to be most sacred."

In Rome, the Pope has continued in the same vein. He says he is flattered that the press of the world shows such interest in the Papacy, but at the same time he is worried about its practices. To a group of magazine publishers he averred that "if there is even one article or one illustration in an issue that might cause scandal to the precious shrine of a single soul, then let us say right now that its other merits are petty indeed and its claims to praise and success are flimsy." It is unfortunately true, John XXIII told members of the Catholic press on another occasion, that a "certain way of behaving and writing, found even in the press devoted to children, is having ever-wider currency, often trampling underfoot the elementary requirements of good manners, of decent reserve and of modesty, using terminology and photographic illustrations which are revolting to any honest conscience."

Both in his first encyclical, "On Promoting, under the Impulse of Charity, Truth, Unity and Peace," and in a special *motu proprio*, His Holiness gave special attention to all forms of mass communications. He is appalled that there are people in this world who "deliberately and wantonly attack the known truth, and in their speech, writing, and action, employ the weapons of falsehood." He exhorts his hearers to be "careful, exact, and prudent" and to denounce those who "disseminate lies, error, obscenity." Many people in this age, the Pope insists, behave as "if they were following an anti-decalogue; it is sufficient to open certain newspapers and see that everything there is treated and discussed as if God did not exist."

To the faults of the press should be added the dangers of the other mass media, especially television, which comes into the home. Granted that much of television is good, "yet often, alas, it can be the source of enticement to loose morals, to a disorderly life, to the snares of error and treacherous vices." The Pope says that "it is necessary to confront evil and erroneous writings with what is right and sound; against broadcasts, motion pictures and television shows which incline to error or the attractions of vice must be projected those which hold truth and strive to preserve wholesome morality."

In his Christmas message of 1960 the Pope was particularly eloquent on this subject. He appealed to all those "who preside over the organization of the civil order—heads of state and of regional and civic administration—to educators, parents, and to teachers—to take a hand in regulating those responsible for public opinion, which is being formed or deformed by means of the press, the radio and television, by the cinema, by meetings and exhibitions of every kind, literary or artistic, by writers, artists, producers, directors, scenery designers."

All signs around the Vatican indicate a crusade-in-the-making on the vital question of the popular audio-visual arts. Considering the Pope's interest, the ecumenical council of 1962 may well deal with this subject.

Journalistic interest in the Vatican is a relatively new development. Fifty years or so ago few newspapers, outside the strictly Catholic press, carried regular Vatican news. Except for such commanding events as the death of one Pope and the election of another, the Vatican was scarcely mentioned from one year to another. Even fairly important Papal pronouncements went largely unreported.

In those days not even the Vatican's own newspaper, *L'Osservatore Romano*, made a regular practice of carrying the Pontiff's speeches. In fact, it was only in May, 1927, that a young newspaperman named Cesidio Lolli, recently come to the Vatican from the ranks of Catholic Action, had the idea of reporting directly the Pope's remarks. He himself was given the assignment and has had it ever since. He is a familiar figure of the Papal entourage. Now an *Osservatore Romano* editor, Lolli has covered virtually every speech that the Roman Pontiffs have made in the last thirty years or more and is thus a mine of information about the speech-making styles of the last three Popes.[1] For a few years he helped Pius XII in the editing of his many speeches; in fact it is sometimes difficult to tell just where the Pope left off and where the Lolli polishing began. In the case of Pius XI, a notoriously bad extem-

---

[1] The speeches of Pius XI were always printed in indirect form in *L'Osservatore Romano*. Those of Pius XII, on the other hand, were invariably printed in direct quotes, while those of John XXIII are half in direct, half in indirect quotes.

poraneous speaker whose greatest trouble was dangling sentences, Lolli was often able to bring them to a graceful conclusion, to the Holy Father's gratification.

The most famous Vatican correspondent of all time was a cleric named Enrico Pucci. Originally one of the editors of a Catholic newspaper of Rome, Monsignor Pucci in the early twenties stopped in every so often at the police station just outside St. Peter's Square and there conceived the idea that there was a future in Vatican news. From then until after World War II his activities both inside and outside the Vatican made him famous and would have made him rich, except for a singular circumstance. Monsignor Pucci's brother died, leaving thirteen children, and Monsignor Pucci manfully assumed the support and education of all of them. One carefully trained nephew is now carrying on the Pucci tradition as the Vatican correspondent of an American news agency.

Monsignor Pucci was a born newspaperman, of the old rough-and-ready school. He knew how to cultivate friends in high places. One of his particular friends was Pius XI's Secretary of State, Cardinal Gasparri, who so enjoyed Pucci that he received him frequently and even gave him occasional on-the-record interviews. In the late 1920's either Pucci or one of his men (by that time he was an employer) would mount guard at the Secretariat of State, much in the manner of the White House corps of correspondents, to buttonhole those who entered and left. Since in those days the negotiations for the Lateran Treaty were proceeding apace, the news he obtained was of interest to all Italians. He was able to sell three different agencies three completely different "inside" stories about how the treaty writing was shaping up. Since Pucci's good friend Gasparri was the Vatican's negotiator, all three versions were widely believed, although all three turned out in the end to be wrong. One version had it that Italy would give the Vatican a corridor to the sea. Another gave the Vatican much of the Tiber's right bank. A third awarded the Vatican a good part of the area and the population of Trastevere.

Vatican authorities, mainly because of the attitude of Cardinal

Gasparri, initially regarded this journalistic activity indulgently. Even Pope Pius XI was not too displeased. But after Cardinal Gasparri died an anti-Pucci tide set in. Cardinal Pacelli, Gasparri's successor, did not like Pucci at all. During the interregnum of 1939 the Pucci office was abruptly removed from the Vatican premises. Not, however, before the conclave of 1939, when Pucci conveyed, through simple hand signals, a half hour before the official announcement, the information that Eugenio Pacelli had been elected to the Papacy. The war was about to start, and in any event Pucci's journalistic days were about over. He lived on until after the conclusion of World War II, but by that time he had so compromised himself with his pro-Axis reporting that the American news agencies declined to use his services.

Thus the gates were shut, never since to be reopened, against newspaper correspondents. Instead, what the authorities call a *servizio stampa* or press service, was set up. Eschewing any thought of press agentry, the new office is attached to *L'Osservatore Romano* and has its primary function the issuance of mimeographed copies of Papal pronouncements and the handing out of tickets for important functions. Once in a while it arranges for conducted tours of parts of the Apostolic Palace where important events are to take place; at least the correspondents can describe the setting. Thus when the Anglican Archbishop of Canterbury was received by the Pope, the correspondents were permitted, the day before, to walk through the rooms where His Grace would also tread. They were not, however, allowed to be on hand the next day when the actual encounter took place.

The press office has never been a place where a correspondent could go to ask questions and get answers; nor can it arrange interviews. In the absence of any such service, the news offices in Rome long ago concluded that other arrangements were necessary. As a result, over the years there has evolved a system of Vatican informers.

All sorts of Vatican employees, including clerics, have accepted gratuities of one kind or another from the Rome news bureaus in return for services rendered. Some of these informers have been put on regular pay rolls, while others are paid according to the job. Quite often higher officials have been aware of and acquiescent to these arrangements. Vatican salaries were at such a bare subsistence level for so long that any attempt to augment them was regarded sympathetically.

The run-of-the-mill Vatican informer is paid little, but the informers for special stories can expect to receive handsome fees. Generous payment can be justified if the result is a half-hour beat on the death of a Pope, or an hour's exclusive on the election of another, especially for a competitive news agency. Risks are involved, however. At the time of the last illness of Pius XII at Castel Gandolfo a group of Italian newspapers came to an agreement with a member of the Papal court, who therefore would be inside the villa, to open a certain window facing the piazza when the Pope died. But the villa became overheated and a servant came along and opened the window. The result: extras in many capitals of the world.

A continental news agency, during the conclave of 1958, devised with the help of an inside informer what was thought to be a good system for signaling the name of the cardinal who had been elected Pope. Nothing could be smuggled out with the conclave in progress, but between the end of the conclave and the proclamation of the new Pope from the loggia of St. Peter's there is usually a good hour. But the signals originally meant for "Roncalli" were mistaken for "Ruffini" (Cardinal Ernesto Ruffini, of Palermo), and papers in many places proclaimed the election of the archbishop from Palermo.

The most notable recent instance of a Vatican exclusive was a photograph taken of the dying Pius XII, with Sister Pasqualina Lehnert and other attendants at the bedside praying. This photograph was published in, among other places, the weekly *Paris Match*. Who took the photograph in question? Undoubtedly somebody high up in the Papal court; otherwise he would not have gained admission to the sick room. But so strict is the rule of silence that to this date no one at the Vatican has spoken on this subject.

Pictorial journalism, both television and still photography, has brought a new dimension to Vatican coverage. To facilitate matters many bureaus have put on their temporary payrolls highly placed officers of the various guards units of the Vatican, with the idea that these men, who normally police the piazza, can insure the photographer a good place from which to take pictures of the mass events in St. Peter's Square. The price for this kind of service is nominal; a 10,000-lire note ($16) goes a long way.

To get permission to take one's camera and equipment *inside* the basilica, however, is complicated, often requiring patient negotiations, generally with the clerics, who are on the whole much more difficult than the military. There are several ways of getting inside, but St. Peter's itself is divided into many small jurisdictions, thus making blanket permission to wander about at will almost unattainable. A good spot within St. Peter's for one of the big convocations is, however, facilitated by the presentation of a fair-sized check with the name of the recipient left blank. The idea is that the prelate receiving this money can decide what charity he should send it to. A consistory, especially if American cardinals are being created, can cost the photographing agency as high as $150. A canonization usually costs less.

Television inside St. Peter's has of late been in the hands of the Italian state monopoly, which then farms the film out to various private bidders. This has proved to be a lucrative business. Pius XII early realized the importance of television. John XXIII, on the other hand, has told his staff that he finds the ceaseless grinding of cameras at solemn functions disturbing to the intimacy as well as the sacred character of the occasion. He wanted to cut it out altogether, but changed his mind when it was argued that only through television could many Catholics see their Pope.

Permission to take special photographs, such as a portrait in color of the Vatican or the Michelangelo frescoes in the Sistine

Chapel can cost, again usually in donations to charities, several thousands of dollars. Naturally, too, in these instances, the photographing outfit must pay for all the necessary scaffolding, for the extra lighting, and for the guards who work during off hours.

Photography in one form or another constitutes a considerable source of revenue for both St. Peter's and the Vatican proper. A few years ago, for example, *Life* paid $15,000 for permission to photograph the latest result of the diggings in the grottoes below St. Peter's, including the spot then believed to be St. Peter's own tomb. Approximately the same amount was paid by the Italian weekly magazine *Oggi* to the Pius XII Institute for a Better World in return for specially posed pictures of Pius XII to illustrate one of his visions. The pictures in question showed the Pontiff in the midst of a small herd of sheep and lambs.

Outside photographers are rarely permitted at Papal audiences. The feeling about pictures inside the Vatican seems to be that one picture can do as much harm as a thousand words of criticism. The Vatican is especially careful about who is photographed with the Pope. During the reign of Pius XII a carefully prearranged routine avoided embarrassment on this score. Many times when a visitor asked to have his picture taken with the Pope, the Master of the Chamber would call the official pontifical photographer, who would arrive breathless, excusing himself because not one bit of unexposed film was left in his camera.

Under the present regime photographs of the Pontiff with such visitors as the Archbishop of Canterbury, the Presiding Bishop of the Protestant Episcopal Church of the United States, and various other non-Catholic religious heads have been firmly outlawed. Asked the reason for this, one Vatican official answered: "Many Catholics seeing the Holy Father cordially receiving the Archbishop of Canterbury would get the wrong idea."

The right to photograph the Holy Father and those being received by him is the exclusive prerogative of the official pontifical photographer, Luigi Felici, the latest representative of a once-humble Roman family that has specialized in pictures for 110

years. The story goes that one of Felici's ancestors was an outrider
on the coach used by Pius IX to flee from revolution-threatened
Rome to Gaeta in 1848. The Pontiff was so grateful to those who
stayed by him in that great hour of need that he extended himself
to think up suitable rewards.

Felici was encouraged to try his hand at the new art of photography. He started by photographing the Zouaves who were then
guarding the Papal States from Piedmontese invasion. Years
passed before Pius IX sat for his portrait. By 1900, however, Leo
XII had appointed a Felici the "pontifical photographer," and successive Popes have invariably renewed that right for succeeding
generations.

Some of Felici's competitors do not consider him a distinguished
photographer. For one thing, his backgrounds seem flat and he
goes in for the posed picture rather than the candid shot. The
Pope and the Vatican court, however, are quite satisfied. Above
all, Felici knows how to behave at solemn functions, which is more
than can be said of some of his colleagues.

Felici's has turned out to be a lucrative monopoly. Not only
does he take pictures of the Pope and some of the many thousand
visitors he receives, but he also photographs the many cardinals
and bishops and monsignori who live in or pass through Rome.
Almost all the seminarists have their pictures taken by Felici, in
groups or alone. An agency that wanted to obtain pictures of
Cardinal Z. from the time he was a seminary student on through
ordination to consecration would begin the search at Felici's studio
in downtown Rome.

Felici is also usually to be found in the middle of every photographic deal of any importance at the Vatican, including the one
with Oggi involving the late Pope's vision. He has begun lately to
dabble also in television, and even at small audiences his television
camera can be heard clicking. Some large picture agencies have
been known to pay up to thousands of dollars merely for the
privilege of assigning one of their men to act as Felici's "assistant"
on important occasions.

The Catholic press in Rome is, of course, a primary source of news material about the Vatican, but it can also be tricky. There are a great variety of publications, each issued for a different purpose and meant for quite different audiences. *Il Quotidiano,* for example, represents Catholic Action in Italy, while *Unitas* is produced for that part of Catholic clergy and laymen primarily interested in Christian unity.

Not everything published under the *nihil obstat* of the Rome Vicariate or even with the consent of the Secretariat of State represents the Pope's thinking. Approval to publish does not necessarily mean complete agreement with the opinions expressed; it merely means that the written material contains nothing contrary to Catholic doctrine and teaching. In the supervision of written and spoken material the Vatican is less heavy-handed than is ordinarily thought. Great leeway is allowed for individual preferences. What control there is is generally exercised, quite loosely, by the chief assistant to the Secretary of State, called the *sostituto.* The Pope himself never gives direct instructions in these matters, and the Secretary of State does so but rarely. The *sostituto* meets with the various editors of Vatican publications and the Vatican radio at regular intervals and hands down general instructions, which can, of course, be used in different ways. For example, early in the last American presidential campaign, instructions were passed down through the *sostituto* not only decreeing impartiality in reporting but also specifying that John F. Kennedy's religion was to go unmentioned.

Occasionally a thorny doctrinal question arises. In this case the Vatican's official theologian may be consulted. This post is presently held by Father Luigi Ciappi, a Dominican, whose official title is Master of the Sacred Apostolic Palace. Catholic publications are likely to be much more careful in doctrinal than in political or social questions.

The only avowedly official publication of the Vatican is a magazine entitled *Acta Apostolicae Sedis* (Acts of the Apostolic See) which comes out twelve times a year. This is written mostly in

Latin and contains the major documents and letters of the Supreme Pontiff, including briefs, encyclicals, *motu proprio*, allocutions, instructions, the routine of *di tabella* audiences, the bestowing of decorations, the appointment of bishops, and the deaths of prelates of the Roman Curia. Important Papal speeches are sometimes also reprinted here. The determining criterion seems to be whether the speech deals strictly with Church matters. Anything found in *Acta Apostolicae Sedis* is of undeniable authenticity. Although this magazine doubtless constitutes required reading for many ecclesiastics, it is not for popular consumption.

The indispensable publication of the Vatican, for journalists as well as for clerics, is the *Annuario Pontificio*, or *Pontifical Yearbook*, an eighteen-hundred-page directory that lists the Church hierarchy all over the world but is primarily a sort of Who's Who of the Curia. This volume has been published since 1716. It is edited in the Secretariat of State and a new edition comes out every January. The Pope himself receives the first copy, after which the yearbook is distributed free to the entire Curia. Besides a careful listing of names and positions, *Annuario Pontificio* also contains invaluable historical notes.

Occasionally a correspondent can discover interesting news items in this directory. A few years ago, for example, *Annuario Pontificio* revealed the fact that the head of the Orsini family, with perhaps the oldest Papal title of Rome, no longer retained his traditional post of "Assistant to the Throne." Correspondents found it easy to guess why: Prince Filippo Orsini, one of Rome's more attractive playboys but still a married man, had been a conspicuous escort of a prominent actress.

The hundred-year-old *Osservatore Romano* is popularly regarded as *the* Vatican organ. In a certain sense this is so. The Secretariat of State, however, for several years stubbornly insisted that *L'Osservatore Romano* was an *unofficial* publication of the Vatican, and kept on correcting correspondents who said otherwise. And in a certain sense that was so, too. It all depended on what pages and what edition of *L'Osservatore Romano* one happened to be reading.

A number of editions of *L'Osservatore Romano* are published. Besides the regular afternoon edition, there is *L'Osservatore Della Domenica* (*The Sunday Observer*), which is a popular illustrated weekly. Still another weekly edition is a summary for the busy parish priests who do not have the time to plow through the regular paper every day. Besides these, there are French and Spanish editions of *L'Osservatore Romano*.

The circulation of the regular edition is at this writing about 40,000. At one time during the last war, when it carried the war bulletins of both sides, which the Italian papers did not, it shot up to 300,000, an increase in readership which embarrassed the Vatican. In fact, the paper's circulation tends to fluctuate greatly, partly depending on how good the neighboring Italian press is. *L'Osservatore Romano* has perhaps more widespread readership than any other newspaper in the world. It is sent to every country, from the Fiji Islands to mission stations among the Eskimos to Tierra del Fuego. Two copies go regularly to the Moscow public library, which has long been a subscriber, and the Soviet government gets ten others.

The status of this Vatican publication was beclouded for some three decades by virtue of its having an opinionated and independent editor named Count Giuseppe Dalla Torre. Dalla Torre comes from an old Venetian noble family which supplied several doges for the *Serenissima*. Although an expert on Gotha and Debrett, Dalla Torre was also a strong believer that the titled should get out and work, and he put his theories to practice from youth on. Graduated with honors from Padua, Dalla Torre soon made his mark as a spirited and able defender of the Papacy in an Italy that was then markedly anticlerical. In due time he was called to Rome and soon appointed editor of *L'Osservatore Romano*.

Here he was supposed to be closely controlled by the State

Secretariat, but often Dalla Torre would go his own way. For one thing, the proud editor was unwilling to take instructions from a *sostituito*. Frequently, too, he did not get on with the Secretary of State. Nor did he see eye to eye with the reigning Pope on all occasions. Pope Pius XII received Dalla Torre in private audience only twice in the last decade of his reign.

At times Dalla Torre had to be called to account. For example, after the last war he became equivocal in his attitude toward what Europe and the West should do were the Communists to force their way into Western Europe. He has always been opposed to an anti-Communist war, believing that the increased misery resulting from any war would inevitably result in the growth of Communism even if Russia were defeated. Dalla Torre also wrote a series of "wave-of-the-future" articles which seemed, vaguely, to favor a Catholic corporate state. Several times the Pro-Secretary of State asked Dalla Torre to retract his defeatist, anti-democratic articles, without success.

It was the Secretariat that finally hit upon the device of calling *L'Osservatore Romano* an "unofficial" publication, thus disclaiming any responsibility for what Dalla Torre published. Even that was unsatisfactory, however; no one really believed it, and besides from time to time Dalla Torre seriously embarrassed the Holy See.

John XXIII, unlike Pius XII, is not one to shirk administrative chores, and he quickly decided that a change at *L'Osservatore Romano* was in order. The Pope was gracious toward Dalla Torre; the count was chosen as one of the first to be allowed to congratulate John XXIII upon his elevation to the Throne. His Holiness was said to have hinted on that occasion that Dalla Torre's superlatives might be modified and went on to say that it was not necessary to refer to the Supreme Pontiff every time by all his titles. "It will be sufficient merely to call me Pope."

The admonition had only a temporary effect, however, and before long Dalla Torre had resumed his old editorial habits. Now the Pope decided to make Dalla Torre a *latore* or bearer of the Papal decoration the Golden Rose. To be a *latore* of the Golden

Rose does not entail much physical labor, but it does entitle one to wear a special uniform on high ceremonial occasions and to march in numerous processions quite near to the Pope himself. Dalla Torre was kept so busy as *latore* that he had little time left for editing. Within a short time His Holiness had named Dalla Torre editor emeritus of the Vatican newspapers, and brought in as chief Dr. Raimondo Manzini, former editor of a Bologna Catholic paper and a deputy in the Italian Parliament.

In a way Manzini seems too much of a layman for the Vatican's clerical atmosphere. He has not, for example, had the classical education that seems so necessary if a man is to hold his own at the Vatican. His theological training is not deep. But possibly the Pope wanted to get away from too much pedantry. In any event, the editor's two chief assistants are well versed in theological and allied subjects.

Slowly but surely Manzini's *Osservatore Romano* has been evolving toward a more readable daily. A typographical change is now in the offing; column widths are being narrowed. The present rather archaic system of headline writing without verbs is due for revision. Manzini has been encouraged to sign and take credit for his own articles. Newspaper correspondents no longer have to guess what part of the paper represents Vatican thinking, and what part represents the caprice of the editor.

The chief criticism of *L'Osservatore Romano* is that it is too parochial. It should be a sort of *Times* of Catholicism, with a universal outlook, but too often it deals with purely Italian and Roman questions. Correspondents at Rome would also like the base of the reporting broadened to include something more than dry summaries of the activities of the congregations and tribunals.

Under Manzini *L'Osservatore Romano* has dropped the old pretense of being an unofficial Vatican organ and has regained its official status.

XII

JOHN XXIII'S
ECUMENICAL COUNCIL

On the morning of January 25, 1959, which is the Feast of the Conversion of St. Paul, Pope John XXIII paid one of his several visits to St. Paul's-Outside-the-Walls, the great Roman basilica where tradition says Timothy deposited the remains of the martyred Paul. After mass the Pontiff repaired to the Benedictine monastery attached to the historic edifice, and for a few moments occupied the pontifical apartment reserved for him on the first floor. After that he went into the capitular hall, normally used by the Benedictine abbot to address the assembled monks, and there proceeded to deliver an important discourse. To the seventeen members of the Sacred College of Cardinals gathered at the spot he announced his intention of holding, as soon as proper arrangements could be made, that rare Church assembly, an ecumenical council.

As is common on such occasions, no member of the press was present. But later that day an official Vatican communiqué, issued from the press office of *L'Osservatore Romano*, quoted His Holiness indirectly as saying that the meeting he proposed would "aim not only at the edification of the Christian people but would also constitute an invitation to the separated communities to seek for unity, toward which so many hearts in all parts of the earth are yearning today."

More than a month later, on February 27, the official Vatican organ *Acta Apostolicae Sedis* published the full Italian text of the original Papal discourse.[1] Few inside or outside the Vatican seem to have noticed that this official version of the Papal address only feebly, if at all, supported the communiqué previously issued. Only in passing, almost at the end of his announcement, had the Holy Father referred to the "separated communities." He had mentioned unity only in passing, and as if he were talking only about Catholic unity.

The Pope began by noting that he had been three months in his new Apostolic Office and that he had therefore been able to form some idea of contemporary spiritual needs. "We are aware," the Holy Father said, "that the new Pope is being watched, in many quarters with friendship and devotion, in others with un-friendliness or with some hesitation, on account of what, because of his essential office, it is right to expect of him." He went on to say that the successor of St. Peter has a twofold task, a double responsibility as Bishop of Rome and as Shepherd of the Universal Church. These, however, were two grants of authority which could not be separated.

"First of all, consider Rome," the Pope continued. "It is a city transformed completely in the course of the forty years from the time we knew it in our youth . . . it is now a veritable human hive, from which issues an endless and confused murmur of voices, seeking for agreement, which come together and fall apart with equal ease, thus rendering laborious and slow the effort to bring about union of minds and of constructive forces for the sake of an

---

[1] The informality of the occasion was stressed by the fact that the speech was in Italian rather than Latin, and that the text of the speech was also later distributed in Italian rather than Latin. Of the seventeen cardinals present, all but two, Agagianian and Jullien, were Italian, and they understood Italian quite well.

order which corresponds to the needs of the religious, civic, and social life of the city."

Rome, the Pope concluded, was badly in need of a more intense spiritual life built around her various dioceses. The Bishop of Rome, however, had also been made responsible for the spiritual government of the world. And when he broadens his vision and looks at the world, "what a spectacle meets his gaze!" On the one hand, portents of spiritual elevation, with the grace of Christ multiplying the fruits of salvation and sanctity; on the other, elements bound to evoke sorrow. He sees human freedom abused and compromised on a vast scale. He sees men who direct all their energy toward one end, "the search for so-called earthly goods," guided by the one whom the Gospel calls the "prince of darkness." Modern progress, the Holy Father continued, "distracts men from their quest of higher goods, weakens the energies of the spirit, leads to a loosening of the structure of discipline and former good order." This results in "serious prejudice to what constitutes the power of the Church and her sons to resist error." Error, according to the Pope, has always in history led to "deadly and fatal divisions, spiritual and moral decadence, and to the downfall of nations."

"To crown the misfortune of the army of the children of God," the Pope continued, "there is added the temptation and attraction toward the advantages in the material order which progress in modern skill—in itself morally neither good nor bad—increases and exalts."

What he had seen, John XXIII concluded, had "evoked a response in the heart of the humble priest whom the manifest will of Divine Providence has lifted, unworthy though he may be, to the heights of the Supreme Pontificate." He had decided that what was needed was to "recall some ancient forms of doctrinal affirmation and of wise decrees touching ecclesiastical discipline." These ancient forms, the Pope said, were efficacious in epochs of renewal in the history of the Church and created a sense of "religious solidarity."

At this point the Pope exclaimed: "Beloved sons and venerable brethren!" and went on to announce, "trembling a little with emotion yet at the same time with a humble resoluteness of purpose," two momentous events: first, the diocesan synod for Rome, which was, in fact, held in January, 1960, and, second, an ecumenical council for the Universal Church, later called for October, 1962.

All this was a far cry from summoning an ecumenical council to discuss Christian unity. The Pope in his speech had said plainly that the higher purpose of the council would be to combat spiritual and moral decadence in the world today; the one concrete result that he expected from such a gathering would be an updating of the Code of Canon Law. True, the Holy Father had added that he would also include in the council agenda "such measures as the Spirit of the Lord may seem to suggest to us along the way." But no hint had been given anywhere in the speech of a program to bring the "separated churches" back to Rome.

What is the explanation of this apparent contradiction? Since Vatican officialdom has maintained silence on the matter, one can only surmise that the stress on Christian unity was a happy afterthought, either of the communiqué writer or, as seems more likely, of the Pope himself. Whatever the explanation, the ecumenical council of John XXIII was quickly projected into the consciousness of the world as a council for Christian unity. Reaction almost everywhere ranged from friendly to enthusiastic. Both the Orthodox churches of the East and the Protestant churches of the West responded sympathetically. The non-Catholics have long had an ecumenical movement of their own, with headquarters at Geneva, and now they welcomed this new sign of an interest and leadership from the Vatican.

Meanwhile, the Vatican followed up the original announcement with a series of speeches, statements, and acts that elaborated and qualified the thesis of Christian unity. Obviously the hierarchy had been surprised at this windfall of favorable reaction, and was determined to make the most of it. Here are some of the new elements which were introduced into the ecumenical picture by Rome on the heels of the Pope's announcement:

• The creation of a Secretariat for the Union of Christians headed by Cardinal Bea with the specific task of handling the Vatican's relations with non-Catholics. No such agency had existed before; it is expected that this Secretariat will become a permanent feature of the Vatican's corporate structure.

• The popularization by the Pope of the expression "separated brothers" and the simultaneous dropping of such terms as heretics, dissidents, and schismatics to describe non-Catholics. Cardinal Bea has vividly explained the reasoning back of this change in terminology. A person who willfully and with full awareness detaches himself from the Church must still be considered guilty of heresy, but one who in good faith finds himself "separated as a result of the heritage received from his ancestors" can only be considered a "separated brother."

• The unprecedented courtesy calls on the Pope of such non-Catholic religious figures as Dr. Geoffrey Fisher, the Archbishop of Canterbury; the Right Rev. Dr. Arthur Lichtenberger, Presiding Bishop of the Protestant Episcopal Church of the United States; and Bishop Hans Lilje, President of the German Lutheran Federation.

• The dispatch of qualified observers with full Vatican credentials both to a conference of Orthodox bishops at Rhodes, in the eastern Aegean, and to the third assembly of the non-Catholic World Council of Churches at New Delhi in late 1961. This followed a series of talks between Catholics and non-Catholics in Germany.

• The several occasions in which John XXIII has presided or been present at Eastern rite masses. At one of these, in St. Peter's, he gave responses in both Greek and several Slavic tongues. On another occasion, in the Sistine Chapel, His Holiness participated in the consecration of a bishop in which the Byzantine rite was used throughout, with the Pope saying the mass in Greek. By thus using rites other than Latin, John XXIII sought to stress the universal nature of the Church and to convey the idea that under the Roman Pontiff many varieties of worship are permissible. This approach, it should be pointed out, is fairly indirect and one can only wonder whether it is sufficiently dynamic to be really effective. The lay public has at best only a vague notion of the differences between one rite and another.

None of these moves is, in itself, important. But taken together they have helped to create a climate of friendliness and mutual understanding between Catholics and non-Catholics that has been almost totally lacking for the past four centuries.

The Pope's original plan of invoking "certain ancient forms of doctrine" and of polishing up ecclesiastical discipline was one thing; to promote Christian unity was clearly another. One was a purely internal matter of the Church, while the other was a question which concerned not only the Catholic part but the non Catholic part of Christendom. An ecumenical council to consider Christian unity would be quite different from an ecumenical council merely to revise canon law.

Here, indeed, was the point which Catholic spokesmen of many degrees were to belabor unceasingly in the months to come. Catholic "integrationalists" had to be satisfied that no changes in Church doctrine or even practice were contemplated at the same time that non-Catholics must be assured that they could again find spacious accommodation within the Roman Church. Those who make it their business to read between the lines of Vatican pronouncements began to suspect that a fierce but—as far as the public is concerned—silent tug-of-war was being waged back of St. Peter's Throne. Should the council be a forthright attempt to reach a reconciliation with the rest of Christianity or should it be chiefly a manifestation to show the superiority of the Catholic faith?

The loudest voices were those who warned that the Vatican had no intention of entering negotiations with the non-Catholic churches. A federation of all Christian churches, with Roman Catholicism forming a part, was early outlawed as even a remote possibility. The chief purpose of the council would be simply ecclesiastical housecleaning; perhaps this effort would make Rome more attractive for the dissidents. The council would thus turn out to be, in a minor key, a repetition of the Council of Trent.

On the heels of the Pope's announcement came the publication in *Quotidiano* of an article by one of the Church's leading ecumenicists, Father Charles Boyer, in which he said flatly: "Of course the Catholic Church cannot change anything substantial in her doctrine. But when our separated brothers, by reason of the free movement of their sentiments and their thoughts, find themselves back in the Catholic Church, they will realize that they have entered, not the house of a stranger, but their own house." Father Boyer then intimated that he had virtually no hope for the quick return of the Protestant churches to Rome, but he did go on to say, in regard to Orthodoxy, that "while the dawn of union has yet to break, we like to believe that the night has not long to last."

Soon Radio Vatican spoke out on the subject in a significant broadcast. For the Roman Church, this broadcast declared, there is only "one road to unity," and that is the road to Rome. All theological discussion aside, the world's "only coherent, total and accepted expression of faith, as well as the sole authority recognized the world over as far as Christianity is concerned, is to be found in the Catholic Church."

Radio Vatican went on to discuss two contending concepts of unity. For the non-Catholic churches unity means the "quest for the greatest common denominator"; to them, the problem is to find a minimum of common ground and stand on that, leaving each church and individual free in all other matters. "But it is obvious," the broadcast said, "that even were this sort of unity to be achieved it would not be a very profound unity."

Perhaps the most authoritative discussion of Christian unity and Catholicism was contained in a series of lectures and articles by Cardinal Bea in 1961. The ecumenical council, the cardinal emphasized, would not be a "council of union" but could "create conditions favorable to union." Like many others before him, Cardinal Bea reminded his listeners and readers that Catholic doctrine and dogma would be safeguarded by the council.

"But that does not mean that nothing at all can be done with regard to the difficulties which exist in the doctrinal field," Cardinal Bea said. "The differences here all too often spring from the fact that the sense of the dogma is not well understood, or has been perverted. It should not be forgotten that mentalities and methods of expressing ideas have changed a good deal with the passage of time. The separated brothers, who have been detached from the Church for centuries, have been under the influence of so many philosophic systems (rationalism, sensism, Hegelism, Kantism, phenomenalism, existentialism) . . . that it is difficult for them to understand properly the dogmatic doctrines expressed in the language of the Church. In this field the council will be able to carry out a useful task of explanation."

In another speech, Cardinal Bea admitted that the dogmas of the primacy and the infallibility of the Pope "as defined after the separation of the Eastern Churches constitute the main obstacles of a doctrinal nature which keep the Orthodox churches from Rome." As regards Protestantism, the situation is complicated by many elements, which include a "different concept of dogma and its immutability," the fact that for Protestants the "constitution and organization of a church do not have essential importance," and, finally, the "lack of an authority in the non-Catholic group with whom it is possible to negotiate." His Eminence added: "In questions concerning the union of churches not even the World Council of Churches is authorized to act in the name of the separate churches."

Nevertheless, Cardinal Bea believed that the council would accomplish much. "The union of all Christians," said His Eminence, "who today total almost one billion would bring a great contribution to the cause of peace and the true values of human civilization."

The Pope's own clarification came by bits and pieces. At one point he warned: "An ecumenical council is not an academy or a parliament, but a solemn meeting of the ecclesiastical hierarchy on questions concerning the ordinary life of the Church and the good of people's souls." In a later address the Holy Father attempted to correct some of the "misinformation" which had been spread. The ecumenical council, he said, was an "internal business of the Catholic Church." Christian reunion was one of the aspirations of the council, but it was not a "council of unity." In simplest terms, John XXIII wished to "restore, rearrange, and embellish" his own house before inviting guests into it.

Perhaps the best Papal speech on the subject was made when he presided over the first plenary session of the "ante-preparatory commission," appointed to make preliminary arrangements for the council. His Holiness began by saying that the council had aroused eager interest and given rise to all sorts of wild "suppositions and conjectures." He continued: "It would be well to remember that the council has been summoned, first of all, because the Catholic Church in her splendid variety of ritual, in her multiform actions and her unshatterable unity, hopes to draw from it new strength for the performance of her divine mission. Eternally faithful to the sacred principles on which she is founded and to the unchanging doctrine entrusted to her by her Divine Founder, the Church, following the path of ancient tradition, hopes to reinforce her own vital consistency, particularly in the face of the many contingencies and situations with which she is faced in this modern world, and for which she will prove capable of establishing workable rules for behavior and activity."

After this, the Pontiff said, almost as an aside, that he hoped the council would result in an upsurge of good works within the Church, adding that perhaps "even those who are separated from the Holy Apostolic See may feel a new and irresistible appeal to unity, that unity which Christ Himself gave to His Church, and to which so many aspire."

Just what is a general council of the Church? Definitions differ at different epochs of history. In theory the Pope can call any kind of a council he chooses. But the Second Vatican Council, as the new gathering will be officially called, promises to be quite different from most of those that went before it, mainly because of the radically strengthened position of the Pope in the last century.

According to canon law, only the Pope can call an ecumenical council, only he can decide what questions shall be discussed, and the council's decisions are binding only when they are ratified by the Pope. These provisions are reinforced by the Church constitution *Pastor aeternus*, passed in 1870, which says that the authority of the Apostolic See "is not surpassed, is to be claimed by no one, nor is any one permitted to pass judgment on its judgment." Therefore, the constitution continues, "they stray from the straight path of truth who affirm that it is permitted to appeal from the judgments of the Roman Pontiffs to an ecumenical council."

In ecclesiastical law, those privileged to attend a general council include cardinals, bishops, abbots, and prelates *nullius*, abbots general of monasteries, and the superiors general of the religious orders. However, an ecumenical council may be considered convened if a "sufficient number of bishops to be representative of the Universal Church" are present. A Vatican release explains:

"The necessary condition is that the bishops represent the Universal Church when they are united with the successor to St. Peter. Only in this way can there be a legitimate college of bishops united with their pastor and the head united with the members. The absolute necessity for agreement of the majority of the bishops is not demonstrable. On the contrary, the Pope may contradict decisions taken by an absolute majority of the bishops.

"The ecumenical council has ordinary and supreme authority within the Universal Church. It is distinguished from that of the Roman Pontiff solely by the number of persons who exercise it. The Pope has the same complete and supreme jurisdiction within the Universal Church. There is a close relationship between the two, in the sense that while the power of the Roman Pontiff is unique, single, universal, and supreme, these same qualities cannot be attributed to the ecumenical council without its union with the Vicar of Christ. This consideration immediately rules out the possibility of appealing to the ecumenical council from a decision of the Pope."

This seems to boil down to the proposition that in this century the properly constituted ecumenical council of the Roman Catholic Church is an advisory body of the Papacy, and little more.

Thus the Second Vatican Council will not be like any of the earlier ones, such as Nicaea (A.D. 325) or Ephesus (A.D. 431), or Chalcedon (A.D. 451), or Constantinople (A.D. 680). For in those times the theory of the absolute primacy of the Bishop of Rome, let alone his infallibility, had not yet been advanced. If the Bishop of Rome attended at all (and generally he did not) he came as just one of many bishops. Generally he sent his legates. He did not control discussion and he had no veto power over the final voting. At these councils the Bishop of Rome held exactly one vote. These were the councils of the early Greek and Latin Fathers, and for them the general council, with decisions freely arrived at, was the Church's highest expression.

The commanding figure at Nicaea was not the Pope, who was then Sylvester I, but rather the Emperor Constantine. In fact, it was the Emperor who had originally convoked the gathering and thus can be said to be the founder of the ecumenical council.

Nor will the new council bear a resemblance to the gatherings at Constance and Basle, which followed the Great Schism of the fourteenth century, when rival Popes reigned at Rome and at Avignon. Catholic historians recognize the Council of Constance, although pointing out that it was improperly convoked, but the official list does not include the Council of Basle. In any event, both these councils went their ways minus Papal guidance. The chief purpose of Constance, in fact, had been to depose two opposing prelates both of whom claimed to have been elected as rightful Popes. Both councils asserted the superiority of a council over the Pope; at Constance it was specifically stated that a "council lawfully assembled by the Holy Ghost" was the supreme organ of the Catholic Church and that even the Pope was obliged to obey its authority.

The fourteenth century witnessed a fierce struggle between the Papacy and those who supported the conciliar theory. Not until 1460 did the Papacy officially prohibit appeals to a general council, and not until a century ago was the conciliar theory finally stamped out of the Catholic Church. For better or for worse, however, conciliarism is still alive in the other Christian communities, especially in the Eastern Orthodox Church, and will doubtless arise in any attempt of Rome to bring the non-Catholic communities back into the fold. One cannot imagine, for example, the Eastern Orthodox Church entering the Roman fold without insisting on the right to convene a council.

The new council will not be similar in any respect to that of Florence in the fifteenth century, the most ambitious council of all, assembled for the purpose of effecting union between the Greek and Latin churches. At this gathering, which started at Ferrara and later shifted to Florence, the Greek Emperor, John VIII Palaeologus, and the Roman Pontiff, Eugene IV, met on terms of equality.

Present-day Catholics insist that the great truths of the Church as contained in dogma are beyond discussion or negotiation, but at Florence the Greek and Roman churches discussed almost nothing but doctrine. They spent months over the question of purgatory, for example. The Greeks thought that purgatory consisted mainly of pain and grief, with little or no fire; the Latins were for fire for unrepentant sinners until Judgment Day. Finally, it was admitted that the two versions of purgatory were without really basic differences. The question of whether to use unleavened bread, as the Latins did, or leavened bread, according to the Greeks, was also a point at issue, finally decided by permitting the Sacrament to be celebrated with either.

The longest dispute of this council concerned the *Filioque*. The Nicene Creed had stated that the Holy Ghost proceeds from the Father, but the Romans added the words, "and from the Son." The Greeks were prepared to say that the Holy Ghost proceeded from the Father *through* the Son, but not *and* the Son; furthermore, they insisted that Rome had no right to add words to a creed properly written in a council. Months were consumed in discussion. A theological duel developed between the Latin prelate, John of Montenegro, and the Greek Patriarch, Mark of Ephesus. Finally, a compromise was written. The Greeks conceded that the Holy Ghost could proceed *from* the Father and *from* the Son provided the Latins recognized that it was "as from one origin and cause." The Latins agreed.

The worst stumbling block at Florence was Papal supremacy. Eugene IV demanded that he be recognized as Supreme Pontiff, successor to Peter and Vicar of Christ, and that the Greeks admit that he judged and ruled the Church both as teacher and shepherd. The Greeks, in no position to bargain, wanted a pentarchy, or rule of five of the ancient patriarchates (Antioch, Alexandria, Jerusalem, Rome, and Constantinople). They were particularly anxious to avoid specific recognition that the Pope alone had the right to convene a council. At long last a compromise formula was written out, the author being the same Cardinal Bessarion, of the Greeks, at whose tomb John XXIII recently prayed. (See Chapter VI.) The text of the compromise is interesting (as well as vague), and might conceivably suggest a pattern for the future: "We recognize the Pope as sovereign Pontiff, vice-regent and Vicar of Christ, shepherd and teacher of all Christians, ruler of the Church of God, saving the privileges and rights of the Patriarchs of the East." This formula was accepted, and union was promptly proclaimed and celebrated in a brilliant ceremony.

The union, though remaining for some time on paper, was never really effective from the standpoint of the Greeks. The cloudiness of its terms caused trouble from the start. For example, for the Orthodox Church divorce is easily granted, for the Latin not so. The monastic orders of Byzantium, as well as the common people, opposed union almost to a man, and later the Patriarchs of Jerusalem, Antioch, and Alexandria issued a joint encyclical describing the Council of Florence as a "council of robbers." The Greeks had come to Florence prepared to sacrifice some of their ancient independence in return for Papal help in the defense of beleaguered Constantinople. In effect, they acknowledged Papal supremacy in return for a few galleys and some three hundred soldiers to hold off the Turks. They could have spared themselves; the Ottomans pressed forward and captured Byzantium in May, 1453. But from the Roman side, the Council of Florence was a victory. Even though the union was never effective, the Greeks had recognized the Pope as the first Bishop of Christendom.

The Council of Trent, in the late sixteenth century, is considered by Catholic historians (as well as by the present Pope) the greatest of them all. It settled more arguments and wrote more statements than all the rest of the councils put together. Trent, however, was at first bitterly opposed by the Popes of the time. They had had enough of general councils, and made every effort to delay and confuse the meeting. That was one reason why Trent dragged on over nineteen years and was spread over five Papal reigns. But because of the Protestant challenge, the Council of Trent finally became unavoidable. Although the Popes' legates attended this council, the Pontiffs themselves hardly controlled it. At every step they had to contend with the strong and opposing views of monarchs such as the Emperor of the Holy Roman Empire and the King of Spain.

The last general council (before this one) was that of the Vatican in 1869 and 1870. This was the council of the primacy of jurisdiction of the Pope and of his infallibility. It was the council to end councils as they had been organized before. Here the Papacy finally won the struggle for absolute power which it had waged since the fifth century, and the old theory of conciliarism was finally and decisively routed. From that time on the Bishops would rule their dioceses not as descendants of the Apostles but at the pleasure of the Roman Pontiff. Any thought of an oligarchic form of Church government went by the boards. The Pope became the ultimate authority not only in government but in doctrine. The constitution *Pastor aeternus* passed at this council states flatly: "If anyone says that the Roman Pontiff has only office of inspection or direction, but not the full and supreme power of jurisdiction over the Universal Church, not only in things which pertain to faith and morals, but also in those which pertain to the discipline and government of the Church, spread over the entire world; or that he possesses only the important parts, but not the whole plenitude of this supreme power; or that this power of his is not ordinary and immediate or over the Churches altogether and individually; Let him be anathema."

The declaration of infallibility was contained in a separate chapter. It is subject to all sorts of limitations. The Pope must be speaking *ex cathedra*. The subject matter must concern faith or morals and must be universal rather than local in application. This, theoretically at least, means that the Pope is infallible in few of his pronouncements. In practice, however, the words "faith and morals" can be stretched to cover many other questions, such as, for example, politics. Moreover, Pius XII held that even his encyclicals were *ex cathedra* pronouncements.

Both the doctrine of primacy and the Dogma of Papal Infallibility stirred up a hornet's nest of opposition, within and without the Church. Noted Catholic theologians inveighed against it, insisting that it would make any reconciliation with Protestantism difficult. History was invoked in vain to prevent the passage of the dogmas; instances could easily be cited where Popes of past centuries had obviously committed error. However, Pius IX was determined. Despite the fact that the council was weighted from the start in his favor, he had to face an opposition of at least one-fourth of the bishops present. Nevertheless, the dogma was eventually pushed through to a favorable vote. It was a remarkable tribute to ecclesiastical discipline that, despite all the blustering, not one bishop was lost to the Church. Thus ended what promises to be the last general council of the Church in which the possibility exists of such outspoken opposition to Papal authority. In fact, many had thought that with the supremacy of the Pope there was no further reason to hold a council. John XXIII has confounded critics by announcing one.

In the past the ecumenical council had been primarily held in moments of crisis, generally to settle disputed points raised by various heresies. Nicaea dealt with the great Arian heresy, Ephesus with the Nestorian heresy, Chalcedon with the Monophysites, and Trent with Protestantism. By ancient tradition, too, the promulgation of dogma had been the special prerogative of a council. This tradition, however, has now been broken in two famous instances, the Dogma of the Immaculate Conception and that of the Assumption. New dogmas can now be proclaimed outside a council. There is, moreover, no crisis in the life of the Church which would warrant the expense and trouble of an ecumenical council today.

Cardinal Montini of Milan recently acknowledged that this would be unlike all former councils. "It is important to note that, from a historic point of view," His Eminence said, "this confirms the complete outdatedness of the theory—justified in the distant past—that the ecumenical councils were, in a certain sense, something to be suffered by the Popes. It also shows that those who thought that the proclamation of the Dogma of Papal Infallibility meant, practically speaking, the end of such councils were wrong."

Instead of meeting to settle questions of doctrine or to discuss matters of gravity, the coming council will "meet in a peaceful and fervent moment in the life of the Church," said the Archbishop of Milan. No internal disorders need healing, but there are other great questions to discuss. "The first is that of the reunion of the separated brothers with the Church of Rome," the cardinal said. He could not hope for an immediate achievement of this reunion, but that did not mean that moves should not be taken in that direction. He personally hoped that there might be friendly talks with dissident Christians. "A great hope has been born within the Church," he added.

On the other side of the fence was the late Cardinal Tardini, who had functioned as head of the ante-preparatory commission for the ecumenical council. He asserted at a press conference that the council would be strictly a family affair. It would not include people from non-Catholic churches. Echoing the Pope's declaration that non-Catholic brothers would be accepted in "sweet reasonableness," the cardinal nevertheless insisted that they would come on their own initiative and that their function would be to hear and not be heard. "The Church has nothing to hide," the cardinal said. "Our plain purpose is to foster the growth of the faith, to renew Christian manners and modernize ecclesiastical discipline according to the needs of the times. It will also provide such a marvelous spectacle of truth, of unity, and of charity as to constitute, even for those who are deeply alienated from the Holy See, an invitation to achieve that unity to which many sincerely aspire."

Most councils have lasted months, and some have gone on for years. But this one, it is predicted, will last a month or a month and a half at most, and will certainly be over by Christmas, 1962, mainly because of the careful preparation that has preceded it. Around 3,500 prelates and theologians are privileged to attend, but in all probability there will be something less than 2,000 actually present. In preparation for the 1869 council preliminary questionnaires were sent out to only 224 prelates and theologians. In preparation for this Vatican council a total of 2,700 letters were sent out, and replies were received from virtually all. Suggestions contained in these replies have been published, but only for secret circulation, in four large volumes.

To prepare for Vatican Council II, John XXIII created brand-new administrative machinery. A central committee of around four hundred members, including sixty cardinals, five patriarchs, twenty-seven archbishops, six bishops, and four superiors general of religious orders, was appointed. This was broken down into ten special committees and two secretariats, each of which was empowered to study special problems and report its findings and recommendations to the Pope.

The ten committees followed the general line of the sacred congregations. Thus there was a Committee on Theology, headed by Cardinal Ottaviani, which was charged with "weighing questions touching Holy Scripture, Sacred Tradition, the faith and its practices." Other committees included a Committee for Bishops and the Government of Dioceses, a Committee for Clerical and Lay Discipline, a Committee for the Religious Orders, a Committee for the Discipline of Sacraments, one for the Eastern Church, one for the missions, one for studies and the seminaries, one for the study of ceremonies, and a Committee for the Lay Apostolate.

The two secretariats include one for the study of questions of the press and of entertainment and the above-mentioned Secretariat for the Union of Christians. The creation of the press and entertainment committee would seem to presage some kind of council statement or decree on the subject of mass media. As for the Secretariat for the Union of Christians, its duties so far have been to answer questions about Catholic doctrine and practice from non-Catholics and to arrange in special cases for the visits of non-Catholic leaders to the Vatican.

This is the first time since the Council of Florence that Rome has actually created machinery to talk with people it formerly labeled heretics and schismatics. Steadfastly over the centuries the Vatican has been wary of contacts with non-Catholics, even to the point of forbidding Catholic laymen to take part in doctrinal discussions. Even now, the Church insists that mixed gatherings can only be held with the sanction of competent ecclesiastical authority and that there must be no common worship. These rules will perhaps be somewhat relaxed as a result of this council.

In one sense Vatican Council II had already started with the convening of the committees. All during 1961 and during the first six months of 1962 these groups met regularly, sometimes under the chairmanship of the Pope, and most of them at this writing have already formulated their recommendations. The council's acceptance of the recommendations is expected to be a formality.

In the case of some committees, the general line of the work accomplished has been made known. The Committee on Theology has submitted a draft of what it calls a "Constitution on the

Sources of Revelation." This draft starts out by saying that it is a proven certainty that God at times has spoken with man, and that man has been able to hear this divine voice. This communication of truth made directly by God to men is called "Revelation." For the Catholics there are two sources from which to take the revealed truths; the Holy Scriptures, also called the Bible, which includes the Old and New Testaments, and tradition. In the Holy Scriptures are contained all those truths which God has consigned to man in order that he might write them down and pass them on to future generations. Enlightening the intelligence and guiding the will of man, God has made use of him as an instrument to make His work known, to make known divine and eternal truths which could not have been understood through the light of human reason alone.

In tradition, too, the draft continues, truths are contained and are revealed by God, but they have been transmitted at first by word of mouth from one generation to the next. These truths are now contained in the documents of the ecclesiastical magistracy and in the writings of the Fathers and Doctors of the Church. The sources of Revelations are, therefore, two, but the fount which generated them is one only: God. And one only is the magistracy which must guard and authentically interpret the truths contained in those sources, in other words the Papacy.

This is by and large a restatement of the Catholic position as defined at Trent. The most fundamental divergence between Catholicism and Protestantism, although not between Catholicism and Orthodoxy, has been in their separate approaches to the Bible. The Reformation insisted on the supremacy of the Holy Word, while the Counter Reformation, as represented at Trent, held that the Bible and Apostolic tradition were of equal force. In recent years a lively back-to-the-Bible movement has developed inside the Roman Catholic Church and some have thought that in the study of the Bible these two great branches of Christianity might draw closer together. The appointment of Cardinal Bea, the Vatican's ranking Biblical scholar, to supervise contacts with non-Catholics suggested as much. But the draft of this Constitution on the Sources of Revelation would not seem to promise much in this direction.

One possible departure that might emerge from the council would be the adoption of some sort of lay ministry. The proposal is often heard for the creation of a new grade of officers called deacons who would be laymen, who could even be married and have children, and who could perform some, although by no means all, of the lesser functions of the clergy. The creation of deacons would help solve perhaps the greatest problem of Roman Catholicism today, the great scarcity of men who want to dedicate their lives to the priesthood. Curiously enough, Protestant countries such as the United States, Great Britain, and Canada give no cause for alarm. The countries that worry Rome the most are the traditionally Catholic ones of Central and South America and the old Catholic centers of Europe. Although the Committee for the Lay Apostolate has made its recommendations, no word of the Pope's thinking on this subject has been forthcoming.

Another issue about which there has been much pre-council discussion is religious liberty. The Roman Church today is the center of a quiet but intense quarrel over this topic. The age-old Protestant charge is that the Catholics simply do not believe in freedom of conscience, and Catholic spokesmen of high degree can be quoted in support of this charge.[2] On the other hand, many Catholic theologians and some Catholic prelates support the principle of freedom of conscience and urge that the Church once and for all take an affirmative stand. Unfortunately, this liberal approach to religious problems does not impress Rome; the odds now seem against any statement in favor of religious tolerance at this ecumenical council.

Christian unity is easily the most exciting topic to be brought up before the Christian community in this century. "Will our

[2] This is the subject of a remarkable booklet entitled *Roman Catholicism and Religious Liberty*, published by the World Council of Churches in Geneva. The author is Dr. A. F. Carrillo de Albornoz, himself an ex-Catholic.

brothers, whose foreheads are signed with the seal of Christ, come back to us?" the Pope asked rhetorically in an informal sermon. "We shall do everything in our power to make them see the error of their ways, and to reform our own bad habits, so that at last all Christians may be at home in the house of the Lord. We know that that house is the Holy Roman Catholic and Apostolic Church. We shall throw open wide the doors of that house, saying to the others, 'Let us join together in peace, in the sincere quest for the Lord. If you will, come and join with us in peace and brotherhood.'"

John XXIII has already taken steps to correct what he called "our own bad habits." For example, from a traditional Good Friday prayer he eliminated the word "perfidious" when applied to the Jews. (Actually, the original meaning of "perfidious" had been "unbelieving" and the word had so been printed in the usual missal.) The Congregation of Rites, doubtless under the Pope's direction, revised the baptismal ceremony for converts to Roman Catholicism so that hereafter they would not have to condemn their former faiths. The Pope also eliminated two paragraphs of a liturgical prayer to the Sacred Heart which he feared might offend Moslems and Jews.

Catholic literature tends to foster the historical illusion that Christendom was united before Martin Luther. Actually the Church has been troubled by division since the days of the New Testament. The first great Christian controversy took place at Antioch, when the uncircumcised Gentiles were not at first allowed to take part in the Eucharist.

Doctrine in the early years was imperfectly defined. Granted that there was no such thing as heresy, there were still many disputes. Unity was more of faith and worship than of organization. The powers of the early patriarchs were still undetermined. The See of Rome was widely respected, mainly because it was at the capital of the Empire, but Rome's claims to world-wide supremacy, advanced fairly early, were never admitted in the East. In fact, historically speaking, these claims perhaps divided rather than unified the early Church.

The Emperor Constantine wanted Christian unity at almost any cost and for that reason summoned Christendom to Nicaea. But even he could not impose unity. During his reign two great schisms developed to threatening size. These early heresies, the Donatist and the Arian, were to die out in the course of the next century (the barbarians took up Arianism, however), but those of the fifth century, such as the Monophysite and Nestorian schisms, are still alive today in the Coptic, Ethiopian, Syrian, and Armenian churches. During many periods of these early centuries the Catholics, as represented by adherence to the dogmas laid down in the first four councils, were in a minority. In many parts of the world bishop was set against bishop. At one time in the fourth century, Antioch knew six bishops, each of whom insisted that he was in the direct line of Apostolic succession.

For the first millennium and more of Christian history the chief opposition to Roman Catholicism came from the East. Protestantism injected a new note only because it was a heresy originating in the West. The exact date of the separation of the Eastern and Western churches has long been a matter of historical dispute. It started with the split of the Eastern and Western empires, and it deepened both with the growth of Greek nationalism and with the development of Papal claims. But it is important to remember that at no time in history did the Roman Pontiff exercise effective jurisdiction over the great patriarchates of Eastern Christianity.

One of the dreams that Rome has pursued for centuries has been that of bringing into the fold—not, it should be stressed, *back* into the fold—the Eastern Christians. Eastern Orthodoxy has an ordained priesthood the validity of which the Latins fully recognize. There has been no break in Apostolic succession. The sacraments are there. The two churches have much the same set of Fathers and, up to a certain point, the same saints. Orthodoxy does not give quite the importance the Roman Church does to

Mary, but the question is one of degree. The Orthodox Church recognizes the weight of tradition quite as much as the Catholics do. Once the two quarreled over the *Filioque* and over purgatory. Today the two have different rules governing the celibacy of the clergy. Divorce, permitted by the Orthodox but denied by the Catholics, might be a problem. But these could with patience be ironed out.

What cannot be passed over is the question of the Papacy. Here is the one great obstacle to East-West, or for that matter to Protestant-Catholic, reunion. And not only the dissident churches stress this question. For the Catholics, too, the Papacy has assumed an importance that easily overshadows every other consideration. Doctrine and dogma revolve around acceptance of the Papal claims. It is not a mere matter of government, not even one of spiritual authority. Most churches, certainly those with an Apostolic hierarchy, would probably agree that there is a residuum of faith which cannot be compromised. But the Catholics make Papal supremacy a part of that residuum.

Father William De Vries, one of Rome's experts on the Orthodox Church, expresses the problem of the Papacy in these terms:

"The main difficulty is, without doubt, the question of the recognition of the universal primacy of jurisdiction of the Pope. This is a psychological stumbling block that will not be easy to get around, since all the Eastern churches have for centuries been used to governing themselves. The problem is to make them understand that the authority of the Pope is a paternal authority; that it is the loving care of the universal shepherd to whom Christ has given the sacred duty of feeding His sheep.

"The Pope does not rule by his own authority. He is the Vicar of Christ, who is and always will be supreme head of the Church. The Pope is infallible not as a man but as head of the Church of Christ, to which Christ Himself promised His present help even unto the end of the world. The authority of the Pope is not the sole authority of the Church, because there is also that of Divine Law, and of the bishops, who are not mere functionaries for the

Pope. The aversion of the dissident Christians is based, at least in part, on certain misunderstandings which can be eliminated. May God grant that the ecumenical council announced by the Holy Father may help bring about the union of all Christians of the East and West in the true Church of Christ."

But this is not quite the way either Eastern Orthodoxy or Protestantism sees the question. To judge from their writings, the crux of the matter is not, as has been so many times suggested by the Romans, merely the primacy of the Pope. The Eastern Church, for one, has admitted officially many times that among the Christian Patriarchs the Bishop of Rome comes first. But he is *primus inter pares*, or first among equals.

Athenagoras I, the present Ecumenical Patriarch of Constantinople and therefore first among the Orthodox prelates, was most explicit on this subject. He and John XXIII have communicated quite frequently of late. Athenagoras professes tremendous admiration for the Roman Pontiff, having congratulated him on his elevation to the Papacy by recalling the text of John I–6: "There was a man sent from God, whose name was John." In return Rome has flattered the Patriarch with attentions, sending various Vatican representatives to call at the Istanbul Patriarchate in recent months. The Patriarch has come to be accepted as the spokesman for Eastern Orthodoxy on the question of Christian unity. Nevertheless, Athenagoras, in a long luncheon interview with the author, felt constrained to say:

"Yes, we want the Pope to lead us to unity, but it must be a unity based on equality. Our churches have been independent for so long that they could not possibly agree to come under another jurisdiction. There are two great obstacles to Christian unity: The Papal claim to infallibility and Papal supremacy."

Nor should the matter be dismissed as a "psychological stumbling block." The big question boils down to the absolutism of the Pope of Rome. It is an absolutism stressed time and again by Catholic theologians. It is an absolutism confirmed by canon law and restated by newly defined dogma. The Pope is supreme even over all the other bishops put together and assembled in a general council.

Granted that the Pope's rule is chiefly "paternal." Granted, too, that tradition and ancient practice make it almost impossible for the Roman Pontiff to act as a real autocrat. Certainly no Pope in the last century has been more benevolent or less authoritative than John XXIII. But John XXIII obviously will not rule the Church forever, while any plan for reunion must be for the centuries. Meanwhile, absolutism is there, clearly written out.

The climate has improved and will perhaps continue to improve. But it is not merely a question of climate or of manners. Before taking the high road to Rome, the "separated brothers" will demand a careful definition of where Papal power begins and ends. The success of any plan for Christian reunion, including that of John XXIII, will depend, not on a re-editing of creed or a restatement of doctrine or a rewriting of the rules of discipline, but rather on a redefinition of the Papacy.

And still there is not the slightest indication of any movement in this direction. In fact, all signs point to the opposite. No Catholic bishop would dare today to suggest a redefinition of the Papacy as a possible council topic. Yet if this question is not considered, Vatican Council II will probably go down as a minor event in the history of Christian unity, however momentous it may be in the history of the Catholic Church.

INDEX